"Think for yourself.
prentice hall
Philosophy—2002

Prentice Hall's *Basic Ethics in Action* series in normative and applied ethics is a major new undertaking edited by Michael Boylan, Professor of Philosophy at Marymount University. The series includes both wide-ranging anthologies as well as brief texts that focus on a particular theme or topic within one of four areas of applied ethics. These areas include: Business Ethics, Environmental Ethics, Medical Ethics, and Social and Political Philosophy.

Michael Boylan, *Basic Ethics*, 2000

Business Ethics

Michael Boylan, ed., *Business Ethics*, 2001

James Donahue, *Ethics for the Professionals*, forthcoming

Dale Jacquette, *Journalistic Ethics*, forthcoming

Murphy, Laczniak, Bowie and Klein, *Ethical Marketing*, 2005

Edward H. Spence and Brett Van Heekeren, *Advertising Ethics*, 2005

Joseph DesJardins, *Environmental Business*, forthcoming

Environmental Ethics

Michael Boylan, ed., *Environmental Ethics*, 2001

J. Baird Callicott and Michael Nelson, *American Indian Environmental Ethics: An Ojibwa Case Study*, 2004

Lisa H. Newton, *Ethics and Sustainability*, 2003

Mary Anne Warren, *Obligations to Animals*, forthcoming

Medical Ethics

Michael Boylan, ed., *Medical Ethics*, 2000

Michael Boylan and Kevin Brown, *Genetic Engineering*, 2002

Rosemarie Tong, *New Perspectives in Healthcare Ethics*, 2003

Rosemarie Tong and Reggie Raymer, eds, *New Perspectives in Healthcare Ethics*, 2003

David Cummiskey, *Global Healthcare*, forthcoming

Social and Political Philosophy

R. Paul Churchill, *Global Diversity and Human Rights*, forthcoming

Seumas Miller, Peter Roberts, and Edward Spence, *Corruption and Anti-Corruption: An Applied Philosophical Approach*, 2005

Deryck Beyleveld, *Informed Consent*, forthcoming

Kai Nelson, *Social Justice*, forthcoming

Please contact Michael Boylan (michael.boylan@marymount.edu) or Prentice Hall's Philosophy & Religion Editor to propose authoring a title for this series!

To Kaye and Margaret

Contents

Preface

The purpose of this book is to offer a critical examination, analysis, and evaluation of key ethical issues that arise in contemporary advertising practice. The book is primarily designed to identify, examine, and evaluate ethical issues that arise in the planning and execution of the advertising process: the process of the communication of advertising messages of persuasion directed at consumers and, as in the case of some types of noncommercial advertising, citizens. With this specific purpose in mind, the book is not designed to address business ethics issues that arise generally and, as a matter of course, within the internal organizational structures of professional institutions, including advertising institutions. Thus the ethical issues addressed in this book are primarily the ones that arise as a result of the planning, production, and communication of messages of persuasion by advertisers to consumers and citizens.

The method of analysis and evaluation employed in *Advertising Ethics* is primarily dialectical, in that it seeks to engage the reader in rational reflective *dialogue* concerning the various advertising strategies and practices that are of ethical concern. The ethical analysis is presented and conducted by way of rational arguments that seek to provide critical reflection on ethical issues that arise with regard to specific advertising strategies and practices in the hope that the reader will feel challenged to think and reflect about the ethical implications and consequences of those strategies and practices. The dialectical method employed throughout the book assumes no prior knowledge of ethical theory or advertising practice and is designed to build the analysis and evaluation of ethical issues that arise in advertising from the ground up, using only certain basic ethical principles that are explained and justified in Chapter 1.

In keeping with the dialectical methodology of the book, the assumed perspective for the examination of the advertisements described in the various case studies throughout the book, is that of a putative rational person: a reasonable person capable of using his or her own critical rational judgment in identifying and assessing the ethical issues that relate to those advertisements for himself or herself. Our own analytical judgments concerning the ethical issues pertaining to those advertisements are ones that can reasonably be ascribed to such a putative rational person.

To assist in the professional and thus practical contextualization of the ethical issues that arise in advertising, the book offers an exposition of the current advertising theory and practice that informs the various advertising strategies currently employed in the advertising industry. Moreover, the ethical analysis and the evaluation of the various ethical issues that follow the exposition of current adverting theory and practice are conducted by reference to actual case studies that assist in highlighting the ethical relevance and significance of those issues, as well as illustrating the practical application of the ethical analysis and evaluation with regard to those issues. Finally, the ethical analysis and evaluation for each relevant chapter is concluded by a summary of instrumental and ethical consequences that emanate either actually or potentially from the advertising strategy or practice under discussion. In a sense, the summaries of instrumental and ethical consequences can be viewed as "ethical balance sheets." Thus the dialectical structure of *Advertising Ethics* comprises four distinct but interrelated components:

1. Case studies
2. Professional practice
3. Ethical analysis and evaluation, and
4. Summaries of instrumental and ethical consequences

The first part of the book (Chapters 1 and 2) provides an introductory account of how ethical principles and codes of ethics are relevant and applicable to professional practice in general and advertising practice in particular. Chapter 1 offers an account of ethical reasoning and ethical decision-making based on ethical principles that are, in turn, justified and supported by contemporary ethical theory. Chapter 2 offers an examination and discussion of codes of ethics relevant to the adverting industry and advertising practice.

The second part of the book (Chapter 3) offers a critical examination and discussion of the relationship of advertising to the community.

The third part (Chapters 4 through 8), which is the major section of the book, offers an account and critical analysis and evaluation of key strategies and practices in contemporary advertising ranging from the place of truth in advertising (Chapter 4); stereotyping (Chapter 5); endorsements and testimonials (Chapter 6); The Ethics of Space and Time (Chapter 7), which examines how advertising infiltrates and colonizes both private and public spatiotemporal spaces; and the digital explosion of advertising (Chapter 8), which examines the introduction and proliferation of digital modes of advertising and their ethical implications.

Finally, the fourth part (Chapter 9) discusses the possibility and desirability of ethical advertising and the way that ethical problems in advertising can and should be addressed and resolved by the advertisers and the advertising industry. The chapter also offers a critical examination and evaluation of the various professional regulation options available to the advertising industry. The preferred option is reflective and effective self-regulation, which is in keeping with our overall view that ethical conduct essentially comprises *ethical self-regulation* at the personal, organizational, professional or institutional, and communal or societal levels.

If, as Socrates claimed, "the unexamined life is not worth living," then it is the responsibility of all individuals to reflectively examine their own lives at all levels and in all manifestations and to determine the best way to conduct their personal, familial, professional, and societal affairs within the parameters and constraints of ethical conduct that, in turn, necessitates an integrated comprehensive and consistent worldview that is good not only for the individual who holds and maintains such a worldview but also for the community at large as required by universal public morality (see Chapter 1).

ACKNOWLEDGMENTS

Edward H. Spence would like to express his heartfelt thanks and deep gratitude to the following people and organizations that in various ways assisted in the completion of this book: The Centre for Applied Philosophy and Public Ethics (CAPPE), Canberra, Australia, for its generous offer of a six-month sabbatical during which time a substantial part of the book was written; Professor Deni Elliott and her Practical Ethics Center at the University of Montana for their gracious invitation and hospitality at the Center in May 2001 when research on the book began in earnest; Michael Boylan, the Series Editor at Prentice Hall, for his tireless assistance, support, and encouragement throughout the duration of the writing and publication process; Kaye Spence for her most generous assistance and advice in formatting the manuscript; and last but not least, Margaret Van Heekeren for her meticulous and comprehensive editing assistance. Finally, many thanks to Andrew Alexandra (University of Melbourne and Centre for Applied Philosophy and Public Ethics), Barbara S. Andrew (William Paterson University of New Jersey), and Mark Alfino (Gonzaga University) for their very useful comments, which have contributed in making this a better book.

Brett Van Heekeren would like to express his deeply felt thanks and gratitude to his wonderful wife Margaret for her support and guidance, and to his children Roan and Anna for giving him the inspiration to succeed, as well as to the School of Communication at Charles Sturt University for its generous offer of a six-month sabbatical that provided the time to write a significant part of the book.

Edward H. Spence
Brett Van Heekeren

chapter one

Ethical Reasoning and Ethical Principles

INTRODUCTION

This chapter will first examine what ethics is. The nature and rationale of ethical principles will be critically examined in the context of contemporary ethical theory. Metaethically, the related authoritative questions of why be ethical and why care about being ethical will also be examined in the context of contemporary ethical theory. This examination is in keeping with the overall tenor of the book of providing justified reasons supported by rational arguments for all the claims made and the analyses offered in the book: that is, claims and analyses that any rational and reasonable person can accept on the basis of his or her own rational reflection. Throughout the book, the practical significance

of the ethical theories and principles examined will be emphasized and, where relevant, will be related to real-life case studies.

Secondly, this chapter will identify and analyze the essential elements that comprise ethical reasoning, as well as examine what constitutes good ethical decision-making in professional practice, including advertising practice.

The rationale informing the ethical model described in this chapter and underlying our analyses and evaluations of advertising ethics as applied throughout the book is as follows:

(1) Insofar as the primary role of a professional practice is determined by its ultimate professional objective, the primary role of a professional practice, in turn, determines the ethical

rules and principles to which that practice is, at least in principle, committed. The ethical principles and rules to which a professional practice is committed by virtue of its primary role is its *role morality*. Thus, for example, the police are, by virtue of their professional role, committed to the principle of justice and to the rule of law, and the principle of justice and the rule of law constitute, among other things, the role morality of policing.

(2) The role morality of a professional practice, including that of advertising practice, is constrained by the requirements of *universal public morality*, which is constituted by principles and rules to which all of us are committed merely by virtue of being rational human agents and members of the social collective that constitutes civilized society. Thus, for example, murder is morally prohibited by universal public morality, even if the "role morality" of one's chosen "profession" as a hired killer sanctions murder. When in conflict, universal public morality always tramps role morality, since the latter is constrained, at least in principle, by the former.

(3) Universal public morality is based on principles that apply *universally* to all human agents by virtue of their common humanity and that are, in turn, justified on the basis of sound rational arguments embedded in contemporary ethical theory that any reasonable person can accept and should accept merely on the basis of his/her rationality.

(4) By identifying the primary role of advertising, we will be able to determine the role morality of advertising and its ethical commitments concerning its various strategies and practices. This analysis will, in turn, allow us to identify and evaluate specific ethical issues that arise in advertising practice in relation to its role morality.

(5) Finally, we will be able, on the basis of universal public morality, to ascertain whether or not certain advertising strategies and practices conform to universal public morality. Insofar as they do not conform to universal public morality, those practices will in principle be considered ethically unacceptable, or at least ethically problematic, even when they appear to conform to the role morality of advertising practice.

Schematically, the Advertising Ethics Model applied in the book is the following: The Role of Advertising determines the Role Morality of Advertising, which is constrained by Universal Public Morality.

WHAT IS ETHICS?

Ethics can simply be defined as a set of prescriptive rules, principles, values, and virtues of character that inform and guide *interpersonal* and *intrapersonal* conduct: that is, the conduct of people toward each other and the conduct of people toward themselves.

Take smoking, for example. If you believed that as a smoker, smoking was harmful not only to your own health but also to the health of other people who were exposed to your smoking; and further, if you believed that with the exception of cases of self-defense, purposely harming others was morally wrong, you would be led to believe in accordance with your own train of thought, that since passive smoking was harmful and that with the exception of cases of self-defense, purposely harming others was morally wrong, then exposing other people to your smoking was morally wrong. On the basis of this kind of reasoning, you may decide and resolve not to smoke in the presence of other people. If you did so, you would be acting ethically on the basis of the principle of not purposely causing harm to other people (for ease of reference, we will refer to this principle as the "nonharm" principle), and your ethical action based on your rational thinking that preceded it would have been determined by *interpersonal* reasons of conduct, that is, reasons for conduct toward other people in relation to yourself.

If in addition you decided to quit smoking on the basis that smoking was causing harm to your own health and if causing harm to your own health was at least equally morally wrong as causing harm to other people, your decision and action to quit smoking, based on your reasoning that smoking was causing you harm was wrong, would have been determined by *intrapersonal* reasons of conduct, that is, reasons for conduct toward yourself.

This way of talking may at first strike us as odd. After all, how can we act immorally toward ourselves? If, with the exception of cases of self-defense, purposely causing harm is wrong, then insofar as we have purposely harmed ourselves, we have acted immorally toward ourselves. After all, self-regret is an instance of the realization that we have harmed ourselves in some way or "let ourselves down." For example, on waking up with a terrible hangover, you may think to yourself, "I shouldn't have had that fourth martini after drinking two bottles of champagne and behaved the way I did—I really let myself down." The expression of self-regret in this simple example would be a realization that in some way not only have you caused harm to your health, at least in the short term, but also you have possibly caused a more long-term harm to your reputation. These kinds of internal monologues that we have with ourselves from time to time illustrate the kind of self-ethical reflection that we apply to our intrapersonal conduct, especially with regard to conduct that results or can potentially result in self-directed harm. It is as if "one's higher self" is taking issue with "one's lower self" over the latter's harmful conduct toward oneself.

The notion of self-moral-wrong, that is moral wrong committed by one against oneself, is important in understanding how personal virtues of character, such as courage, moderation, prudence, and justice, sometimes referred to as the *cardinal virtues,* are important not only in motivating ethical conduct for the sake of others but also equally in motivating ethical conduct for the sake of oneself. For the ancient Greek philosophers of the fifth and fourth century B.C., including Socrates, Plato, and Aristotle, and later the Hellenistic philosophers of the third century B.C., especially the Epicureans and the Stoics, acting morally was ultimately in one's self-interest because moral behavior emanating from a moral character was a necessary condition for one's well-being and happiness.

According to these philosophers, since everyone wants to be happy, for who wouldn't want to be happy, and since moral behavior and a moral character are a necessary condition for happiness, it is clearly in one's self-interest to be ethical and moral. (Throughout this chapter and the rest of the book, the terms "moral" and "ethical" will be used interchangeably, in keeping with the custom in moral philosophy where no material or meaningful distinction is made between these two terms.) According to Socrates, in acting unethically, not only does one harm others, but also equally and perhaps more importantly, one harms oneself in corrupting one's character, which according to Socrates is the most valuable thing that each person possesses.

If the Greek philosophers are right in claiming that unethical conduct toward others harms oneself just as much as, if not more than, it harms others, then unethical conduct involves a *double moral jeopardy.* It is a moral jeopardy that a prudent person will try to avoid incurring by conducting oneself ethically both in one's personal life as well as in one's professional dealings with other people. We will say more about the ethical importance of a virtuous and moral character, for interpersonal and intrapersonal relationships, when we come to discuss the topic of *integrity* in Chapter 9.

The Structure of Ethical Reasoning

Ethical reasoning comprises three main components: justification, motivation, and compliance.

Justification provides valid and cogent reasons for the rational acceptance of ethical principles, rules, values, and virtues that guide ethical conduct through the medium of rational sound arguments provided by contemporary ethical theories.

Motivation for acting ethically on the basis of justified ethical principles, rules, values, and virtues is provided by the same rational sound arguments that provide validity for the ethical principles, rules, values, and virtues as noted in the preceding paragraph. Thus a good argument provided by a particular contemporary ethical theory not only must provide rational justification for the ethical principles that it promotes but also equally and just as importantly must provide psychological motivation *capable* of motivating normal, rational persons to act ethically in accordance with those principles.

The key word in rational motivation is "capable" because no theory can be expected to actually motivate each person to act ethically in every instance, irrespective of the prevailing circumstances. Circumstances can be such that certain individuals at certain times through weakness of character or weakness of the will, for example, might fail to do the right thing even when they know that they are required to do the right thing and moreover know that the ethical requirement to do the right thing is justified by reasons that they rationally accept. It is just that in a particular case, they may simply fail through moral weakness or weakness of the will to do the right thing. For example, a person might know and accept that smoking in an enclosed public place can harm others through passive smoking and that harming others is wrong but might still smoke because in a moment of weakness of the will, the person just gives in to an impulsive craving for having a cigarette.

Equally, one might know that drinking and driving is not a good practice, since it might potentially harm others and oneself if involved in an accident caused under the influence of alcohol. However, for convenience and in a moment of weakness of the will, one decides to drive one's car, although knowing that in an inebriated state, one should not do so. Both examples illustrate that a justified principle *capable* of motivating rational persons to act ethically in accordance with that principle under normal circumstances, may at times and in particular circumstances fail to motivate particular people to act ethically even when those individuals accept the validity of that principle. That outcome is no fault of the motivating capability of the principle, however, but rather the fault of the person's ability in particular circumstances to act ethically in accordance with a reasonable principle of action whose justification and validity the person both acknowledges and accepts.

It is because of the importance of motivation in ethical decision-making and action that the virtues of character, as we shall see when we come to discuss personal integrity in Chapter 9, play a crucial role in enabling individuals to act ethically even under difficult and challenging circumstances. Like a good and an effective training regimen that prepares and enables one to keep running the last eight miles of a marathon race even though one's body just wants to stop running, analogously the inculcation of the virtues can help one through habituation to develop a moral character that is not easily swayed from doing the right thing under difficult and morally challenging circumstances. Like a well-trained runner, a morally trained person can hopefully be better prepared to meet the challenge of acting ethically under very difficult and demanding circumstances, both personally and professionally, than can a person who is not similarly adequately prepared. The analogy between physical health and fitness, on the one hand, and moral "health" and "fitness" on the other, is one that the Greek philosophers, especially Plato and Aristotle, as well as the Stoic philosophers, often make.

Compliance for acting morally is necessary for converting one's recognition, acknowledgment, and intention to act ethically into ethical action. We will refer to this type of compliance as *internal compliance.* Insofar as one has justification and adequate motivation for acting ethically then, in the absence of any external coercion that might preclude one from acting ethically, one would normally act ethically. The dual recognition and acknowledgment that there are good reasons, in accordance with some justified principle(s), for acting morally, together with adequate motivation generated by that rational recognition, will, under normal circumstances, suffice to render a person predisposed to act ethically; and in the absence of any external precluding coercive factors, the person would act ethically in compliance with his or her ethically informed and motivated intention to do so.

However, individual internal compliance in accordance with justified principles sufficient for providing adequate motivation for ethical decision-making and ethical action may prove inadequate or ineffective within a corporate or professional environment. This could be the case either because there is an absence of adequate ethical awareness through adequate programs that actively support and promote ethical education within an organization, or because there is a dominant amoral or even an immoral work environment that does not encourage and that even actively discourages ethical reflection and appropriate ethical action with regard to the organization's operations. In such an amoral organizational environment, an individual's ethical internal compliance may not suffice to allow the person to act ethically in compliance with justified ethical principles. Even if the person chooses to act ethically in every instance, the amoral organizational culture may frustrate and

override the effectiveness of the person's ethical decisions and actions. For example, an ethical individual may find it difficult to operate ethically within an advertising organization that did not support or promote ethical decision-making practices. Similarly, at the organizational level, an ethical advertising company may also find it difficult to always act ethically within an amoral institutional and business environment that not only did not support such ethical conduct but also, by contrast, rewarded, at least financially, unethical behavior.

Under such amoral organizational and institutional circumstances, *external compliance* becomes necessary in order to compel the amoral organization or institution to comply with professionally acceptable ethical standards and principles. Such external compliance can take the form of either (a) institutional or professional *self-regulation* or (b) *legislative regulation* imposed from without the institution or the profession by the government.

Institutional self-regulation will be adequate and effective only if there is an established adequate ethical institutional environment that is effectively monitored and policed by the institutional body. The effectiveness of institutional self-regulation would be measured by how effectively the institutional regulatory body can appropriately reward or punish ethical conduct by its individual members. An institution than cannot adequately or effectively monitor and control the ethical conduct of its individual members would lack adequate and effective self-regulation. This lack would render it both necessary and desirable either to revise and overhaul that institution's self-regulative policies and practices, making them more adequate and punitively effective, or to introduce effective legislative regulation by the government to ethically and legally monitor and control the work practices of that institution.

In sum, ethical reasoning consists, at the individual, organizational, and institutional levels, of the ethical components described in the following sections.

At the Individual Level

Justified ethical principles are capable of providing motivating reasons for ethical action that can result in ethical action through voluntary and internal ethical compliance. Such ethical compliance is internal because it is motivated and brought about by an individual's ethical decision-making process.

Justification—Motivation—Internal
Compliance—Personal Ethical Conduct

At the Organizational and Institutional Levels

(A) *Where there are* ARE *adequate and effective institutional self-regulation monitoring and reward/punitive controls for encouraging ethical conduct and discouraging unethical conduct within the institution there should be the following:*

Justified ethical principles that are capable of providing motivating reasons for ethical action that can result in ethical action through the individual members' own internal ethical compliance AND the members' collective compliance with the institution's self-regulating codes of ethics and codes of conduct that accord with the justified ethical principles that regulate and motivate individual conduct; for individual ethical internal compliance will in turn contribute to and enhance the collective ethical organizational and institutional compliance.

Justification—Motivation—Internal
Self-Regulated Compliance
(Individual + Organizational +
Institutional)—Professional
Ethical Conduct

(B) *Where there are* NO *adequate and effective institutional self-regulation monitoring and reward/punitive controls for encouraging ethical conduct and discouraging unethical conduct within an institution there should be the following:*

In the short to medium term, the introduction of external legislative regulation to provide adequate and effective monitoring and reward/punitive ethical controls over the practices of the institution and its members.

Legislative Ethical Regulation—External
Government Compliance—Professional
Ethical Conduct

In the medium to long term, the introduction of adequate and effective self-regulating ethical individual, organizational, and institutional ethical structural practices as in section (A).

TYPES OF RATIONAL ARGUMENTS: DEDUCTIVE AND INDUCTIVE

Ethical principles are principles that are designed to guide ethical thinking and conduct, both interrelationally and intrarelationally, and are rationally justified by valid deductive or valid inductive sound arguments provided by contemporary ethical theories. A valid and sound *deductive argument* is an argument whose conclusion follows logically from a set of true premises. For example, take the following argument:

1. Xanthippe is a woman.
2. All women are mortal.
3. Therefore, Xanthippe is mortal.

In this simple argument, the conclusion follows logically from a set of two true premises. If one accepts the truth of the premises of the argument, one is compelled by one's own reason to logically accept the truth of the conclusion. This argument is a valid *deductive* argument because the conclusion of the argument follows by logical necessity from the argument's premises. Given the truth of the premises, the conclusion follows as of logical necessity, for if one accepts the premises of the argument but denies its conclusion, one involves oneself in self-contradiction, a sure test that the argument is a valid deductive argument. This argument is *valid* because the conclusion follows from the premises of the argument, and it is *sound* because all the premises of the argument are true. Validity and soundness, however, do not always go together. Consider the following variation of that argument:

1. Xanthippe is a woman.
2. All women are immortal.
3. Therefore, Xanthippe is immortal.

This variation of the argument leaves the original argument still valid just because the conclusion of the original argument follows by logical necessity from the argument's premises. However, unlike the original argument, this new argument is not sound, because premise (2) of this argument is false. Women, being human, are not immortal, at least not physically.

Sometimes the conclusion of an argument would not follow by logical necessity from the premises of an argument but would follow with *inductive probability*. That is, given the truth of the premises of an argument, its conclusion would follow inductively but not deductively, if it is the most likely because most probable outcome or conclusion. Consider the following *inductive argument:*

1. From what we know, the sun has risen and set every morning for millions of years in the past, including yesterday.
2. Therefore, the sun will rise and set tomorrow.

Given that the premise is true, then the conclusion follows not by logical necessity but by inductive probability. The conclusion does not follow deductively because the acceptance of premise (1) and the denial of the conclusion of the argument do not involve a self-contradiction. Even if the sun has risen and set for millions of years in the past, it could be destroyed by a supernova between now and tomorrow, thereby stopping the sun from rising and setting tomorrow; this is a highly unlikely but not an impossible event. However, the conclusion follows by inductive probability from the premise of the argument, for insofar as we have adequate evidence that the sun has been rising and setting for millions of years as well as the evidence of our own personal testimony, that the sun has been rising and setting for as long as we can remember, then it is highly probable, but of course not certain, that the sun is likely to rise and set again tomorrow.

Sometimes ethical theories will employ a combination of deductive and inductive arguments in support of the principles that they promote. Starting from simple empirical observations that people will assent to on the basis of their own experiential knowledge of the world, such arguments then proceed to deduce further self-evident premises that ultimately lead to a conclusion that a rational person will accept either because the conclusion follows logically from the preceding premises or because the conclusion, though not logically deducible from those premises, nevertheless follows from those premises by inductive probability. Alan Gewirth's argument for the Principle of Generic Consistency (PGC) that we examine later, is an argument that combines a series of interconnected inductive and deductive arguments within the argument structure of an overarching single sound deductive argument, the argument for the PGC.

The preceding elementary comments about argument structure, validity, and soundness were merely introduced to alert the reader to the *dialectical methodology* employed in this book, which seeks to support all ethical claims, opinions, and judgments made in the book, by rational arguments that appeal to the reader's own rational thinking and empirical experience of the world. The methodology is primarily "dialectical" in that it seeks to appeal to the reader's rational judgment by engaging the reader in a kind of notional rational dialogue about ethics generally and advertising ethics specifically. The reader should accept our claims, opinions, and propositions about advertising ethics in this book only insofar as the reader finds the arguments that support those claims, opinions, or propositions reasonably persuasive on the basis of their cogency and soundness.

ETHICAL PRINCIPLES: DEONTOLOGICAL, TELEOLOGICAL, AND CONSEQUENTIALIST ETHICAL ARGUMENTS

Having offered some preliminary comments about the structure of two main types of rational argument, we can now examine in more detail some of the ethical principles offered by contemporary ethical theories by way of rational arguments for the justification and support of those principles.

For simplicity and economy, we have opted to present the ethical principles discussed in this chapter in terms of the generic metaethical arguments that support them, without giving a detailed exposition of the various contemporary ethical theories in which those arguments are embedded. Apart from the theories that are specifically mentioned in this chapter, other theories that support one or more of the deontological, teleological, and consequentalist ethical principles mentioned here, are, among others: Hobbesian Contractarianism (Thomas Hobbes's seventeenth-century classic *Leviathan* and David Gauthier's 1986 *Morals by Agreement*); Kantian Contractarianism (John Rawls's 1972 *A Theory of Justice*); and Utilitarianism (R. M. Hare's 1981 *Moral Thinking: Its Levels, Method and*

Point). An excellent and comprehensive text on contemporary ethical theory is Michael Boylan's 2000 *Basic Ethics,* by Prentice Hall.

As with immorality in general, unethical advertising practices can be shown to be wrong on either the basis that they are inherently wrong, that is, wrong in themselves irrespective of their consequences; or wrong simply because of their consequences. Under the former, unethical advertising is wrong because of some inherent wrongness in the advertising practice itself; and under the latter, unethical advertising is wrong if it results in harmful consequences for other people, oneself, and one's profession. If it is stated that unethical advertising is inherently wrong, independently of its consequences, the reasons adduced in support of that statement could be various. They could be either *deontological* reasons or *teleological* reasons. Deontological reasons are ones that pertain to the action considered by itself, independently of the purpose, goal, or end for which the action was performed. So with the exception of justified self-defense, physically harming someone by hitting the person over the head with a blunt object would normally be considered to be morally wrong by virtue of a deontological principle to the effect that, with the exception of justified self-defense, physically harming people is wrong.

By contrast, teleological reasons pertain to the purpose, goal, or end of an action. Thus if one hit someone over the head with a blunt object for the purpose of defending oneself against an unjustified and unprovoked assault, then the action might be morally justified by virtue of the teleological principle to the effect that injuring an attacker for the purpose of justified self-defense is morally permissible. If, on the other hand, it is stated that unethical advertising is wrong only because of its bad consequences, the reasons adduced in support of that statement would normally be *consequentialist* reasons. "Deontological," "teleological," and "consequentialist" are three terms used by philosophers to refer to three different sets of reasons offered in support of the moral evaluation of actions. The following deontological, teleological, and consequentialist arguments can be adduced to show why unethical advertising is morally wrong.

Deontological Arguments

Universal Laws and Moral Rights

The Categorical Imperative (CI)

According to the German philosopher Immanuel Kant (1724–1804), a moral rule must be one that is capable of being a universal law—a law that applies to everybody in all places and at all times without exception. Kant referred to this moral principle as the *Categorical Imperative.* According to Kant's principle, we must act only according to rules that we can at the same will that they become universal laws. Kant thought that an essential feature of moral rules or principles is their *universalizability,* that is, their capability of being applied universally under relevantly similar conditions. Two formulations of the Categorical Imperative (CI) are worth noting:

(i) Always act in such a way that you can also will that the rule or maxim of your action should become a universal law.

And

(ii) Act so that you treat humanity, both in your own person and in that of another, always as an end and never merely as a means.

Although the preceding formulations are formally equivalent, the first illustrates the need for moral principles to be universalizable, that is, being capable of being applicable to everyone at all places and at all times without exception under relevantly similar conditions. The second formulation, which draws a sharp distinction between *things* and *persons,* emphasizes the necessity to respect persons for themselves and not *merely* for what they can do for us. Under this formulation, the categorical imperative is designed to show that treating other people as a means for the advancement of our own self-centered ends is morally wrong.

Applying the first formulation of the Categorical Imperative, can we consistently will that (say) theft or telling lies became universal laws? It would seem not, since we could not consistently will that theft or telling lies become universal laws. For such laws would be detrimental and impractical both for oneself and for others, since if everyone engaged in theft, then the right to property would be undermined; and if everyone lied, the process of communication would be undermined, since no one would believe what anyone else said.

In sum, Kant's CI principle is designed to show that actions such as telling lies and committing theft are inherently unethical because they are inherently irrational. And they are inherently irrational because they cannot be consistently willed, by anyone, as universal laws. According to Kant, therefore, it is only universal laws that can form the basis of moral conduct.

The Principle of Generic Consistency (PGC)

According to the contemporary American philosopher Alan Gewirth,[1] we all have natural rights to freedom and well-being by virtue of being purposive agents. Because as human beings we all possess the natural property of being purposive, that is to say, being in possession of a natural disposition of having purposes or goals that we, both individually and collectively, want to pursue and fulfill, we have by virtue of that natural disposition of purposiveness the rights to freedom and well-being. And we have these rights by virtue of the fact that freedom and well-being are essential conditions for all purposive action, that is, action required to pursue and fulfill our individual and collective purposes as human beings.

Moreover, because these rights emanate solely by virtue of a common natural disposition of having purposes or goals that we want to fulfill, one that we all naturally share by virtue of our common humanity, rights to freedom and well-being are essentially universal rights, since they arise out of our common shared property of human purposiveness. Accordingly, the Principle of Generic Consistency (PGC) is formulated as follows:

> Act in accord with the generic rights of your recipients as well as of yourself.[2]

The PGC essentially states that rights to freedom and well-being are universal human rights that should be respected in others as well as in oneself. Moreover, like Kant's moral laws, Gewirth's moral rights to freedom and well-being are universalizable simply because they are capable of being applicable to everyone at all times and in all places without exception, under relevantly similar conditions.

Promises and Contracts

The fact that people have promised, contracted, or agreed to do something typically means that they have put themselves under a moral obligation to do that thing. Accordingly, it is morally wrong for them to fail to do what they promised or contracted to do. Naturally, there are circumstances under which failing to fulfill a promise or contract would not be morally wrong, for example, if one was coerced into making the promise or the contract in the first place, or if some overriding and unforeseen moral consideration came into play.

Teleological Arguments

Teleological arguments focus on the ethical or moral goal or ends of a process, a practice, a profession, or an institution. Thus the purpose of the criminal justice system is to deliver justice,

that of journalists to unearth and communicate the truth, and so on. Moreover, these ends or goals are held to be in part definitive of the process, practice, profession, or institution in question. Accordingly, to undermine or obstruct the realization of these goals or ends is to strike at the heart of the process, practice, profession, or institution. Thus a teleological argument might be available to show what is wrong with unethical advertising in endorsements, for example, if it could be shown that deceptive endorsements undermine the role of advertising in providing credible and reliable information through endorsements to consumers.

Moreover, any act carried out by a person or group of persons that undermined the purpose of a particular practice, profession, or institution, to whom that person or group of persons was committed by virtue of a preestablished professional or institutional duty toward that practice or institution, would be self-defeating and thus irrational—irrational because inconsistent with the preestablished purpose of the relevant practice, profession, or institution.

Note that Gewirth's Principle of Generic Consistency has the features of both deontological and teleological arguments discussed before. On the one hand, the PGC is a deontological principle because, like Kant's Categorical Imperative, it purports to be a universal moral law based on the dual principles of universalizabilty and logical consistency. On the other hand, the PGC is a teleological principle because it is derived from the property of purposiveness, a disposition that we all share in common simply by virtue of our goal-orientated human nature.

Role Morality

The preceding teleological reasoning leads us on to the realization that every practice, profession, or institution has its own *internal* **role morality**—a morality that is determined by the specific overarching role of a particular practice, profession, or institution. Thus the role of a police officer is to uphold law and order and to provide assistance in the criminal and judicial process; the role of a journalist is to inform the public truthfully and fairly on matters of public interest; the role of a doctor or a nurse is to provide medical care to the patients for the benefit of their health; the role of a priest or a minister is to provide pastoral care to members of the congregation; and the role of a politician is to provide good and just government to the electorate.

The role morality of a particular practice, profession or institution sets in turn its own internal rules and codes of conduct for the ethical regulation of that practice, profession, or institution. Thus, typically, the code of ethics for a particular profession, industry or institution, would reflect and be constitutive of the role morality of that profession, industry or institution. To the extent that a profession's code of ethics does not reflect or is constitutive of that profession's role morality, that code of ethics is inadequate. It is therefore of paramount importance that before establishing a profession's, industry's or institution's code of ethics, the role, determined by the ultimate goals and ends of that profession, industry or institution, are well understood and accurately ascertained.

Consequentialist Arguments

According to the consequentialist argument, sometimes also referred to as the *utilitarian argument,* the morality of an action depends exclusively on its consequences. Thus an action is moral if it results, overall, in good consequences for (say) the greatest number of people affected by that action. To put it another way, an action is moral if it results in a maximization of utility (utility understood as preference satisfaction or happiness or pleasure or something equally desirable) for the greatest number of people

affected by that action. Similarly, an action is immoral if it results, overall, in bad consequences, especially harm, or overall reduction of utility, for the greatest number of people affected by that action. According to the consequentialist argument, therefore, unethical advertising is morally wrong only to the extent that it results, overall, in bad consequences for the greatest number of people affected by unethical advertising practices.

In contrast to the deontological argument, the consequentialist argument does not focus on the inherent moral wrongness of any particular form of unethical advertising. According to the consequentialist argument, unethical advertising would be counted as unethical only if it resulted overall in bad consequences or in a reduction in overall utility for the greatest number of people affected by the unethical practices of advertising. In fact, under consequentialism, a generally considered unethical advertising practice that involved deception, for example, would be considered ethical under consequentialism, if it resulted overall in good consequences for the greatest number of people. With regard to the hypothetical example, it is difficult, however, to imagine that in practice, deceptive advertising would ever result in the greatest satisfaction of utility for the greatest number of people. Though of course conceivable, such a scenario seems from a practical perspective to be highly unlikely.

Universal Public Morality

Before we proceed to examine more closely and generically what might be wrong with unethical advertising, it is of vital importance to say something about *universal public morality:* universal, because like Kant's Categorical Imperative and Gewirth's Principle of Generic Consistency, it applies universally to everyone without exception in all places at all times under relevantly similar conditions. Thus, everyone is worthy of moral respect simply by virtue of being a human being; and likewise, everyone has rights to freedom and well-being simply by virtue of being a purposive human agent; moreover, universal public morality is public, because it applies individually and collectively to members of the general public in their role as citizens both locally and globally. Thus if it can be shown that unethical advertising practices are, according to universal public morality, morally wrong, it would also be the case that it is morally wrong in all places at all times under relevantly similar conditions. If that is the case, universal public morality will show that unethical advertising is universally morally wrong, both locally and globally, and not merely morally wrong relative to local customs, or to cultural, religious, social, or political norms. Thus advertising practices that deceived consumers about the products or services advertised would count as unethical irrespective of the idiosyncratic and specific cultural, social, religious, or political norms of the country in which the deception takes place. Such deceptive practices would simply be unethical because deceiving people is morally wrong both in accordance with the deontological principles of Kant's Categorical Imperative and of Gewirth's Principle of Generic Consistency, as well as in accordance with the consequentialist principle that it might result in overall bad and harmful consequences for all the stakeholders, including the profession of advertising itself, as well as in accordance with the teleological principle of the role morality of advertising that precludes, at least in theory, false and deceptive advertising.

Universal Morality and Role Morality

Sometimes the role morality of a particular institution or profession may come into conflict with universal public morality. When that event happens, universal public morality will always take precedence over role morality for the simple reason that universal public morality as foundational, is more fundamental, and applies equally to everyone irrespective of the particular personal or professional interests or commitments, including those required by the role morality of a particular institution or profession.

Since role morality acquires its moral authority derivatively from universal public morality, it stands to reason that when the two come into conflict, universal public morality should take precedence, because the role of a particular institution or profession which generates that institution's or profession's role morality must first be morally justified and thus morally acceptable on the basis of the principles of universal public morality. Universal public morality, which is universal and public, applies equally to every member of the public (thus it is public) at all times and in all places without exception (thus it is universal).

The fundamental rights to freedom and well-being that are justified by the Principle of Generic Consistency, which as we saw earlier apply to every individual person just by virtue of being a purposive agent, must be respected and protected against practices that may be allowed by the role morality of a particular institution or profession but not allowed by universal public morality because such practices may involve violations of the rights of freedom and well-being of particular individuals or groups of individuals, that are morally not permitted by universal public morality. For example, under no circumstances would deceptive advertising be morally acceptable even if it were allowed by the role morality of advertising simply because deceptive advertising would involve the violation of the individual as well as the collective rights of freedom and well-being of members of the public. Similarly, some forms of stereotyping would be morally objectionable and unacceptable if they involved the violation of the individual as well as the collective rights of freedom and well-being of a particular gender, ethnic, or racial group that was being stereotyped. Advertising that targets children and encourages them to develop undesirable habits such as eating junk food, may also fail the requirements of not violating the children's rights to freedom and well-being even if such a practice was considered acceptable by the role morality of advertising.

Ultimately, the role morality of every institution and profession is answerable to the principles and hence the requirements of universal public morality because it is universal public morality that provides the foundational justification of any particular role morality. It would be self-defeating, then, to allow role morality to overrule the very principles of universal public morality that provide the initial and foundational moral justification of institutional or professional role morality. Hence, role morality will always be trumped by the requirements of universal public morality where the two moralities come into conflict, as they can do from time to time.

To be sure, often institutional and professional ethical transgressions will also violate the moral requirements of institutional or professional role morality, such as when a police officer falsifies evidence in an effort to secure the conviction of a suspect. Such falsification of evidence is a violation of both the requirements of police role morality, which demands that police officers uphold the law and the criminal justice system, as well the requirements of universal public morality, which demands that the citizens' rights to a fair trial are not violated by the police through the fabrication and falsification of evidence in an investigation. Deceptive advertising is an example of an advertising practice that would be precluded by both the role morality of advertising, which requires that advertising information communicated to consumers is not misleading or deceptive, as well as by universal public morality, because such deception would constitute a violation of the consumers' rights to freedom and well-being.

In sum, universal public morality places restrictions on institutional or professional role morality in at least two ways. First, there are good instrumental and pragmatic reasons for an institution's or a profession's role morality not to be allowed to violate the rights of citizens or consumers that are required and supported by universal public morality, because such ethical violations may prove self-defeating through loss of public trust in the role of an institution or a profession that is seen to violate citizens' and consumers' universal rights to freedom and well-being. Such loss of trust could harm the reputation of the institution or profession whose role is seen by the public to violate the requirements of universal public morality.

Second, the violation of the requirements of universal public morality by an institution's role morality goes against the public good if it harms other people by violating their rights to freedom and well-being. This violation is rationally and ethically self-defeating, since members of an institution whose role morality is allowed to undermine the public good are by extension also harmed as citizens, because they are also committed to the overall public good of the society in which they live by the requirements of universal public morality that apply to everyone, including themselves.

THE GENERAL RUDIMENTS OF ETHICAL ANALYSIS AND ETHICAL DECISION-MAKING

The deontological, teleological, and consequentialist arguments discussed in the preceding section provide two essential methodological functions. First, they provide a *metaethical* justification for various ethical principles that demonstrate that there are good cogent and rationally sound reasons for being ethical that any reasonable person would and should acknowledge and accept, thus providing a reasonably definitive answer to the authoritative question of morality, "Why be moral?" These arguments essentially demonstrate morality's (ethical) authority over human affairs. Second, those arguments provide the means for enabling the application of *ethical normative analysis* to relevant ethical issues that arise in professional practice through the application of justified ethical principles to specific relevant cases.

In advertising, deontological, teleological, as well as consequentialist ethical principles can be used to determine the presence of an ethical issue that arises as a result of some specific advertising practice and then to demonstrate on the basis of ethical normative analysis that employs any or all of those principles, why a particular advertising practice is ethically problematic or ethically unacceptable.

For example, deceptive and misleading advertising that has the tendency to deceive consumers is ethically unacceptable on the basis of all three types of principles. It is deontologically unacceptable because deception is precluded by Kant's Categorical Imperative as well as by Gewirth's Principle of Generic Consistency, which require that the rights of every person be respected. Deceiving people is unethical because it violates those rights. Specifically, with regard to the PGC, it violates people's rights to freedom and well-being. Cosequentially, deception is ethically unacceptable because it results in bad consequences by way of causing harm, at least potential harm, to consumers and the general public who might rely on deceptive advertising to make informed decisions about consumer products or services. Finally, teleologically deception is unethical because the role morality of advertising that is itself justified on the basis of teleological reasoning precludes deception as an unacceptable professional practice. Moreover, deceptive means that are used for the end of persuading consumers to feel predisposed toward particular products advertised cannot be justified, since those means are unethical. Deception is generally considered a moral wrong unless it is used, under very restricted and special circumstances, to preclude a greater ethical harm from occurring, one that cannot be

precluded through any other ethical means. For example, lying to a Nazi officer in order to save a Jewish family who are taking refuge in your cellar would be considered justified deception because the capture and death of the Jewish family by the Nazi would be a much greater ethical harm than deceiving the Nazi officer by lying to him.

Some forms of stereotyping in advertising could also be found to be unethical under at least deontological and consequenstialist principles if it were shown that those forms of stereotyping treated certain gender, ethnic, racial, or other social groups with disrespect or violated their rights to freedom and well-being, thereby causing them harm. Treating people with disrespect by diminishing or degrading them in some specific way through stereotyping can just as surely cause them harm as can sticks and stones, and in some cases, even more so, since the harm, though less tangible, can be greater and more enduring. Generally, it would be a bad consequence for society overall if certain groups within our society were maligned or misrepresented through stereotyping in adverting, for it would be an affront to our whole system and sense of justice conceived as fairness.[3]

As we will be presenting ethical analysis of relevant ethical issues that arise as a result of different practices in advertising, we will not be offering an exhaustive ethical analysis of those issues here but will do so in the specific chapters that address those issues in greater detail. This chapter is merely intended as a general examination of the various ethical principles and the arguments that support those principles through rational justification, and the chapter's objective is to indicate initially the general structure and methodology of how those principles may be applied in providing ethical normative analysis of specific advertising ethical issues in the rest of the book.

Finally, to conclude this chapter, it is important to consider briefly the concept of "worldview."[4] Every individual has his or her view of the world that acts as a filter through which a particular individual perceives the world. An individual worldview is largely determined by one's familial, religious, educational, racial, ethnic, professional, and other social factors that contribute in shaping our personal, as well as collective, social identities as people. Ethical analysis and ethical decision-making do not take place in an abstract theoretical vacuum devoid of the influences that an individual's view of the world at both the personal, professional, and communal levels brings to bear on that ethical analysis and the resulting decisions ensuing from that analysis. Thus an individual's worldview plays, and must play, an integral part in the ethical decision-making process.

According to Boylan, a person's worldview should be holistic and integrated, one that eschews fragmentation that can result in dissonance. On the contrary, what is recommended is consonance between one's thinking and one's motives and actions as informed by one's holistic, comprehensive, and consistent worldview. Central to this recommendation is the view that one should be critically reflective about one's life in keeping with Socrates' famous dictum that "the unexamined life is not worth living," meaning that an unexamined life is not worthy and thus not becoming of a thinking human being whose nature is at least partly defined by his or her ability to think rationally and reflectively about everything one does or does not do.

The preceding short exposition forms the background of Boylan's "Personal Worldview Imperative" (PWI): *All people must develop a single, comprehensive, and internally coherent worldview that is good and that we strive to act out in our daily lives.*[5] According to Boylan, "every agent acting or potentially acting in the world falls under the normative force of the Personal World View Imperative."[6]

According to Boylan, "many people reside in several self-contained worlds that dictate how they should act in this or that situation. These worlds are often contradictory." As we saw earlier, one's Role Morality, as a practitioner in a particular profession or other institutional practice, may involve one in a potential conflict with Universal Public Morality by whose requirements everyone, including the professional practitioner, is required to abide. Thus when such a moral conflict arises, Universal Public Morality will always trump the narrower requirements of one's role morality and will require the professional practitioner to act in accordance with the requirements of Universal Public Morality over those of his profession's role morality. The "Instrumental and Ethical Consequences" summaries that function as ethical balance sheets at the end of the relevant chapters in this book highlight how the instrumental requirements dictated by the narrow requirements of the role morality of advertising get trumped and are overridden by the wider ethical requirements of Universal Public Morality.

How can the moral conflicts that may potentially arise between an individual advertiser's role morality and Universal Public Morality be accommodated and resolved within that individual advertiser's worldview? Boylan correctly suggests the following:

> The Personal Worldview Imperative calls for us to create a single worldview, meaning that a person who holds multiple worldviews that refer, in turn, to multiple and contradictory practices must work to create unity and coherence among these worldviews. By integrating these various beliefs and general attitudes and life values, the individual confronts the world more authentically.[7]

What is required, according to Boylan, to render the creation of a single comprehensive and consistent worldview possible, is a process of integration:

> The process of integration involves relating the empirical world (in which a person lives and makes sense of the world by continually struggling and striving with these issues) to more abstract principles in such a way that life becomes rationally comprehensible.[8]

Continuing, Boylan correctly suggest that

When we accept the fact that we must examine our lives to develop a single, comprehensive, internally coherent worldview that we must strive to adhere to, we have self-consciously agreed that this exercise of autonomy and freedom is what we should do. Such behaviour defines us as humans in a more comprehensive way than saying that we are rational animals. This is so because the Personal Worldview Imperative specifies the manner of executing our rationality. It is holistic and ties people to abstract and atemporal logic, to an intellectual tradition, and to various cultural and personal values that jointly describe who we are.[9]

The dialectical methodology employed throughout this book that seeks to engage the reader in a dialectical dialogue concerning the various ethical issues and problems that confront advertising theory and practice, is in keeping with the process of worldview integration though dialectical interaction as described in our preceding exposition of Boylan's theory. In particular, the "Instrumental and Ethical Consequences" balance sheets provided at the end of relevant chapters in the book reflect the type of dialectical interaction that is designed to encourage and hopefully to bring about a process of integration between the empirical and the ethical analysis offered throughout the book with the reader's own worldview. This worldview can be rationally modified, if necessary, to reflect the need for achieving a single comprehensive and consistent worldview that is holistic in outlook and seeks to avoid dissonance and to achieve, on the contrary, maximal consonance between reflective ethical analysis and ethical decision-making on the one hand, and professional practice on the other, both at the individual, organizational, and communal domains within which a person operates.

Finally, it is worth noting that Gewirth's Principle of Generic Consistency discussed earlier in this chapter is, as Boylan puts it, "worldview engaging."[10] This is the case because the structure of the argument that supports the derivation of the PGC is *worldview friendly*. Its initial appeal to the subjective perspective of the individual agent engages and helps integrate the agent's own worldview in the structured dialectical process of the argument, since the essential conditions for all purposive actions to which the argument refers, namely freedom and well-being, are the same invariable and universal conditions that underlie any worldview, irrespective of its particular subjective content, which of course would vary across different individuals.

Moreover, the dialectical interaction between the agent's own recognition of his prudential interests and generic rights to freedom and well-being and the agent's subsequent rational recognition that those rights are not merely self-regarding prudential rights but also other-regarding moral rights (which apply not only to him or her personally but to all other similarly placed agents as well) leads to an unavoidable rational recognition that his or her own worldview is constrained by the ethical requirements that the moral rights of other agents place upon him or her in the form of concomitant moral duties and responsibilities. Such a rational recognition is capable of leading, formally to begin with, but practically over a period of more dialectical reflection and rational engagement, that includes the cultivation of the moral sentiments and the inculcation of the moral virtues (see Chapter 9), to an integration of the agent's own worldview and the universal ethical perspective and normative requirements of the PGC.

It is because we care deeply about our fundamental rights to freedom and well-being that we should also care about engaging in critical self-refection and examination of how our particular personal worldview is or is not comprehensive and consistent and above all good in being in accord with the ethical requirements of Universal Public Morality as supported through rational justification by a direct application of the PGC.

chapter two

Regulating the Advertising Environment: The Role of the Codes of Ethics

INTRODUCTION

The advertising environment is a complex and an ever-changing dynamo. It has developed from a simplistic statement of services (anecdotally, some of the earliest known advertising is believed to have been scrawls on Roman brothels detailing what was available within) to a multibillion-dollar, global industry.

This environment has developed in parallel to the growth of consumerism. The more products that are available dictate a greater need for the diversity of these products to be known, thus steps in the communication device known as advertising and the advertising practitioner. Put simply, it is up to the advertiser to communicate to the consumer that a particular brand or product is the most worthy of purchase. The pressure, therefore, on advertisers is immense. Accounts worth millions of dollars can be withdrawn from one agency and placed with another, sometimes leading to financial ruin. At its best, this pressure for survival can be the birthplace of exhilarating creativity and ingenuity. At its worst, it can lead to advertising campaigns that not only push the boundaries of societal acceptance but also go beyond acceptable norms, thus creating ethical problems and dilemmas. As society evolves, so too do the standards deemed acceptable, thereby necessitating an equally adaptable regulatory environment.

The current codes of ethics and the current practice in advertising will be examined and discussed in relation to the general ethical principles established in Chapter 1. The justification and ethical adequacy of those codes will then be assessed. Various codes of ethics and practice will be compared in order to establish whether or not there is a set of universally accepted ethical rules and principles that apply in the advertising industry globally, or at least in the West.

This chapter will also address the notion and practice of self-regulation in the advertising industry—how it works and whether it works adequately. In Chapter 9, the issue of self-regulation will be revisited and addressed again in the light of the ethical explorations, evaluations, and conclusions of the book. The general position taken in the book will be that professional self-regulation should reflect ethical self-regulation at the personal, organizational, institutional, and societal levels respectively. This position is in keeping with our philosophical conception of ethical conduct as ethical self-regulation and the philosophical notion of "worldview" developed by Michael Boylan in *Basic Ethics* (2000), namely, the view that "all people must develop a single, comprehensive and internally coherent worldview that is good and that we strive to act out in our daily lives."[11] In adopting this principle, this part of the book, but also the book generally, will

show that one's personal beliefs and convictions, whatever they happen to be, must accord and be consistent with the ethical principles and practices to which one's profession commits him or her. Moreover, those commitments must also accord and be consistent with the fundamental ethical and social standards of society that in turn, must be justified according to some rational and reasonable ethical principle(s) in accordance with the requirements of Universal Public Morality, which was examined in Chapter 1.

In Chapter 9, this notion of a four-way consistency—personal, organizational, professional or institutional and social or communal—is used to develop a notion of integrity that is also in keeping with the principle of worldview as well as with our principle of ethical self-regulation. It is only on the basis of a consistent and comprehensive view about the world, one that is both ethically right and good, that people can develop and maintain their personal, organizational, professional, and social integrity.

By examining the concept of professional self-regulation, the chapter will also examine and discuss different types of regulation by exploring current regulatory structures and their effectiveness. It also examines the role that codes of ethics and conduct play in maintaining self-regulation as a tool for achieving the goal of building a framework for ethically acceptable advertising.

CASE STUDIES

CASE STUDY 2A   Windsor Smith—Shoe Company Sidesteps Regulators[12]

In Australia, outdoor advertising is in the frontline in the war against "unacceptable advertising" because of its attributes of being indiscriminately accessible to the public eye and not monitored by any particular regulatory body. These attributes—and indeed self-regulation—were put to the test in 2000 through a campaign produced by shoe company Windsor Smith. The company produced

a series of sexually suggestive campaigns culminating in a series of outdoor billboards headed with the words "Windsor Smith" and divided into two halves. The right-hand half comprised a photograph of three different types of shoes with the left side featuring a photograph of a seated woman next to a standing man. The man is dressed in black trousers and shirt, whereas the woman is wearing a black jacket, bra, high-heeled sandals and miniskirt, with underpants revealed as a result of her spread-legged pose. The man is cupping the woman's face in his hand, which is held in close proximity to his groin area.

Complaints about the poster were made in the popular media and to the Advertising Standards Bureau (ASB)—the Australian body responsible for managing the dispute resolution process—regarding the content and prevalence of the material. Although Windsor Smith stood by their belief that the billboard campaign was not inappropriate and the advertising agency responsible rejected claims that the material was sexist, that it was demeaning to women, and that it offered any suggestion of sexual activity, the ASB responded to complaints by reviewing the material.

The ASB held the view that the portrayal of the men and women in the advertisement was in breach of part of Section 2 of the Advertiser Code of Ethics. This code provides that "Advertisements shall treat sex, sexuality and nudity with sensitivity to the relevant audience and, where appropriate, the relevant program time zone."[13] The ASB subsequently requested that Windsor Smith withdraw the material.

In making its determination, the ASB noted that the location of the advertisement on prominent outdoor sites effectively placed it on general exhibition to the public at large. The board further regarded the image, in its overall context, as conveying a strong theme of sexual suggestiveness that was inappropriate for such an audience and, accordingly, upheld the complaints.

As a result of the voluntary nature of compliance in the Australian system, the advertiser exercised its right to continue to run the campaign and lapped up the related publicity. Ultimately, the material was withdrawn, not by Windsor Smith, but by Australian Posters, the media owners. This voluntary move by the outdoor company to replace the contentious posters was made in support of the ASB's ruling and was seen as a victory for the cooperative nature of advertising self-regulation in Australia. But it had also demonstrated that a system of voluntary compliance was inadequate. Windsor Smith had gained much from the media coverage and publicity, acquiring a competitive advantage over those advertisers who endorsed and supported the industry codes

of conduct. This case highlights the problems with a system of voluntary self-regulation, in which weak sanctions and a lack of a statutory role in the process allowed an advertiser to challenge social values and at the same time to gain competitive advantage.

CASE STUDY 2B   Fcuk—French Connection UK Shock Tactics Ignite Self-regulation Debate[14]

Since its first use of the letters *fcuk* for a logo as part of an advertising campaign in 1997, French Connection UK has continually presented contentious material that has remained under the microscope of the UK's Advertising Standards Authority (ASA).

But in April 2001, the ASA imposed the toughest measures that it can on the advertiser by ruling that the company not be allowed to exhibit advertising posters for two years without prior approval. This ruling meant that future advertising material produced by the company must be vetted by the Committee of Advertising Practice (CAP), whose approval will be required before placement.

The French Connection UK logo—fcuk—is an obvious acronym for the company's British division but is not what immediately comes to mind when the abbreviation is first sighted. This overtly connotative symbol has been a constant flashpoint between the company and the regulators since its launch.

In 1998, the ASA rejected ads sporting taglines such as "fcuk fashion," "fcuk fear," and "fcuk advertising." Instead of putting posters up in public, the company ran them in store windows, which the ASA does not regulate.

In 1999, the ASA considered complaints about a poster campaign in which the letters *fcuk* were set alongside phrases like "my place now" and "all night long." The authority rejected the complaints, accepting the company's explanation that "my place now" was meant to indicate that the French Connection store "is the place for me."

In 2001, the company found itself in conflict with the ASA on numerous campaigns. In January, they ran an ad in the *London Evening Standard* headlined "World's biggest fcuk." Again, there were complaints, but since it was a one-off placement to promote the new London store, the ASA confined itself to reminding French Connection that it should not use its trademark in a sexually suggestive manner and that it should not repeat the approach.

By the middle of the year, the company had really crossed the line in the authority's view. The authority banned French Connection's multimillion-pound television campaign, which featured a couple peeling each other's clothes off. The company responded by plastering signs on its posters and store windows urging people to visit its website, which featured the commercial in full.

The press ad (placed in the *Evening Standard*), which was headlined "sorry," claimed "but the powers that be have decided our new TV commercial "kinkybugger" contains an unacceptable level of sexual innuendo and is therefore unfit to be screened on national television. See you in cyberspace . . . fcukinkybugger.com."

The ASA considered that the combination of words used together could be read as "fuck kinky bugger.com" or "fucking kinky bugger.com." Also, the ASA considered that the advertisement was likely to cause serious or widespread offense. It told the advertisers not to repeat the website address in broad-based media and advised them to consult the CAP advice team before using the website address again in an advertisement.

Moreover, the ASA ruled on objections to a poster that stated "fcukinkybugger.com." The ASA was concerned that the poster used ambiguous words that could be seen by children and was likely to cause widespread offense; that it was irresponsible; and that it brought advertising into disrepute. The ruling by the ASA ensured that French Connection would not be allowed to put up any new advertising posters for two years without prior approval.

Although it can be argued that this ruling on taste and decency sent a message to the industry that authorities will crack down on ads deemed offensive (particularly those placed in the public domain), it can also be argued that the sanctions and the related publicity have worked for French Connection by delivering a constant audience to the brand as well as fueling the brand's image of being challenging and naughty.

This scenario has exposed inherent weaknesses in a self-regulatory system. An advertiser was able to place overtly offensive material designed to achieve "multiplier effects" by stirring up controversy, with the regulatory authority's being unable to prevent the material from being exposed to the general public. The authority was also unable to curb the usage of the offensive material in the company's own space and other domains (such as cyberspace). It is only in a true self-regulatory environment where individual, organizational, and institutional commitment to codes of ethics and conduct is exercised that such practices can be averted. The alternative is a more regulated environment. Industry practitioners and critics are still debating the ideal solution.

PROFESSIONAL PRACTICE

*To thine own self be true—self-regulating
the advertising environment*

The notion of a self-regulated media is a necessary component of a society that hopes to call itself democratic. A self-regulated environment provides industry with the capacity to control its own operating condition, free from government or state interference or from externally imposed rules of behavior. It is an inclusive process that provides a foundation for accountability and acceptability of advertising to its users. This ethos of self-determination tends to promote good practice and allows for the flexible targeting of specific problems within the industry. In this way, effective self-regulation can help bypass the often overly prescriptive nature of regulation and can allow industry to be responsive to changing consumer needs and expectations, in effect empowering them in the process.

But There Are Degrees of What Is Perceived to Be Self-regulation

Regulation is essentially a social control mechanism. In that case, self-regulation could ultimately be perceived as self-control that is in keeping with our conception of ethical conduct as a form of ethical self-regulation. It is this notion of self that is often ignored in a discussion of "what self-regulation is." Most definitions of self-regulation take a more macro view of this notion of control, describing degrees of control that are driven by industry bodies, generally in partnership with government and users or consumers. Quantifying the role of each of these main stakeholders is often the basis of the discussion of self-regulation at the expense of the realization that the key stakeholders are "selves"—the individuals that make the whole. When an understanding of this notion of self-regulation becomes universal within an industry, then it has the potential to reach its ethical zenith. In the Windsor Smith case, if the advertiser truly believed in this notion of self-regulation, it would have immediately complied with the ruling of the "standards" authority or would have acted in an even more socially responsible manner by proactively avoiding council judgment altogether. But in the highly profit-motivated and competitive environment of business, this outcome is probably a little too much to expect.

Three Models of Regulation

There are three generally accepted stages or forms of regulation ranging from *self-regulation,* in which government involvement is minimal to nonexistent; a *semiregulated environment* in which a catalogue of standards, mechanisms, and rules is drafted by government and that businesses are expected to comply with; and finally, *absolute government regulation.*

Regulation fosters an environment of legislative-based control, which is policed by a statutory authority with the potential to be intrusive, restrictive, and costly to administer. A semiregulated or coregulated environment exists where the government and industry body, in partnership, determine the ethical and regulatory framework in which industry will function. This model is more inclusive and is able to provide industry with more reactive power than a totally voluntary self-regulated environment. This model often involves the consumer in the process who is the user of the communication—the product of advertising.

In most advertising environments, administrators have embraced what they label a self-regulatory model, in effect establishing a situation in which the industry or profession is doing the regulating with varying degrees of contribution from other stakeholders, including government. In the Windsor Smith case, it was the involvement of the media owner that forced the removal of offensive material and upheld the established standards of conduct in the Australian advertising environment. This action supports the definition of self-regulation as a form of coregulation that recognizes the need for input from multiple sources.

So in summary, it is proposed that self-regulation is an environment where the government or the state formally hands over the power to regulate, so that the industry itself is doing the regulating, in effect empowering the industry or business community to establish its own standards of behavior through the creation and maintenance of some formal codes of conduct, ethics, standards, or principles. This definition also acknowledges that government may not be totally divorced from participation in the process, therefore creating a coregulatory form

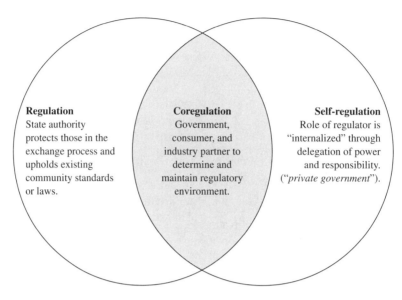

Regulation
State authority protects those in the exchange process and upholds existing community standards or laws.

Coregulation
Government, consumer, and industry partner to determine and maintain regulatory environment.

Self-regulation
Role of regulator is "internalized" through delegation of power and responsibility. ("*private government*").

of self-regulation. Jean Boddewyn[15] proposes the colorful notion of self-regulation as a form of "private government" in that industry peers rather than outsiders formally control or dominate the establishment and enforcement of self-imposed and voluntarily accepted rules of behavior. A product of this notion is a self-regulation mechanism that is limited to professional or institutional codes of conduct and practice, with an obvious legislative tone supported by a sophisticated dispute resolution process, a common model in most advertising and market environments.

The Model in Action

The coregulated advertising and media environment is multilayered by nature, with each stakeholder, organization, or body driven by its own codes or standards. This arrangement creates a complex web of guidelines and rules that are far too complicated for most practitioners to understand, and this situation is a real problem for effective self-regulation. But aside from this, a common structure in "developed" media environments includes some government control through acts or laws coupled with industry control through the establishment of industry bodies working to self-generated codes. These codes are developed, maintained, and upheld through the establishment of specific bodies charged with regulatory responsibilities.

For example, in Australia, the Australian Association of National Advertisers (AANA) is charged with the role of managing the self-regulatory system through the adoption of an Advertiser Code of Ethics and of the maintenance of these codes through an Advertising Standards Board (ASB) and an Advertising Claims Board (ACB). These boards have been developed to resolve complaints by members of the general public in regard to taste and decency (in the case of the ASB), and truth, accuracy, and legality (in the case of the ACB).

Determination of complaints is dependant upon whether or not the boards deem these as breaches of the AANA's Code of Ethics. These bodies are also assisted in the regulation process through government legislation via acts such as the Broadcasting Services Act of 1992, the Trade Practices Act of 1974, the Tobacco Advertising Prohibition Act of 1992, the Therapeutic Goods Act of 1989, and many others. Also assisting are the specific media whose representative bodies enforce their own codes of practice. So here we have a tiered system of coregulation whereby government, the advertising industry body, and the other media industry bodies effectively support each other in an attempt to propagate consistently ethically acceptable advertising.

Similarly, in the United Kingdom, the Advertising Standards Authority (ASA) operates as the independent, self-regulatory body for non-broadcast advertisements. The authority administers the British Codes of Advertising and Sales Promotion to ensure that ads are legal, decent, honest, and truthful. The authority works in partnership with media bodies such as the Independent Television Commission (ITC) to enforce compliance to codes and can refer offenders to the Office of Fair Trading for legal action.

In the United States, a coregulatory system operates. The Federal Trade Commission (FTC), which is the primary regulator of deceptive advertising, offers advertising guidelines and upholds trade laws. Operating in partnership with this legislative body is the industry-sponsored National Advertising Division (NAD) of the Council of Better Business Bureaus (CBBB), which operates the National Advertising Review Board (NARB). The NAD is the investigative body, whereas the NARB is the appeals body of the system. This two-tier structure was established to sustain "truth and accuracy" in national advertising, to minimize government intervention, and to foster public confidence in the credibility of advertising.

The Role of Stakeholders in Advertising Self-Regulation

As the fcuk case demonstrates, it is only through the cooperation of multiple bodies and organizations that a self-regulatory system can effectively enforce compliance to its codes. The threat of having material vetted or embargoed from publication or broadcast is one of the most effective sanctions, since it deprives the advertising message from being experienced, which at the end of the day is self-defeating, since the advertiser is paying for the advertising message to be experienced.

So how do the key stakeholders in the advertising environment—the media, the industry bodies, and the consumer—contribute to its effectiveness?

Media's Role in Self-regulation

As we have seen in both the Windsor Smith and the fcuk case scenarios, the media has functioned as a screen between the advertiser and the consumer, and their commitment to upholding their own industry's code of conduct has served the cause of self-regulation.

Although advertisers and advertising agencies are the key drivers of the self-regulation processes, it is clear that they require the participation of all stakeholders to be truly effective. One of the key stakeholders is the media through which advertisers convey their persuasive communication. The media is the final and the regular point of contact between the consumer and the advertiser. The media, therefore, plays a significant role in delivering and giving life to the advertisers' message. Because of the relationship that audiences have with their core media—a relationship built on trust and habit—their role in supporting a self-regulatory environment is critical.

Media organizations and bodies construct and maintain their own set of principles and guidelines on the type of advertising they will accept. This practice is particularly evident when it comes to advertising to children. Restrictions on the amount of advertising, the type of advertising, and the times of day that advertising will be delivered to children are some of the key policies administered by media industry bodies.

Media trade organizations, such as the National Association of Broadcasters (NAB) in the United States or the Independent Television Commission (ITC) in the United Kingdom are examples of bodies that regulate advertising in their media. These organizations establish codes and standards to use as a benchmark for approval of material to be published or broadcast through their media. But the explosion of media options makes their role a little more difficult, with new media and more innovative means of connecting with consumers becoming more common strategies for advertisers. Media such as ambient-postcards, scooters, skywriting, body-painting, and the like, lack the industry maturity and jurisdiction to be effectively regulated, posing potential problems for an effectively self-regulated advertising environment.

The media is important in that it provides regulating bodies with a sanction tool for advertisers that choose not to comply with industry codes and guidelines. Refusal to place potentially (or proven) offensive advertising material is a useful "last straw" for advertising industry regulators. In Australia, self-regulation was rescued by outdoor company Australia Posters when it replaced material deemed offensive by the Advertising Standards Board despite the advertiser's refusal to comply to the Board's determination (see the preceding Windsor Smith case study). This action reinforced the role of a cooperative environment in an effective self-regulation process.

Industry Bodies and Consumer Orientation

Effective self-regulation calls for the development of a commitment to the wider community, not just to an industry's current customers. In this regard, a process of consultation between industry, consumers, and government is established as each has a role to play to make the system work. Government offers a public policy perspective, whereas industry bodies offer the alternative view to a regulatory environment. It is the number of willing industry participants involved in the self-regulatory system that will determine its ability to provide proactive and effective self-regulation. Just as important is consumer input into the process in order to maintain relevance and confidence in the system.

The key factor here is communication with consumers and the education of both creators and receivers of advertising messages. Communication to all stakeholders is critical to self-regulation to ensure that there is both an industry understanding of the key principles and processes of the system and a consumer understanding of the complaints processes and of the industry's commitment to "acceptable advertising." The usual practice of industry regulatory bodies is to create avenues of communication to its practitioners and to the general public that both inform and educate about the self-regulation process. Industry bodies maintain public websites, conduct industry training and education programs, and produce regular media-releases that provide coverage and publicity of the self-regulation mechanisms and adjudications.

As most self-regulatory systems are reactive in nature, an effective dispute resolution process is critical to successful self-regulation. Such processes allow the consumer a voice in determining acceptable advertising standards through complaints and representation on complaints boards. It is the accessibility and profile of these dispute resolution processes that will generate consumer confidence in the self-regulation system.

Codes—The Mechanics of Self-regulation

In their most basic form, codes of ethics and codes of conduct are both a set of guidelines to which an industry is expected to adhere and a framework for regulators to test the value of a complaint. In this light, we could frame codes as a reactive tool that act as a benchmark for establishing industry standards and for measuring degrees of compliance. This interpretation of codes places them predominantly within a determination environment As discussed, one of the key roles of self-regulation is to manage the consumer redress or dispute resolution process, and codes are the foundation for that function. But codes should be viewed as more than this. They should also be held up as the regulators' mission statement that publicly declares an industry's commitment to a certain moral standard and that plays the important role in influencing an individual's ethical disposition (character) and ethical conduct, as well as serving to provide an ethical and a professional collective spirit within an organization and institution or industry.

In this way, a code of ethics can play some role in influencing people's ethical dispositions or characters and can give people a reason—perhaps a decisive reason—to act in one way rather than another. A code of ethics or conduct can get people to behave differently than they might otherwise do in the absence of the code, as well as to motivate them to declare their commitment to a certain moral standard. This role is in keeping with our conception of professional self-regulation as a form of ethical self-regulation, which in turn defines our overall conception and understanding of ethical conduct as being essentially a form of ethical self-regulation or ethical self-control. In order for such a high-profile industry like advertising to develop and maintain the trust, confidence, and credence of society, a relevant, inclusive, and fluid system of codes of ethics is imperative.

Essentially, codes bring professionals together as a group that supports common aims and interests and that accepts some responsibility to the public. They form a collective public commitment to acknowledged ethical principles and standards.[16] But the most overt demonstration of codes is their disciplinary function that outlines a set of requirements and prohibitions and the subsequent sanctions for breaches. Their compliance serves as the most obvious benchmark for measuring acceptable advertising, thereby reducing codes to a reactive rather than a proactive tool.

There are two key components of a codes system: one is aspirational, the other consequential. The aspirational, or ideal, elements of the code are generally referred to as prescriptions that are concerned with what professionals ought to do or not to do and what they as a profession as a whole ought to aim at.

The consequential elements, or *sanctions,* refer to what actions, if any, should follow noncompliance of the prescriptions. The consequences of noncompliance vary according to the type of self-regulation structure that the industry has developed. Usually a process of persuasion and consensus forms the first phase of remedy, but as in both the Windsor Smith and fcuk cases, this process was not adequate. Stronger sanctions are sometimes required to force an advertiser to comply. These sanctions include adverse publicity, which can have a multiplier effect that gives the advertiser a competitive advantage; cooperation with media organizations to remove offending material or to refuse space for an offending advertisement; and in some instances, ensuing legal proceedings. Advertisers that push sanctions to the extreme bring the industry into disrepute and often suffer the pressure of public opinion.

Generic Codes

There is no one standard model of self-regulation; subsequently, there is no standard set of codes of ethics operating globally. However, a survey of four codes reveals some core commonalities. From studying the basic principles inherent in the Australian Advertiser Code of Ethics (administered by the Advertising Standards Bureau http://www.advertisingstandardsbureau.com.au/industry/aana_code_ethics.html); the British

Codes of Advertising and Sales Promotion (administered by the Advertising Standards Authority, www.asa.org.uk); the Better Business Bureau (BBB) Code of Advertising (administered by the National Advertising Division of the Council of Better Business Bureaus, http://www.bbb.org/advertising/adcode.asp); and the Canadian Code of Advertising Standards (administered by Advertising Standards Canada), a generic set of codes can be derived. There appears to be a common commitment to the following principles:

1. A sense of responsibility to consumers, community concerns, and society.
2. Decency, honesty, and truth.
3. Avoidance of misrepresentation and deception.
4. A sense of fair competition.
5. The protection and promotion of the reputation of the advertising industry.

These five principles will serve as a reference point for discussion of acceptable advertising behavior throughout this book.

Ethical Practice

As we saw in Chapter 1, our ethical reasoning and decision-making model, comprising justification, motivation, and compliance, places the responsibility for moral action ultimately on the individual who, on the basis of ethical principles justified by sound arguments capable of motivating moral action, is required to comply with those principles in acting ethically.

However, as we also stated in Chapter 1, it may prove difficult for a moral individual or organization to always operate ethically, even with the best of intentions, if such an individual or organization finds oneself or itself in an amoral environment that not only does not encourage or support ethical conduct but, on the contrary, also rewards unethical conduct where such conduct

is perceived to be professionally or commercially successful.

In general, with regard to professional practice in which professional actions impact not only on individuals but also on professional organizations and professional institutions, as well as more on the community as a whole, the responsibility for ethically regulating the professional environment becomes a *collective ethical responsibility* that encompasses the individual practitioners, the organizations, the institutions or professions, and equally importantly, the whole community. In the two cases discussed earlier, it was the conjoint action of the advertising industry, of the government regulative bodies (particularly in the case of fcuk), of other media organizations (particularly in the case of Windsor Smith), and of the community at large through complaints made by individual members and other communal groups that the offensive advertising campaigns in both the fcuk and the Windsor Smith cases were finally terminated.

The very successful antismoking campaigns in many parts of the world, especially in the United States and in Australia, in which smoking has been banned from all public places including public buildings, airports, public transport, and restaurants in Australia in 2002, to name but a few, is a prime example of collective and conjoint action in regulating a socially perceived harmful and undesirable activity by not only banning smoking in public places but also banning the promotion of smoking through advertising and corporate sponsorships. Public pressure and pressure from various government and communal health-related groups, including the medical association in Australia, has initiated a debate around the world concerning the harmful effects of junk food on health that are indicated by the alarming rise in obesity generally, but child obesity in particular. Given that the problem of obesity, which is possibly related, at least partly, to the consumption of junk food, like the problems of smoking and alcohol abuse, is a communal problem. Its solution requires collective and conjoint action involving individuals, the manufacturers and distributors of junk food, the retail outlets of junk food, the government, as well as the marketing and advertising industries that promote junk food through their campaigns.

Insofar as the advertising industry wants to be perceived as ethically responsible by the community at large and insofar as the relationship between the rise in obesity and the promotion of junk food through advertising can be established with a reasonable degree of probability, then the advertising industry has an ethical responsibility to actively contribute to any policies and information and education campaigns that may be instantiated and applied in an attempt to redress the problem of obesity in the community, especially as it affects children. Such action may require, as in the case of smoking, the reduction, if not outright elimination, of ads that promote the indiscriminate consumption of junk food, as well as the elimination of sponsorship deals that allow the promotion and sale of junk food in schools in return for books or computers to those schools. This issue will be discussed at greater length in Chapter 3. At this juncture, we merely want to use the problem of obesity to which advertisers may be contributing in order to emphasize the collective nature of ethical responsibility with regard to professional practice. Such collective responsibility will also be applicable in other ethically problematic areas of advertising, such as stereotyping (Chapter 5) and invasive advertising techniques that violate people's personal as well as public privacy and spaces (Chapters 7 and 8).

Insofar as ethical decision-making that leads to ethical action requires compliance, informed and inspired by rational justification and psychological motivation, then professional self-regulation conceived by us as ethical self-regulation (see Chapter 1) must be supported and assisted *motivationally*, not only at the individual level through the inculcation of certain moral virtues of character discussed in Chapter 9, but also at the organizational and institutional levels through the instantiation and application of appropriate and adequate self-regulated controls that reward ethical professional conduct as well as penalize unethical professional conduct in keeping with the principles of universal public morality as reflected in the principles of professional ethical morality.

The preceding five basic ethical principles, which are extracted through a comparison of a sample of various advertising professional codes of ethics from around the world, indicate that the adverting industry is committed, at least in principle, to ethical principles that are supported and indeed required by universal public morality, as we saw in Chapter 1. This is an important discovery because it demonstrates the ethical responsibility that the adverting industry has to the whole community at large, as well as demonstrating the community's ethical responsibility in actively engaging in the professional self-regulative process of the advertising industry as one of the key and major stakeholders.

Ultimately the ethical buck stops at every individual citizen, both individually and collectively. If we as citizens deserve the governments we elect, we also deserve the kind of advertising we get on screens, radios, billboards, buildings, print, and all the other media channels of advertising communication. Insofar as the professional self-regulating process in advertising involves the community as a key and major stakeholder, as the process ought to, then the community has an ethical responsibility to be part of and contribute actively to that process. Equally, the adverting industry has an ethical responsibility to actively involve the community in its regulative process and be ethically responsive to the community's concerns regarding unethical advertising practices.

chapter three

Advertising and the Community

INTRODUCTION

Advertising addresses people primarily as consumers, whereas people are primarily regarded, at least according to the philosophical and political principles of democracy, as citizens. Are the two concepts compatible or incompatible in advertising? Informing people as citizens on the one hand, and informing them as consumers on the other, may rely on inherently conflicting objectives and principles. As citizens we have certain responsibilities to other citizens and the state, as well as certain responsibilities to the natural and social environments in which we live. The chapter examines in what way, if any,

these ethical responsibilities are addressed by the advertising industry's mission of persuading us to consume ever more products and services. Are the community values that we share as citizens compatible with the desired, but perhaps not always desirable, commodities we are actively encouraged by advertising to consume or to aspire to consume as individual consumers? Is advertising turning us into hedonistic lotus-eaters whose primary concern in life is the constant pursuit of pleasure through the ever-increasing consumption of commodities? Is free trading the same as fair-trading? Do we care under what working conditions our Nike shoes are made?

CASE STUDIES

CASE STUDY 3A   Consuming Children[17]

Brand Loyalty

The main goal of target advertising is to create brand loyalty. The aim is to develop lifetime customers for products. The goal is not just to get people to try a product but to get them to experience *a relationship to a brand*. With children, for example, brand loyalty begins early. Advertisers and marketers spend billions of dollars annually to get their messages out to kids. In 1999, corporations spent approximately $12 billion in U.S. money on such efforts.[18]

Children are targeted in at least three ways:

(a) Persuading them to spend their own money
(b) Influencing parental spending
(c) Creating a steady stream of new customers.

*Brand Sharing: Toys and Burgers,
Books and Cereal*

> "Our strategy is to deliver added value. We know for a fact that kids will come to Burger King because of Nickelodeon toys."
> *(Richard Taylor, Burger King U.S. Marketing Executive)*[19]

> "The great thing about a fast-food company is that they have 8000 places where our audience can experience our brand every day. Burger King does a tremendous job of partnering."
> *(Pam Kaufman, Senior VP—promotions marketing for Nickelodeon)*

Books that spotlight brands appeal, according to the advertisers and the marketers, to both kids and parents. General Mills has sold millions of copies of Cheerios-branded books, including *The Cheerios Counting Book* and *The Cheerios Play Book*. Similarly, Kellogs is on bookshelves with

its *Froot Loops! Counting Fun Book;* M&M and Mars with *The M&M's Brand Counting Book;* Kraft Foods with *Oreo Cookie Counting Book;* and Campbell Soup Co. with Pepperidge Farm's *Goldfish Counting Fun Book.*[20]

No Downside

> "For the marketer it's creating affinity for the brand. For parents, the kid is learning to count. There's no downside."
> *(Julie Halpin, CEO of WPP Group's Geppeto Group, New York)*[21]

Best Interest

But such product branding strategies have their critics, especially those strategies aimed at young children. Allen Kanner, clinical psychologist at the Wright Institute, Berkeley, California, says young children, below the age of eight, don't realize adults wouldn't be acting in their best interests. "It is unfair to be using these techniques on developmentally gullible kids. There's an explosion of childhood obesity that parallels junk food being advertised and the problem of marketing violent products to children." [22]

CASE STUDY 3B   Generation Next Is Generation O[23]

The next generation of world citizens is in danger of being known as "Generation O"—that's O for obese, a term that refers to people who are considered by medical authorities to be carrying an unhealthy amount of fat in proportion to their ideal body weight. Advertising is in the firing line as one of the causes of the obesity problem.

The World Health Organization estimates that a billion people worldwide are overweight or obese, contributing to an increasing incidence of diabetes, heart disease, and other chronic illnesses.[24]

In America, the story is not pretty, with obesity seen as the nation's leading health problem. A report in the October 9, 2002, *Journal of the American Medical Association* found that 30.5 percent of Americans are obese, up from 22.9 percent a decade ago. And 64.5 percent, or nearly two-thirds, are overweight. The researchers also found that 15 percent of children aged 6 to 19 are overweight. The problem accounts for about 300,000 deaths a year, second only to deaths from tobacco.[25]

In Europe, Weight Concern (a UK organization that addresses problems of obesity), claim the United Kingdom is officially the fattest nation in Europe, with one in five U.K. adults—about 8 million—clinically obese, three times as many as in 1980. Weight Concern also claim that more than one million kids under 16 are obese.[26]

In Australia, the research indicators are that the country has the second-highest rate of obesity in the world (behind the United States) and that around 18 percent of children are overweight.[27]

It is the calculated targeting of children that has most critics calling for action—and that the action should be banned or regulated advertising of junk food to children.

The food industry in the United States spends an estimated $33 billion a year on ads and promotions.[28] With so much advertising weight, the message is clearly to eat more, and the focus of that message is children. Advertising during children's TV programs is on the rise. In the United States, the number of commercials during Saturday morning cartoon hours rose from 225 in 1987 to 997 in the mid-1990s.[29] However, children are not targeted just by mainstream media strategies; they are also targeted through fully integrated campaigns using television, radio, and print media; by trade shows, with coupons; and through product placement in films and books.

The food industry now links food with entertainment, especially with movie and cartoon characters. Brand-name foods and drinks appear on toy cars and helicopters, and fast-food chains issue "educational" card games. Following suit, advertising campaigns also link food, soft drinks, and sports beverages to entertainment (movies, videos, video games, and celebrities) and toys. One can buy Spiderman cereal and limited-edition toaster pastries. Children can make their own McDonald's Happy Meal, using Play-Doh and plastic molds for each component; a coupon for the real thing is included with the set. The toymaker Mattel sells a Barbie doll who works at the McDonald's Playset drive-through. There, most ironically, that slender icon can take your order for "all your fast-food favorites." Toys and books that either are actually food or are packaged with food now abound. Children can play chekers (draughts) with fruit-flavored gummi candies (sweets) and can learn to count in various calorie-filled and sugar-filled ways, through books that use sweets and cereals to teach math.[30]

To make it even more difficult to find sanctuary from the junk food pitches, soft-drink companies have pouring rights contracts, and fast-food chains sell burgers, tacos, and the rest of their fare in schools.

A group called Stop Commercial Exploitation of Children Coalition (SCEC) claims that one of the biggest contributors to the surge in childhood obesity, including such complications as type-2 diabetes, is the aggressive marketing and advertising by the food industry.

U.K. food policy watchdog Sustain (a UK based, independently funded alliance for the promotion of better food and farming) published research showing that 99 percent of the food advertised on children's TV contains high levels of fat, salt, or sugar.[31]

In Australia in 2002, academics and health experts speaking at a Childhood Obesity Summit said that advertising had a role to play in the obesity debate and called for action, including the banning of fast-food ads targeted at children.[32] But advertisers defend their tactics by suggesting that parental modeling and the home food environment are far more critical factors in determining eating habits.

An Australian study of 2,000 people over the age of 18, by the research company Australia SCAN, revealed that the majority of respondents (64 percent) felt that parents should be primarily responsible for the personal health and eating habits of children and for teaching them skills and behaviors needed to accomplish that goal.[33]

Many of the solutions offered around the world include the creation of advertising campaigns that educate the community about healthy eating. If they can be as effective as the campaigns produced by junk-food manufacturers, then obesity problems should see a dramatic turnaround.

Case Study 3c Drink Till You Drop

(i) At the top-left corner, the print ad shows four smiling young men in black tuxedos standing abreast in a church at a friend's wedding. Next to the picture, the caption reads: "The honeymoon won't be the same without them." At the right-bottom corner, a full bottle of "Jim Beam" stands alone. To the left of the bottle, the caption reads: "Real friends. Real bourbon. Since 1795."

(ii) The whole print ad is a picture of the inside of an open refrigerator. All the shelves of the refrigerator, including those on the inside door, are stacked with cans and bottles of Fosters, Victorian Bitter, and Crown Lager beer. Each of the six-packs and the cartons of beer are labeled with the names of various football games and other sports: USPGA + USLPGA, NRL, Major League Baseball, American Football, Premier League Rugby, US Open Tennis, TRI Nations Rugby, and World Motorcycle Champs. At the bottom-right corner, the caption reads: Fox Sports: The Game Never Ends."[34]

Case Study 3d Nesquick Bunny Makes Brand Loyalty Leap[35]

After a hard day at the child-care center, your loved one throws his or her bag on the kitchen table and declares, "I've got a letter for you, it's from the Nesquick Bunny." You shake your head and say, "That's nice, darling," and take the letter and begin to peruse its content. "Nesquick Bunny and his team loved meeting your child today! Be sure to try all the yummy Nesquick flavors available at your local supermarket."

You open your child's bag to find a Nesquick sample bag containing a range of Nesquick products. The penny drops: your child has just experienced a sophisticated marketing communication practice. That's the tactic that Nestle adopted in Australia in 2002, a sponsorship arrangement with entertainment acts that tour child-care centers, targeting children under 5.

The Nestle Nesquick Bunny performs for 40 minutes free of charge, sings a song that includes the lyrics "I'm the Nesquick Bunny," hands out milkshakes and sample bags, and then moves on to the next gig.

Children under 5 have been introduced to the brand, tested the product, and made to laugh at the same time—an ideal brand experience. The trouble is that the under-5 is a vulnerable target who has now been introduced to a range of products that would be considered "unhealthy" and has been encouraged to employ his or her "pester power" to ensure that the products remain in the house.

Case Study 3e Culture for Sale[36]

In her book *No Logo,*[37] Naomi Klein proposes that the intent of "advanced branding is to nudge the hosting culture into the background and make the brand the star. It is not to sponsor culture but to *be* the culture."[37] Her point suggests that branding is in a stage of cultural expansionism, looking for new territories to conquer and to take ownership. This expansion has pushed the advertising boundaries to the point where the line between the advertiser and the vehicle for the advertising has become obscured. The new vehicle for advertising and for brand messages is now the "communication-created" culture itself.

From the moment when the "superbrand" Michael Jordan teamed up with Bugs Bunny to create the film *Space Jam,* the lines between culture and promotion became obscured. When brands such as fashion label Benetton and coffee giant Starbucks also became magazine publishers, when a beer brand such as Molson became a rock music promoter, when actors and pop stars created their own fashion labels, the branding of culture became fair game. It is difficult to find a cultural experience that is not branded in some way.

Product placement in movies has become commonplace, with blockbuster experiences such as James Bond's becoming a commercial franchise parading an array of brands that have paid for the privilege to piggyback on the James Bond brand. Even the successful Sundance Festival documentary *Dogtown and Z-Boys,* which portrayed skateboarding culture, was financed by the skateboard shoe company Vans.

In television, brands are strategically integrated into the content of the programs. In the United States, the variety show genre is about to be transformed by a program that features no commercial interruptions but, instead, advertising incorporated into the show with comedy routines and sets built around sponsoring products and brands. A consortium of advertisers called the Family Friendly Programming Forum Mission fund scripts and development of TV programs that will serve as appropriate "platforms" for their advertising. Products of this venture to date have included *The Gilmore Girls, Sabrina the Teenage Witch,* and *American Dreams.*

In Australia, STW Communications has set up a division to devise TV programs for their advertisers. In 2000, one of their products was a reality TV program called *The Band,* which followed a rock band on a 7-week tour. The band drank XXXX beer, a key brand in Lion Nathan's stable (the client that the series had been created for).

Music festivals are a branded experience with sponsors overtly placed throughout venues. At a prominent music festival in the height of a Sydney summer—*The Big Day Out*—brands involve themselves in the experience. In the 2003 festival, Levi's gave away drinking water, Durex gave out free condoms, and brewer Tooheys (an Australian beer company) set up an eye-catching inflatable bar.

In radio, integration of advertising with programming is a regular occurrence, with presenters reading live scripts or consuming products on the air and commenting on their features.

Even music has become a vehicle for promotion. As described earlier, in Australia the multinational confectionary company Mars produced a jingle for their product Starburst and released it as a pop tune. Radio stations played it, and it became a hit single. Similarly, musicians are employed by advertisers to write songs to promote products. The Australian group "The Scared Little Weird Guys" was approached by the Sydney advertising agency Maverick to write songs for its clients. The songs would be performed by other artists alongside noncommercial music to the difficult-to-reach youth market.

Even literature is not sacred space any more, with the precedent set by jewelry brand Bulgari, which commissioned writer Fay Weldon to mention the brand in a fiction novel. The result was the book *The Bulgari Connection,* a Bulgari brand experience as much as a bona fide piece of literature.

In their attempts to get under the "detectors" of media-savvy consumers, advertisers have infiltrated the boundaries of culture by masquerading as culture itself. As Naomi Klein suggests, advertisers are ". . . transforming culture into little more than a collection of brand extensions-in-waiting."[38]

Case Study 3f   Slip Slop Slap[39]

Slip Slop Slap—slip on a shirt, slop on the sunscreen, and slap on a hat: that's been the advice for bronzed Aussies for over twenty years. And this advice has successfully targeted a critical problem facing Australians residing in a harsh and dry continent. Australians are eight times more likely to develop common *skin cancer* than any other form of cancer, with more than a quarter of Australians being treated for skin cancer each year. The iconic figure of the "bronzed Aussie" is a difficult image to dispel. However, over the years, a carefully targeted campaign has significantly increased the understanding of and has highlighted the concern about skin cancer. More than 90 percent of Australians know what skin cancer is, and of those, more than 95 percent believe that it is a serious disease. Also, there has been an annual decrease in the number of people who desire a tan. Sunscreen sales in Australia have increased exponentially over the past 10 years.[40]

Launched in 1981, Slip Slop Slap has been one of Australia's most successful public awareness campaigns. Based on a catchy jingle sung by the tap-dancing, board shorts, and floppy-hat-wearing Sid the Seagull, the campaign was an immediate success with the real target audience of kids, who would be developing a system that they would live with forever. The message became institutionalized, with kindergartens, schools, and local councils around the country becoming the premier sun-protection program in the world.

In the past 5 years, male mortality from melanoma has fallen by 4 percent; and in the past 10 years, female mortality has fallen by 8 percent.[41] SunSmart reports a 50 percent reduction in the number of people getting sunburned today compared to 1988.[42]

In 2000, the Anti-Cancer Council of Victoria resurrected the well-known slogan with a campaign called "Timebomb," but the contemporary campaign was much tougher than its predecessors. The television *advertising* campaign targeted at 15- to 24-year-olds (predominantly males) shows skin cancer being removed from a patient. These shock tactics were seen to be necessary because "slip slap slop" by itself just doesn't cut it any more.

Today Australian beaches have become tent cities in the summer, filled with children wearing long-sleeved clothing, a far cry from the early 1980s vision of oiled and tanned bodies exposing all but the areas covered by bikinis and Speedos.

PROFESSIONAL PRACTICE

The practice of targeting in the advertising process is one that is designed to create both efficient and effective marketing communications. The process involves identifying where the core business comes from in the community, defining this segment or fragment of the community on the basis of a combination of common characteristics they possess, and creating and delivering precise messages to that segment. The result is the prevention of wastage in the communication process and, hopefully, more relevant communication for the target.

In Chapter 5, we will discuss how this process both creates and perpetuates stereotypics in the community. In this chapter, we are concerned with the notion of identifying vulnerable and impressionable community members and institutions, and of designing advertising strategies that take advantage of these vulnerabilities.

In this context, the key issue regarding the ethics of targeting lies in the question of whether the targeting practice is responding to the target's genuine needs or is exploiting consumer vulnerabilities to the gain of the targeting marketer.

As stated previously, the advertising practice of targeting communication at particular segments serves the purpose of avoiding the wasteful "scattergun" approach of disseminating messages and promotes the more efficient method of customizing messages to match the wants and needs of particular types of people. The foundation of this approach is an understanding of what those consumer needs actually are and responding appropriately to meet them. It is when the consumer insight gained from research identifies a vulnerability that can be exploited that the practice becomes ethically questionable. Here the practice is engineered primarily for the benefit of the advertiser rather than for the benefit of the consumer. In this way, advertising is seen as a process that creates or exaggerates needs, particularly among vulnerable target groups, the most prominent of which are children.

In Case Study 3b, there is clear evidence that suggests that the tactics of fast-food advertisers have had a detrimental effect on the health and well-being of members of the community, particularly children, with obesity rates growing exponentially in the last decade. The tactic of advertisers to surround their targets with a variety of communications from traditional means such as TV and radio, as well as covert product placements, in films, books, and the educational environments of schoolchildren, is a great example of effective execution of Integrated Marketing Communication (IMC). The side effect is an obese generation.

This tactic of IMC is a standard advertising practice that is designed to strengthen the relationship that brands have with their targets, so that a pervasive presence in the life of the target increases the likelihood that the brand will be salient in the mind of the target and that the target will establish some loyalty to that brand, and ultimately will be a lifelong customer.

In this regard, children are a critical target, since their loyalty will ensure that a product or brand has a long life whether it is bought directly by the child or by the parents as a result of the significant pester-power influence of the child. In Case Study 3d, we are introduced to the covert tactic that Nestle Australia adopted to introduce children to Nesquick in an entertaining manner that engages the child with the brand. The problem is, however, that it occurs in the sanctuary of the child-care environment and occurs without the child's really knowing what is happening: the child is receiving persuasive communication dressed as entertainment.

In the current consumer environment that features a plethora of competing brands and a more consumer-savvy consumer, brands need to be more creative in the ways in which they converse with their targets. Thus we find contemporary brands being far more fluid in their relationship with their customers. A presence in the media is essential, but so too is a presence in the life and community of the consumer. Advertisers therefore attempt to develop associations between brands and institutions, culture, and issues of importance to their targeted audiences of consumers. Brands such as Nike and McDonald's have developed relationships with universities and charities, as part of this integrated strategy, and the sponsoring of sporting and cultural events plays an important role in this strategy.

This is the "New Branded World" that Naomi Klein refers to in her book *No Logo.* "Advertising and sponsorship have always been about using imagery to equate products with positive cultural or social experiences. What makes nineties-style branding different is that it increasingly seeks to take these associations out of the representational realm and make it a lived reality."[43] She believes that the intent is "not to sponsor the culture but be the culture," and this strategy has been "so successful that the lines between corporate sponsors and sponsored culture have entirely disappeared"[44] (see Case Study 3e).

The evidence is everywhere. In Australia (where the national sport is cricket), the major domestic cricket competition is called the Pura Cup (Pura being a brand of dairy products), which replaced the iconic Sheffield Shield that carried 107 years of tradition and culture. This example would be similar to the U.S. World

Series Baseball competition being rebranded as the Wal-Mart Baseball Series. This level of cultural ownership by modern brands was never more prominent than the "Coca Cola–lisation" of the Atlanta Olympics.

The contemporary brands must be flexible and fluid to adapt to the multiple environments that they must cohabit with their customers. They are "less concerned with uniformity, more with diversity. It is less about dominating the visual landscape with an iron hand and more about providing a rich, multi-sensory experience which speaks with consumers, instead of shouting at them."[45]

Brands must understand that if they aren't tuned in to their local environment and their users' needs, they risk being viewed at best as irrelevant.[46] Therefore, they must understand the community that they live in, whether that is an on-line community or an off-line community. As we discuss in Chapter 8, both worlds play critical roles in the contemporary consumer environment, as both worlds have a role to play in targeting the multifaceted interests of their customers. This is the strategy of Integrated Communication or 360 degree branding, which targets consumers and permeates their world.

ETHICAL ANALYSIS

As we saw in Chapter 1, we as individuals have, in accordance with the Principle of Generic Consistency (PGC), personal rights to freedom and well-being and concomitant ethical responsibilities to respect the rights of freedom and well-being of other people. We also have under Kant's Categorical Imperative principle ("The Kingdom of Ends" formulation) a moral obligation to treat other people always as ends in themselves worthy of respect in their own right and never merely as a means in the pursuit of our own self-interested ends.

The same two principles, however, also bestow upon us certain moral obligations that we have toward our respective communities— moral obligations that we all share collectively as members of those communities. For example, we all have a collective moral responsibility to obey traffic regulations, to avoid smoking in public places where nonsmokers may be adversely affected through passive smoking, to pay our taxes, to reduce speed when driving through residential and school areas, to not drink and drive, to not pollute the environment, to participate in the electoral system, to save water when advised to by the government during times of drought, and to help our neighbors and fellow citizens when they need our help when we can do so with minimal cost to ourselves. The driving idea behind these collective moral responsibilities is that their fulfillment leads to the overall greater good of society, an idea that it is in keeping with the consequentialist moral considerations that we encountered in Chapter 1: namely, that an action is morally determined by either the overall good or happiness for the greatest number of people that results from a particular action or the overall harm for the greatest number of people that can be avoided or reduced through the commission or omission of a particular action.

As we also saw from Chapter 1, professionals have certain ethical commitments emanating from the role morality of the profession or institution of which they are members. For example, police officers have the right to, and are indeed required by their role morality, to apprehend, arrest, and take into custody persons suspected of having committed a crime, a right that is not available to ordinary citizens. However, as we also saw in Chapter 1, the role morality of any profession or institution cannot overrule the demands of universal public morality to which all people are committed regardless of their personal or professional role morality and must in fact give way to universal public morality when the two moralities come into conflict. So, for example, police officers cannot fabricate evidence and obtain false confessions for the purpose of securing convictions of suspects, for doing so would constitute a violation of the suspects' rights to a fair trial, as well as corruption of the criminal justice system that recognizes that suspects have a right to a fair trial and are presumed innocent until proven guilty.

Similarly, by parity of argument, advertisers also have moral obligations to their respective communities that may require them to avoid certain professional or institutional practices, even if such practices are allowed by their role morality, if such practices undermine the public good and violate the requirements and interests of universal public morality.

In determining what are the ethical obligations that advertisers and the advertising industry generally have to the community, we will examine the moral obligations that advertisers have with regard to the advertising strategy of targeting, as this is a manifold strategy that targets various groups within the community and thus has ethical relevance and consequences for the whole community.

In ethically analyzing the strategy of targeting, we will first look at what might be ethically problematic about targeting from a deontological perspective. We will then examine why targeting might be ethically objectionable from a consequentialist perspective (for deontological and consequentialist ethical considerations, see Chapter 1) by exploring the ways in which particular vulnerable groups of individuals can be harmed by targeting that ultimately undermines the overall good of the whole community. Insofar as it can be shown that certain targeting strategies are not only harmful to individual persons or groups of persons but also harmful to the whole community, such strategies should be abandoned or regulated, either internally by the advertising industry itself, or externally by government regulation through appropriate sanctions.

However, as indicated in Chapter 1 and reinforced in Chapters 2 and 9, the preferred option is professional self-regulation, since this is in keeping with our overall conception of professional self-regulation as a form of *ethical self-regulation* that ultimately is what defines ethical conduct: ethical self-regulation of the individual, of an organization, of an institution, and of society. Conceived as a form of ethical self-regulation, professional regulation becomes self-administered and internal as ethical motivation provides its own internal ethical compliance that when maximal, obviates the need for any external regulative compliance (see Chapter 1).

So what is wrong with target advertising? By examining the issues in Case Study 3a, "Consuming Children," we can make the systematic ethical observations that follow.

Brand Loyalty, Ethical Disloyalty

Conceptually, the association of "loyalty" with consumer brands is a perversion and corruption of the aspirational value of loyalty. Loyalty is a highly valued relationship like love and affection that exists or can exist between people and perhaps between people and other sentient beings like, for example, domesticated animals that people keep as pets. Being in a reciprocal relationship, as most relationships are, people can be loyal to other people and/or to their pets in the expectation and hope that other people and/or their pets will be loyal to them. An inanimate consumer product or brand, by contrast, is incapable of being "loyal" to its owner, and it is conceptually difficult, if not absurd, to see how people can, in any real sense, be loyal to consumer products. This kind of "loyalty" has very little or nothing to do with the robust notion of the aspirational and reciprocal value of loyalty, as socially understood. Moreover, loyalty to an inanimate "brand" has similarly no real significance, since a brand is just a name or a logo that stands as a placeholder for certain particular inanimate consumer products.

Perhaps, however, we have been too literal and harsh about the use of the term "brand loyalty." "Loyalty" with regard to brands may be used in a metaphorical and loose sense to signal a relationship of pseudoloyalty or quasi-loyalty that advertisers and marketers aspire to implant and engender in consumers with regard to certain products they wish to promote. On the positive side, it can be understood as the implicit promise communicated to the consumer by the advertiser that there exists a certain consistency of content, quality, and price between products or services of the same brand. "Brand loyalty" used in this sense could simply mean a fixed disposition to purchase goods or services of a particular brand that the consumer perceives to be of a certain reliable and trustworthy quality. On the negative side, it could be understood as the attempt by unscrupulous advertisers and marketers to implant and engender an uncritical commodity fetish or an impulsive and perhaps compulsive fixation to certain products and services in impressionable and vulnerable groups of consumers, such as teenagers and children, through manipulative branding.

Hence, the application of the term "loyalty" to brands that merely stand for certain inanimate consumer products has no evaluative or ethical resonance in itself, and it is merely a perversion and corruption of this significant aspirational value for purely commercial and instrumental reasons. The term can, however, be used in a metaphorical and quasi-sense in the manner indicated before, either in a positive or in a negative way.

"Loyalty" may be created to brands of products that may not be good for the consumers themselves. For example, creating loyalty in children to junk food may cause obesity in children, which is not good for the children themselves, their parents, and the community at large

(see Case Study 3b). This practice is ethically wrong for at least two reasons:

1. In general, advertising that specifically targets certain vulnerable social groups, such as children, treats those groups as consumers, not as ends in themselves, but merely as means for the advertisers' and their clients' primary end or objective of promoting consumer products. Insofar as it does so, advertising treats those people with a lack of moral consideration that they are owed by virtue of being human beings who are inherently worthy of respect as ends in themselves. This practice violates Immanuel Kant's Categorical Imperative (CI), namely, to "treat humanity in your person or in the person of any other never simply as a means but always at the same time as an end" (The "Kingdom of Ends" formulation of the CI—see Chapter 1).

2. An issue related to the one above is that the attempt to create brand loyalty to products that may be harmful to the consumers targeted does not have the consumers' *best interest* at heart. Quite on the contrary, the attempt to elicit the consumers' loyalty to products that may be harmful to them undermines the consumers' interest, and by extension that, of the whole community. Previously, advertising tobacco campaigns that targeted young people in the hope of aligning them to a particular brand of cigarettes is a case in point. Equally, insofar as advertising of junk food and confectionery that targets children leads to obesity, as children may be encouraged by these ads to adopt a high fat and sugar diet that is in the long term detrimental to their health, then such ads not only do not have the children's best interest at heart but also, on the contrary, undermine their interest by undermining their health. By undermining the children's interest in health, an interest that is not only restricted to the children themselves and their families, but as Case Study 3b indicates, an interest that concerns the whole community (as obesity generally and children's obesity in particular is a communal health concern), advertising undermines the interest of the whole community.

Similarly, advertising that targets young men, as in Case Study 3c, and that encourages them to consume ever more alcohol through associating the consumption of alcohol to good friends and sport is ethically irresponsible if it results, as sometimes it may, in drinking and driving offenses, other antisocial and violent behavior, and other criminal alcohol-induced violations.

The crucial point, as before, is that these alcohol ads that target young men and young people generally through associating alcohol with things that young people generally value, such as friends and sport, do not have the best interest of the targeted group at heart but rather the interest of the profit-orientated promotion of consumer products—alcohol in this case—regardless of how those ads and the products they promote may or may nor serve the best interests of the targeted groups. Simply put, advertising as described here does not display any care about the effect that these ads may have on the interests of the targeted groups and, by extension, on the overall interest of the community at large that has to deal with the harmful consequences of obesity and alcohol abuse.

Government advertising of the sort illustrated by Case Study 3f does, by contrast, have the best interest of the targeted audiences at heart even when it uses shock tactics as in some of the Road Traffic Authority ads discussed in Chapter 9. These ads seek to encourage drivers to drive more safely and thus to avoid harm to themselves and to others, which is in the interest not only of the targeted groups but also in the collective interest of the whole community, since road accidents can, potentially at least, adversely affect everyone.

In Case Study 3f, the Slip Slop Slap ad, which targets the Australian community, including children, unlike the junk food and alcohol ads discussed earlier, treats the members of its targeted audience not merely as means but as ends, since they are primarily aimed to benefit the interests of the citizens themselves. Unlike the unethical advertising that targets children with junk food and young people with alcohol consumption—ads that may not be in their interest or the interest of the community—government advertising, by contrast, that seeks to educate its citizens about the dangers of skin cancer or unsafe driving practices that can result in injury or death, is ethical advertising because it is conducted with the interest of the targeted audience at heart, namely the citizens.

This discussion so far illustrates the fundamental difference between persuasion and information as communication strategies, a difference that lies at the heart of the hybrid nature of advertising that is, as indicated throughout this book, inherently ethically problematic. On the one hand, commercial advertising seeks to *persuade* consumers through various tactics to feel predisposed to various consumer brands by approaching people as mere *consumers,* whereas on the other hand, government advertising that seeks to *inform* people about matters of public interest approaches people as *citizens.* The ethical problem with commercial advertising is that the persuasion that it sometimes provides under the guise of "information" is not only misleading and deceptive, but also, as in the case of the targeting of vulnerable groups such as children, it can have harmful consequences both for the targeted groups as well as for the community as a whole. And that is ethically objectionable and thus unacceptable.

Brand Sharing: Children Beware When Advertisers Come Bearing Gifts

"For the marketer it's creating affinity for the brand. For parents, the kid is learning to count. There's no downside"
(Julie Halpin, *CEO of WPP Group's Geppeto Group, in New York*).

In addition to the ethical problems with brand loyalty examined earlier, there are a few related ethical problems associated with brand sharing (see Case Study 3a). The association of bad, at least potentially bad, products such as junk food with good products such as books to encourage kids to consume more junk food is particularly ethically objectionable because it is dishonest, since it is intended to manipulate and deceive.

1. *Manipulation:* Children are manipulated to go to certain outlets such as Burger King to consume junk food through the lure of toys or to purchase and consume sugar-saturated cereals through the lure of books, with a likely result in obesity. Alternatively, children as in Case Study 3d are targeted by advertisers in the sanctuary of their play pens with gimmicks like Nesquick, which are primarily designed to entice children to consume more candy. Again, this practice is not for the children's good but for the commercial good of the advertisers. This double-dealing—offering something good like books for the primary objective of enticing children to consume something potentially bad like junk food that can result in obesity and poor health for the primary interests of advertisers and the junk food manufacturers—is ethically objectionable.

2. *Deception:* Like the intentions of the makers of the Trojan horse, the intentions and motives of the advertisers do not match their deeds, which are designed to benefit not the children but themselves. And like the Trojans who fell for the Greeks' deceit to their ultimate doom, so too the unsuspecting children fall for the advertisers' deceit to the potential detriment of their health. Children, beware when advertisers come bearing gifts!

Both manipulation and deception are morally wrong deontologically because they treat others merely as means and not as ends, in direct violation of Kant's Categorical Imperative, as well as in violation of the Principle of Generic Consistency, since manipulation and deception violate the generic rights of freedom and of well-being of those who are manipulated and deceived. Moreover, the targeting strategy of enticing and

encouraging children to consume junk food that may potentially lead to obesity is also consequentially morally wrong, since the consequences of obesity for the children, their parents, and society at large are harmful. So all in all, there is a serious downside to enticing and manipulating children to consume junk food, and the downside is morally significant enough to warrant the regulation of such practices either internally by the industry itself or externally by government regulation through actionable sanctions, as in the case of tobacco advertising.

Deception in adverting also violates, as we saw in Chapter 2, one of the five basic universal principles of the adverting industry, namely, the avoidance of misrepresentation and deception; therefore, deceptive advertising practices generally, and specifically the ones discussed in this chapter, not only violate the principles of universal public morality but also violate the principle of the advertising industry's own role morality. For both these reasons, deception in advertising is ethically unacceptable and should thus be avoided.

A SUMMARY OF INSTRUMENTAL AND ETHICAL CONSEQUENCES

Desirable

1. Targeting is an effective advertising strategy because, like a heat-seeking missile, its communication messages are tailor-made to fit and track the marketing profiles of its targeted consumer groups. As such, it is, from a technical and professional perspective at least, instrumentally desirable. Moreover, in the case of government-sponsored advertising campaigns, such as the "slip slop slap" campaign that we examined in Case Study 3e and others like it that are designed to inform citizens of the harmful consequences of various habits and activities like smoking, drinking and driving, speeding, and

alcohol abuse, target advertising is, insofar as it is effective, also ethically desirable, since it can result in overall good consequences for the whole of society.

Undesirable

1. The targeting of vulnerable and impressionable groups such as children with the marketing promotion of high fat and sugar-saturated foods that have little nutritional value and whose consumption has been steadily leading to alarming levels of obesity in children (see Case Studies 3b, 3c, and 3d) and the targeting of young people with attractively packaged and seductively named alcoholic drinks that look innocuously more like soft drinks and that have the effect of encouraging young people to binge-drink beyond moderation, are ethically undesirable advertising practices.

   Even if such practices as effective advertising strategies are from a business perspective instrumentally desirable and in keeping with the ultimate goal of advertising of favorably predisposing the targeted audiences toward the advertised products, these practices are ethically undesirable if they have a tendency to actually or potentially result in harmful consequences for the targeted audiences. Moreover, insofar as obesity and excessive alcohol consumption are harmful to people's health, they are also harmful to society at large, not least because of the financial health costs that society as a whole has to shoulder.

2. The targeting of vulnerable and impressionable groups such as children and young people by advertising and marketing is effectively using the members of these groups merely as means to the end of promoting the sale of consumer products whose consumption is potentially harmful to those targeted groups. Both deontologically and consequentially this practice is ethically unacceptable and thus ethically undesirable. Even if the exploitation of vulnerable groups of people through targeting is allowed by the role morality of advertising, universal public morality that trumps role morality when the two come into conflict (see Chapter 1) precludes the exploitation of people as means merely for the end of promoting the sale of consumer goods. Because people are clearly inherently more valuable than commodities, advertisers as members of the community should desist from exploiting the vulnerabilities of their fellow citizens merely for their own financial self-interest.

3. Moreover, the exploitation of people by advertisers though targeting that can potentially harm them can also harm the instrumental interests of the advertisers themselves by creating an image of corporate moral irresponsibility in the public mind. Insofar as the exploitation of the targeted groups is designed to enhance the instrumental interests of the advertisers engaging in these types of potentially harmful targeting, this is a self-defeating and thus an instrumentally undesirable strategy that is best avoided both for instrumental and for ethical reasons.

In conclusion, the preceding ethical balance sheet indicates that overall, the advertising strategy of targeting vulnerable and impressionable groups of people that can potentially result in harming them in some way and, by extension, in harming society at large, is both instrumentally and ethically undesirable and should thus be avoided.

chapter four

Truth in Advertising

INTRODUCTION

What role, if any, does truth play in advertising? Insofar as the role of advertising is to present consumer products or services in a way that persuades people to buy them or at least feel positively predisposed to those products or services, advertising often seeks to persuade primarily by an appeal to sentiment rather by an appeal to intellect. Some examples are ads that associate products with feelings of well-being, fun, humor, freedom, romance, glamour, and friends and family, such as those ads used by Coca-Cola and Pepsi, some beer and other alcohol producers, McDonald's, and car and cosmetics manufacturers.

If that is the role of advertising and if it can achieve that role without having to be truthful, why be truthful, especially since on the whole, most people do not perceive ads as truthful depictions of reality. Often they are not truthful and are not designed to be so. Quite a few ads operate at the fictional and metaphorical levels. Others work by the association of disparate and incongruous images. In those cases, the ads are not intended as true representations of reality or as narratives that correspond to the truth, but rather as rhetorical and metaphorical evocations that are designed to appeal to the consumers' emotions and aspirations for the purpose of creating positive and alluring images for the products in the minds of the consumers.

This chapter will examine the relevance and scope of truth in advertising. The absence, suppression, manipulation, subversion, or mere suspension of truth through suspension of disbelief in advertisements that use fictional and fantastic images or metaphorical images will be addressed.

Perhaps truth is simply not relevant in such advertisements. By contrast, truth in "real-life" ads, endorsements, testimonials, and straightforward product description intended to convey accurate information about a product or service, is relevant and ethically necessary. The relation and difference between deception and suspension of disbelief and its ethical impact with regard to some specific typical advertisements will be examined and illustrated.

CASE STUDIES

CASE STUDY 4A   British Airways, "The World's Favorite Airline"[47]

"The World's Favorite Airline" is one of the most famous slogans in advertising, but is British Airways really the world's favorite airline? How can BA make this claim? And from a consumer's perspective, does it really matter? Well, it certainly mattered to competitor Virgin Atlantic. In 1999, Richard Branson's airline attempted to have two key U.K. regulatory bodies, the Advertising Standards Authority (ASA) and the Independent Television Commission (ITC) ban the slogan on the basis that it was untruthful.

The slogan has been part of BA's brand armory since 1983 and is a registered trademark. The company therefore continues to present an ownership argument, that the phrase is synonymous with British Airways and that its usage no longer requires justification.

The UK's advertising regulatory body ASA has consistently supported BA's argument that the fact that it flies more international passengers than any other carrier justifies its continued use of the slogan but rejected the argument that the claim did not require justification.

During the 1999 complaints process, BA substantiated its claim of world's favorite airline by citing figures to support the fact that it carried more international passengers than any other airline. They used International Air Transport Association figures showing that BA flew 28 million passengers in 1997, 5 million more than Lufthansa, the second biggest international carrier.[48] They also pointed out that they flew to more countries than any other airlines. Because the claim's context was the world, domestic markets and figures were considered not relevant to the claim and were not considered. The authority acknowledged that BA carried more international passengers than did any other airlines and considered that the claim was justified and thus did not object to the advertiser's continued use of the claim.

British Airways's slogan connotes that passengers have a preference for their airline, and this subjectivity is difficult to qualify. For example, how many BA passengers use the airline simply because it offers the right flight at the right time? How many passengers on competitor airlines would prefer to be on BA, but situational factors such as flight availability and fare costs are a barrier?

The bout between Virgin's and BA's use of puffery became one of semantics with the ASA as referee, and in the end, rational facts were skewed to support a subjective claim. Such is the "adjudication minefield" that upholds truth in advertising.

CASE STUDY 4B   Reading the Fine Print[49]

In May 2000, the Advertising Standards Authority (ASA) in the United Kingdom upheld a public complaint against a national press advertisement for Daewoo cars. The press advertisement featured the headline "Daewoo Admits Price Fixing." The copy stated, "We're proud to admit our prices are fixed up to 30% lower than competitors' models with the same specification." The complainant challenged whether the advertisers could substantiate the claim. In their defense, the advertisers stated that they had calculated the price differential between their cars and other cars available in the United Kingdom, using independent data on price and specification.

The ASA conducted their own comparisons and noted that the advertiser's cars were often more expensive than those of some manufacturers and that buyers could negotiate price reductions with car dealers for other manufacturers' cars but not with the advertiser's. Because one manufacturer's cars were cheaper than the equivalent Daewoo, the authority considered that the claim was misleading and asked the advertisers to change it.

In April 2001, the ASA addressed a public complaint against a national press advertisement for Fiat cars that pictured the Fiat Multipla. The ad stated, "Fiat On The Road Prices Lowered By Up To 13%*" next to a ticked box. A footnote stated, "*Up to 13% reduction on standard on the road (OTR) prices effective from 1st December 2000, 13% reduction applies to Fiat Barchetta 1.8 16V. Car shown Multipla ELX reduced by 1%." The complainant objected that the price reduction claim was misleading because it did not relate to the car pictured in the advertisement. The authority considered that to feature a car that was eligible for a price reduction of 1 percent below the claim "prices lowered by up to 13%" was misleading. It told the advertisers not to use the advertisement again.

During 2001 in Australia, retailer Target experienced the embarrassment of having to run corrective advertising as a result of being found guilty of breaches of the Trade Practices Act. The breaches involved a television campaign in which Target advertised 25 to 40 percent off "every stitch of clothing" but in small print excluded underwear and socks, which it classified as accessories. Another ad involved 15 to 40 percent off housewares but excluded manchester (household linen). The fine print exclusions were considered to mislead consumers, many of whom were enticed to the stores by sales, only to find that the sales were heavily qualified.

Australian Competition and Consumer Commission (ACCC) chairman Allan Fels expressed concern about the "too common a practice in retailing to have big, bold, spectacular ads that are qualified but with the qualifications typically invisible to the ordinary customer." In their corrective advertising, which ran nationally throughout Australia on television and the print media, Target agreed that their advertisements were misleading in that they failed to adequately inform consumers.

These are three examples of acknowledged misleading advertising, in which advertisers had not made the full story obvious to consumers. Fine print, irrelevant images, and just plain incorrect facts are all examples of the types of transgressions that consumers have grown to become wary of when studying persuasive communications. These misrepresentations of the truth are overt and can be rationally adjudicated upon. Their tendency to mislead and deceive consumers has unwelcome and undesirable consequences that provide regulatory bodies with most of their controlling activity.

Case Study 4c Nothing Real about Reality Advertising[50]

The advertising agency Mojo Partners bought film footage of the San Antonio floods in Texas and used it to dramatize a Telstra (the largest national telecommunication company in Australia) commercial featuring the 1997 floods at Katherine in the Northern Territories, Australia. In particular, they used the image of Melanie Finley, a 14-year-old girl who died in the U.S. floods several years before the Katherine disaster. Permission to use pictures of Melanie Finley was not obtained, nor was permission to use pictures of Katherine residents. Understandably, Melanie's parents were distressed to find that their daughter's picture, taken just moments before her death, was used in an advertisement for commercial purposes. So were the residents of Katherine whose pictures were taken and used in the same commercial without their permission. The advertisement was subsequently removed from circulation by Telstra. Mojo Partners issued a public apology and claimed that they weren't aware of Melanie's subsequent death. In Australia, there is no legal obligation to obtain consent before using a person's picture in a publication.

PROFESSIONAL PRACTICE

Introduction

Seventy-four percent of American consumers either "strongly" or "somewhat strongly" believe that "most advertisements deliberately stretch the truth about the products they advertise," claims an article in *Adweek*.[51] This is a statistic that wouldn't really surprise most consumers around the world, since advertising is a form of communication that does its best to make truth a minor criterion for judging its worth. As a communication genre, it wants you to believe and dispel belief in the same breath.

In this chapter, we look at the critical elements in the advertising process that push the boundaries of social responsibility in terms of producing "truthful" advertising. We also propose what is considered to be the critical parameters of acceptability for truthfulness in advertising. What harm is there in British Airways's claiming to be "The World's Favorite Airline" as opposed to Target's claiming a particular "price off" without qualifying the conditions, or a weight-loss company's guaranteeing a weight reduction result in the order of "44 pounds in 30 days" as per their testimonial claims?

There is a definite distinction between problematic untruth and harmless untruth.

Message Strategy and Advertising Claims—The Context for Truth in Advertising

The proliferation of brands and advertisers competing for space in the consumer's mind has meant that achieving communication breakthrough and brand preference has become a more difficult task. Similarly, the advertisers' quest for a sustainable point of difference for their brands has become more demanding. For some it is a calculated decision to use an emotional battleground, whereas for others, rational territory becomes the competitive frame. Advertising strategists and architects ask the question, to achieve breakthrough, will we appeal to the heart or the head? For each of these battlefields of competition comes a particular message strategy and associated claims about brands. These claims will be either subjective or objective. For example, Volvo's rational claims are founded on the objective arguments of safety. These claims are supported by qualified evidence that safety benefits are a key feature of Volvo cars. The claims are supported by proofs such as armored plating applied during the body painting process, independent research on automobile safety records, and so on. This message strategy is designed to firmly position Volvo in the consumer's mind as a safety-first automobile company.[52]

If a clear, rational sustainable point of difference cannot be established for a product or brand, then a more intangible set of arguments is presented to consumers that appeals to more emotive triggers. Nike's "just do it" appeals to the emotional connection with sporting endeavor rather than to the pursuit of the ultimate athletic footwear—a choice to position the brand as one that knows what it takes to win. In this situation, proof or support for claims becomes less critical in the eye of the consumer and the regulator.

The type of message strategy or advertising claims that an advertiser adopts sets the context for compliance to ethical (and legal) codes relating to truth in advertising. An objective claim obviously requires substantiation in order to be accepted by regulators. Only some consumers will actually seek out this substantiation. A subjective claim based on more intangible arguments, such as image and attitude conveyed in the communication, will provide a more tenuous reason to believe the claim.

Advertising tactics have become more complex and covert as a result of a number of competitive factors, including proliferation of new products and brands, proliferation of media options, growing product parity, and more communication-savvy consumers. Advertising strategy is being pressured to break the existing boundaries, and regulators constantly observe, adjudicate, and adjust.

Guidelines and Measures for Truth in Advertising

As a result of the pressures on advertisers to gain a competitive advantage, regulatory bodies over time have developed sets of codes and practices to make advertisers comply with a set of community standards. In essence, these are intended and designed to protect consumers from misleading claims, by diminishing the degree of claim exaggeration, or puffery, in advertising messages. The following excerpt from the British Codes of Advertising and Sales Promotion is representative of the parameters established to create a more truthful and socially acceptable advertising environment.[53]

Advertising Code

Principles
(2.1) All advertisements should be legal, decent, honest, and truthful.

Truthfulness
(7.1) No advertisement should mislead by inaccuracy, ambiguity, exaggeration, omission, or otherwise.

Honesty, truth, and accuracy are key factors in the adjudication of misleading claims in advertising. As demonstrated in the British Airways case, there was no intention to deliberately mislead consumers, and the advertiser offered substantiation for its debatable claim. On the other hand, the advertisers in Case Study 4b fell foul of their regulatory bodies because of the inaccuracy and ambiguity overt in their claims that ultimately deceived consumers and posed far more harmful consequences.

In the United States, the Federal Trade Commission (FTC) (the consumers' protector from unfair or deceptive acts) has been particularly proactive in weeding out deception in advertising, ensuring that objective advertising claims be truthful and substantiated. In 2002, the commission deliberately targeted dubious claims made in weight-loss advertising and identified a surge in commission challenges to claims made in advertisements over a 10-year-period.[54] The commission elected to direct magazine publishers to prescreen weight-loss advertising. It is the factual and "real-life" context of weight-loss advertising that makes its claims even more harmful and problematic to consumers.

According to the FTC's Deception Policy Statement,[55] an ad is deceptive if it contains a statement or omits information that

- is likely to mislead consumers acting reasonably under the circumstances; and
- is "material," that is, important to a consumer's decision to buy or use the product.

From this statement it is clear where the FTC draws the line in terms of the type of untruth it deems to be most harmful and the consequence it perceives to be most critical.

When Truth Is a Problem

An advertisement that is not literally true is not the key issue, but an advertisement that is designed to deceive or mislead a consumer is a different matter. This is the situation in which the use of puffery in advertising comes under scrutiny. Puffery, which is a common practice in advertising, is not considered illegal. It is the key reason why consumers have the expectation that advertising will stretch the truth rather than express the truth.

In essence, the notion of puffery refers to exaggerated claims, comments, commendations, or hyperbole, and in its most common usage, puffery is based on subjective views and opinions. It is generally considered to be part of the artfulness and playfulness of advertising and as such is not considered to be taken very seriously by reasonable consumers. It is for this reason that most regulatory bodies disregard it as a code-violating activity. In the United States, the FTC makes this view clear in its own definition of puffery or puffing[56] as "an expression of opinion not made as a representation of fact," and as a result, puffery is generally not acted upon by the commission.

Metaphors, similes, and exaggerations are considered to be accepted by consumers, who are now more than familiar with the genre, as less than harmful. Misinformation and unsubstantiated claims pose a more critical set of problems that have made the practice not only unethical but also illegal.

The advertising process is based on strategic thinking, which by definition connotes a sense of warfare and aggressive competitive activity. This strategic approach involves an understanding of the competitor environment, the consumer environment, and the product environment. From this understanding, a plan of attack develops. This plan is generally communicated via a strategy statement or brief from which creative executions are created.

As previously discussed, a strategy sets the direction or focus for the advertising, from which the "creatives" apply their trade and devices to achieve the communication's objective(s). It is at this stage of the process at which truth is really tested. The creative framing of the advertising proposition will establish the environment upon which consumers and regulators will often judge the message's authenticity.

The advertising architect's role is to bring a claim to life or even to bring it to larger than life, as the case may be. A basic principle or technique of creative strategy is to dramatize the benefit offered by the product. This principle, by its very nature, challenges the notion of truthfulness in advertising.

Nike's "the wall" advertisement from 1994 uses an animated sequence in which a London poster of a famous soccer player comes to life and strikes a ball that arrives in Paris, where it is received by another animated poster of a famous French player who comes to life and who then strikes the ball to Berlin, and so forth. This is clearly a dramatization that stretches the truth and plausibility, but the frame that is set by the animation genre allows the puffery or exaggeration to be accepted by the audience.

In Australia, a print campaign for a dog-obedience-training center called Adelar simply featured the image of a dog standing on two legs at a public urinal. It is a clearly untruthful image, but one that represents the advertiser's claim that Adelar understands that some people treat their dogs like humans and that Adelar does also. The overt exaggeration in this image dramatizes a benefit rather than attempting to mislead, and this communication intent is unquestionably recognized by its audience.

In contrast, the campaign by Australia telecommunications company Telstra, which featured dramatic footage of floods in the central Australian region around Katherine, thereby establishing a real-life context for their claim "making life easier," provided both the claim and the brand with the desired credibility, while dramatizing the benefit of that claim. Unfortunately, as mentioned earlier, the footage featured actual material from Texas floods, in particular the footage of a young girl who later drowned in those floods.

This creative execution was produced in a form in which truth was important, and thus the dramatization was in itself a deception.

This example also raises questions about the role of visuals in advertising and their potential to deceive. Images of models with stunning hair quality as a result of using brand X shampoo may dramatize the benefit of the product and lend credibility to the brand's claim (particularly if the model is a celebrity), but is the stunning hair quality representative of the general results achieved using the brand? Also, the before-and-after images of the typical person who has undertaken a particular weight-loss program may dramatize the advertising claim, but is that result representative of the general results achieved using that program?

As demonstrated in Case Study 4b, Fiat's use of a particular model of vehicle in its advertising imagery would certainly attract attention to the advertising claim, but the fact that the image had little relationship to the advertising claim became its fatal flaw in a clear case of deception.

ETHICAL ANALYSIS

Before we examine the ethical relevance of truth in advertising, it is important to get clear about what we mean by "truth." At least since the time when Pontius Pilate asked Jesus what truth is, philosophers have written volumes in trying to answer that question. Luckily for us, we do not have to go that far, since we can simply accept, for our purposes at least, the common garden variety of truth, namely, the notion of truth that relates to facts. That Washington, D.C., and Canberra are the present capitals of the United States and Australia respectively are two indisputable facts. People can, of course, argue whether they *should* be the capitals of those two countries and may wish that, contrary to fact, New York and Sydney were the respective capitals of the Unites States and Australia. However,

wishing that something were so does not make it so. The fact remains that at present and until such time that there is a change, Washington, D.C., and Canberra are, whether we like it or not, the respective capitals of the United States and Australia.

Generally, facts are what they are irrespective of our wishes, subjective opinions, or judgments about them. They are true by virtue of their relation to an independent reality—by how things just are in the world. And facts can be true simply by virtue of their relation to the physical reality, such as that water comprises two molecules of hydrogen and one molecule of oxygen; or by virtue of their relation to a conventional reality, such as that traffic stops at a red light and moves at a green light. A philosophical definition of "truth," one that is in keeping with our common garden variety notion of truth, is known as the correspondence theory of truth. According to that theory, "truth" is a relationship between sentences or propositions in language and the world or reality. For example: "Canberra is the capital of Australia" (sentence "S") is true just because sentence "S" corresponds to reality. It corresponds to how things are in the world. In Australia, the city called Canberra is, as a matter of fact, the capital of Australia. It is because of that very fact that the sentence "S" is true.

Truth plays a central role in the communication of information, because by its very nature, information must be true to be valuable and useful. Information that is not true, like a pen that doesn't write, has no value; moreover, if information is untrue or false, it can potentially cause harm to people who rely on that information. But what exactly is information? By definition,

*"Information is communication
of instructive knowledge."*

Notice, however, that though simple, this definition has provided us with an answer to our question "what is information?" in terms of another undefined term, namely, "knowledge." So what is knowledge? For a definition of knowledge, we now have to refer to philosophy. A philosophical definition of knowledge—one that is found in Plato's dialogue *Theatetus*—is the following:

"Knowledge is Justified True Belief."

According to this definition of knowledge, a knowledge claim or any statement or proposition must be attended by the following three necessary conditions, otherwise it wouldn't be knowledge:

1. It must be believed by someone.
2. The belief must be justified.
3. The belief must be true.

For a statement, an opinion, a claim, or a judgment to qualify as knowledge, all three conditions must be present.

A belief that is justified, on the basis of some plausible account or explanation, but that is not true, would not qualify as knowledge. Take, for example, the statement "The sun moves up and down (rises and sets) in relation to the earth." If you believed this was the case, you would no doubt believe this statement on the evidence provided by your own eyesight. It does, after all, seem as if the sun rises and sets: that evidence would provide some initial justification for your belief. Moreover, if you had no other available information regarding this matter (and people prior to Copernicus and Galileo didn't have), then the justification for your belief, based on the evidence of your senses, would seem reasonable. But, of course, your belief would not be true, and therefore your belief, though justified to some degree, would not qualify as knowledge, since contrary to appearances, it is the earth that moves in relation to the sun and not the other way around.

Alternatively, you may hold a true belief that doesn't qualify as knowledge, because your belief, though true, is not justified. For example, you may have dreamed that the horse Firecracker will win the third race. On the basis of your dream, you place a bet on Firecracker, and he wins. Did you have knowledge that Firecracker would win? You certainly believed that he would, and as a matter of fact, he in truth did win. However, your true belief does not qualify as knowledge because dreams as a rule are not *reliable* and *credible* sources of knowledge and cannot, therefore, provide adequate epistemological ("epistemology" is the philosophical term for the "science of knowledge") justification for one's opinions, claims, or judgments.

Alternatively, you still may be a skeptic or an agnostic and thus entertain no beliefs about anything. In the absence of any beliefs, you would have no knowledge, since you would lack one of the necessary conditions of knowledge, namely, belief. Or like Socrates, you may entertain the one single belief that you know nothing.

Given the preceding definitions of truth, information, and knowledge, *is truth relevant to advertising?* To answer that question, we first need to ask another question and then offer the following for our answer: What is the ultimate role of advertising?

Simply put (and hopefully not too simplistically), the ultimate role of advertising is the presentation and promotion of consumer products and services for the purpose of persuading consumers to purchase them or at least to persuade them to think favorably of them.

What does instrumental rationality counsel with regard to fulfilling that role?

Advertisers should employ the most effective persuasive means or strategies in fulfilling that goal (unless specified otherwise, we use the term "advertisers" to refer to both the advertising agencies and their advertising clients, usually the manufacturers of the products or providers of the services advertised). The more effective the persuasive means, the better.

What are possibly some of the most persuasively effective means or strategies that advertisers can use in conveying information about a product or a service to consumers?

1. Provide complete and true information about the product or service advertised.

2. Present the product or service advertised in the best and most attractive possible light. Maximize the appeal of the product or service to the consumer.

3. Instead of focusing on the product or service, advertising should focus on the consumer. Create in the consumer positive feelings and thoughts about the product or service advertised. This outcome could be achieved by creating an association of positive feelings in the consumer between the product or service and the consumer. Alternatively, it could be achieved by creating an association of negative feelings between the consumer and the absence or lack of the consumer product or service—the feel-good or feel-bad strategy.

Example: Advertisements of Cosmetics:

"Use the product and you will look as beautiful and youthful"

or

"Use the product and you will get rid of ageing wrinkles. Wrinkles are bad because they make you look old, and therefore they should be made to vanish. This product makes vanishing possible."

These types of statements may not, of course, be specified explicitly but merely suggested by the images and associations in the advertisements.

Let us consider each possible persuasive strategy in turn:

1.1. Works only if the product is up to it and the statement is actually true. Advertising Rolls Royce as the most luxurious and prestigious car in the world, for example, could be persuasive because, as a matter of fact, it happens to be true; or for the sake of argument, since this is only an example, let us assume that it is true.

1.2. Won't work for products that are not up to it, and the statement is not true or cannot be made to look true with any degree of credibility. For example, advertising that a Big Mac is the most nutritious and low-fat food in the world and that eating a lot of them is good for your health won't work because most people will know that this claim is not in fact true. They will at least know that it is a blatant exaggeration of the truth.

1.3. The presentation of complete and accurate information can be time-consuming—ads, especially TV ads, are expensive and thus have to be short, usually no more than 30 seconds long. Moreover, complete and accurate information may exceed the attention span of most consumers.

1.4. Some people may find complete and accurate information about a product to be boring. They will switch off the TV, or even worse, they will associate the product with boredom.

Therefore, strategy 1, on the whole, does not appear to be an effective persuasive strategy.

2. This strategy is directly in keeping with the role of advertising, because presenting the product in the best and most attractive possible light does not require complete and true information, thus overcoming the problems under strategy 1. But how can this be done?

- Exaggerate the merits of the product, and underplay its shortcomings.
- Invent merits that the product does not possess, or leave out most, if not all, of its shortcomings.

However, exaggerating or inventing the merits of a product while not mentioning its shortcomings may amount to deception. Setting aside any ethical problems, the pragmatic problem is that if the deception is found out, the product will lose credibility, and consumers won't buy it. Moreover, advertisers may lose peer respect and face self-regulating discipline from the advertising industry. Also, advertisers may face legal sanctions.

3. This strategy avoids the problems under strategies 1 and 2 by not saying very much about the

product itself. It doesn't provide complete and accurate information, nor does it exaggerate the merits of a product or downplay its shortcomings. Rather, it merely creates a positive image for the product by associating the product with values that consumers instantly recognize and consider worthy, like love, freedom, independence, family, friends, comfort, pleasure, security, happiness, humor, imagination, and fantasy. For example, two car manufacturers associate their cars with the notion of happiness or joy. An advertisement for Hyundai boldly declares that "Happiness is Hyundai," and a stock advertisement for Toyota has as its theme slogan the catchy phrase "O what a feeling . . . Toyota!" accompanied by someone jumping for joy in the air. Over a period of time, these pervasive images of Hyundai and Toyota cars become associated in the minds of consumers with the positive values of happiness and joy, at least subconsciously. Other examples are advertisements of cars associated with the notion of freedom and of perfumes associated with the notions of independence, romance, and even of truth.

So how relevant to advertising is truth, and by extension, information as instructive knowledge? From the preceding analysis, it seems that truth is only marginally relevant to advertising. Truth is certainly relevant in advertisements that purport to provide accurate information about a product or service as under strategy 1; but it is hardly relevant to advertisements that either exaggerate the merits of a product or service or that downplay its defects and shortcomings as under strategy 2, or that provide almost no information about the product or service itself, but rather appeal to the sentiments of the consumers by associating products and services to values or lifestyles to which most people aspire.

Often advertisements will use fictional modes of communication that consumers readily recognize as a form of communication that is fictional, metaphorical, or fantastical, and thus they are willing to suspend disbelief. For example, an advertisement in Australia shows a young man asking the "cookie genie" to grant him the wish of conjuring up an exotically beautiful woman. The cookie genie grants him his wish but either by accident or by design transforms the unfaithful young man into a packet of Tim-Tams, Australia's iconic chocolate cookie. His girlfriend, upon returning to their apartment, finds her boyfriend missing, but she is consoled by the packet of Tim-Tam biscuits that have miraculously turned up in the refrigerator.

This particular advertisement—which is not untypical of advertisements of this kind that promote products not by accurate description but by an association of the product with values, metaphor, fiction, and fantasy—has effectively used fiction, fantasy, and humor to advertise the well-known chocolate cookie. The descriptive truth, by way of information about the product itself, was almost entirely absent from the advertisement. Truth in this advertisement and similar ads is *irrelevant,* since the advertisements do not in any way purport to provide descriptive information about the product itself but rather attempt to invoke certain positive sentiments about the product by associating it with those sentiments through the use of humor, fiction, and fantasy. As the suspension of disbelief is called for through the fictional and fantastical mediums used, there is no deception, since no deception was ever intended.

However, when deception in advertisements is intended or at least when proper care has not been taken to avoid advertisements that are likely to mislead or deceive, those advertisements are ethically objectionable. With regard to Case 4c, "Nothing Real about Reality Advertising," the advertising agency Mojo Partners and/or their client Telstra, either (a) knew that the film footage of the floods used in the Telstra advertisement was that of the Texas floods or (b) didn't know and were under the mistaken impression that the film footage was in fact that of the Katherine floods in Australia, as purported to be. If (a), then either Mojo or Telstra or both acted deceptively and thus acted unethically, since deceiving others in the way that Mojo and/or Telstra deceived the Australian public is unethical and morally objectionable. If on the other hand (b), Mojo and/or Telstra acted negligently; and their action, or rather their omission to act in exercising due care in ensuring that the film footage was that of the Katherine floods, is also morally objectionable, though in the absence of intended deception, less so than in the case of outright deception as in (a).

What is particularly problematic in this particular case is that the advertisement in the genre of "reality advertising" was intended to depict reality in accordance with our preceding correspondence definition of the truth. That is to say, the film footage of the floods in the "reality advertisement" for Telstra should have *corresponded* to reality and the corresponding facts regarding that reality. Namely, the film footage of the floods should have been that of the Katherine floods as the Telstra "reality advertisement" purported to depict and not of the Texas floods to which the advertisement misleadingly, and possibly deceptively, actually corresponded.

The further ethical problem in the Telstra case was that the picture of Melanie Finley in the Texas floods and the pictures of the Katherine residents in the Australian floods were taken and used without the consent and permission either of Melanie's parents or that of the residents of Katherine depicted in the Telstra commercial. Melanie's parents were particularly distressed to find that their daughter's picture, which was taken just before her death, was used in an advertisement for commercial purposes. Although there is no legal obligation, at least in Australia, to obtain consent before using people's pictures in a media release or publication, there was nevertheless an ethical obligation upon Mojo and Telstra to do so, especially since the "reality" advertisement was intended to show how Telstra cares about the harm that people suffer as a result of natural disasters such as floods. Mojo's and Telstra's "caring" should have included caring about obtaining the prior consent and permission of the people whose images were used in the commercial.

The general ethical problem in the Telstra case is the problem concerning *advertorials*. An advertorial is an advertisement that masquerades as editorial comment or opinion, usually on a matter of public interest. In the Telstra case, whether deceptively or merely negligently, the Telstra commercial in the guise of a "reality advertisement" was used to create a dramatic effect that seemed intended to associate the depiction of the floods in Katherine with the caring attitude of Telstra, "making life easier," in the minds of the Australian public. It's a pity that Mojo and/or Telstra did not show as much care about the truth, which was deliberately or at least negligently sacrificed for the sake of a "reality advertisement."

The general problem of advertorials ensues from the underlying potential conflict between the principle of persuasion and the principle of information. The potential conflict between the principle of persuasion and the principle of information, which is inherent in advertising, can result in a situation such as the Telstra case, in which a "reality advertisement" deceptively or negligently presented information that purported to have the epistemological credentials of knowledge about a "real" event to which the advertisement referred primarily as a persuasion strategy intended to create a positive opinion about Telstra in the minds of the Australian consumers.

The potential conflict inherent in advertising between, on the one hand, the *principle of information,* which requires information as a form of knowledge to be both true and justified through independent corroboration and verification, and, on the other hand, the *principle of persuasion,* which does not necessarily require the information communicated to be either true or justified, can give rise to advertisements that use information merely as a vehicle for persuading consumers to purchase certain products or services, or at least to create in consumers' minds a pro-attitude toward those products or services.

Of course, information that is both true and justified can, and often is, persuasive. However, persuasion in itself need not necessarily be achieved through information that meets the conditions of knowledge, since misinformation, half-truths, lies, or simply omission of the facts can just as easily be persuasive if they are presented in the right format. Successful propaganda is a case in point.

If the primary role of advertising is the successful persuasion of consumers to purchase products or services, or at least to render them favorably predisposed toward the products or services advertised, should advertising use *any* effective means in pursuit of that goal, especially if that goal is in keeping with the role morality of advertising (see Chapter 1)? Even if the means of persuasion are those described earlier in strategies 2 and 3? Does the end of successful persuasion always justify the means used to persuade others?

The answer, of course, is that the end of successful persuasion for the ultimate purpose of selling consumer products or services does not justify any means used for that end. As we have been discussing, means of persuasion that mislead or deceive consumers by intention or through negligence, as the Telstra and the Target and Daewoo cases illustrate, are morally objectionable and should always be avoided. Also, as we saw in Chapter 1, the role morality of a profession or practice should as far as possible always be congruent with Universal Public Morality; and when a conflict arises between the two, Universal Public Morality, to which everyone, including advertising practitioners and other professionals, are by rational necessity socially committed, should always take precedence. Hence, insofar as Universal Public Morality prohibits deception and the promulgation of

misleading information either by commission or omission, then deception and misleading information, irrespective of their possible persuasive and rhetorical merits, are ethically objectionable and should be avoided.

In conclusion, truth is relevant in advertising only when advertisements are intended by their context and mode of communication to provide accurate and factual information to consumers, as in the case of the Telstra, Daewoo, and Target advertisements previously discussed. As we shall see, to the extent that advertisements are meant to be informative in a certain way, as in endorsements and testimonials, and to the extent that ads must not misinform through stereotyping, then truth is also relevant to those types of advertisements. Truth, on the other hand, when fictional and metaphorical modes of communication are used and the consumer is required by convention to suspend disbelief, is not relevant, or not nearly as relevant to advertising.

A SUMMARY OF INSTRUMENTAL AND ETHICAL CONSEQUENCES

Desirable

1. "Reality advertising" can be an effective persuasion strategy even if there is very little or no reality about certain "reality advertisements," and thus from a purely pragmatic perspective the untruthful though persuasive "reality advertising" may be perceived as instrumentally desirable as in keeping with the ultimate role of advertising of persuading consumers to feel favorably predisposed toward the advertised products.

Undesirable

1. However, the use of truth and reality in advertising as an effective persuasive strategy can backfire if misused or abused, as the examination of Case Study 4c illustrated. Insofar as the misuse

or abuse of truth or reality in advertising carries the heavy penalty of loss of credibility and of trust by the consumers if the misuse or abuse is discovered, it is potentially a self-defeating strategy, since it could result in loss of persuasion rather than persuasion, and thus the misuse or abuse of "reality advertising" is an instrumentally undesirable strategy.

2. Since the misuse or abuse of "reality advertising" or "truth in advertising" is a form of deception, it is ethically undesirable, since deception in advertising is, either by negligence or by design, unethical and should be avoided. This observation applies to all forms of deception in advertising, including the use of advertorials as well as the use of exaggerated and inflated claims that cannot be objectively and independently verified. "The World's Favorite Airline" marketing slogan used by British Airways in Case Study 4a lies on the borderline of credibility, since the subjective and unquantifiable veracity of the claim renders it not untruthful as such, but "nontruthful,"

namely, an unverifiable claim whose truth or untruth cannot in principle be established with any degree of certainty. This observation applies generally to all claims that may qualify as mere puffery. The consumer must guard against putting any epistemological weight on such puffed-up claims.

In conclusion, the misuse or abuse of reality or truth in advertising in all its forms is both ethically and instrumentally undesirable, at least potentially instrumentally undesirable, and should thus be avoided. If advertisers cannot get right the truth or reality in their advertisements without misusing it or abusing it, they should leave it out of their advertising campaigns and should resort to other advertising strategies whose use of metaphor, fantasy, or fiction, which requires suspension of disbelief, renders irrelevant the use of truth or reality with regard to those strategies.

chapter five

Stereotyping—The Commodification of Identity

INTRODUCTION

What is stereotyping, and what is wrong with it? This chapter will examine types of stereotyping in advertising that are centered around sex, race, ethnicity, religion, age and other societal types, and the ethical problems involved in stereotyping. Because advertising is maximally constrained by time, so that most TV and radio ads run for 30 seconds, some degree of stereotyping is inevitable. To the extent that some degree of stereotyping is unavoidable in advertising, the chapter will examine what constitutes acceptable and unacceptable forms of stereotyping.

Apart from stereotyping by commission, there is also the more insidious stereotyping by omission. By focusing on certain types of people and

individuals—for example, white, young, beautiful, and slender people with immaculate hair, teeth, and complexion—advertising may be presenting a very biased and very partial view of society, one that excludes many groups of individuals who do not fall into those selected advertising types. If, as we are often told, advertising is a reflection of society, then it is a very limited, partial, and biased reflection. In fact, it is a reflection that is itself a grand stereotype, and one from which certain groups of ordinary citizens are rendered absent or invisible through exclusion from the very public sphere of advertising. Or if they are included, they are usually, like the Mexican bandits with the stereotypical sombrero hats used in commercials to advertise anything from burgers to beer, portrayed as figures of ridicule or amusement.

Case Studies

Case Study 5a   Women Take Portrayal into Their Own Hands[57]

In 2001, outdoor advertising in Australia was under the microscope for the way in which it appeared to support the negative portrayal of women. In the state of Victoria, a sequence of highly publicized complaints about advertising content on billboards, in particular the portrayal of women, prompted the government to establish the "Portrayal of Women Advisory Committee" to submit a discussion paper on the improvement of the portrayal of women in outdoor advertising, with a view toward discussing the possible further regulation of the advertising industry.

In partnership with industry associations, the committee set about reporting on the impact of outdoor advertising on community perceptions of women and to offer strategies to achieve improved representation of women in outdoor advertising. A key strategy was to propose a set of Gender Portrayal Advertising Guidelines that could be initially focused on outdoor advertising but that could also be used across all media.

The guidelines were formulated on the basis of research findings about adverse advertising images, their impact on community perceptions of women, their impact on women and girls, and an understanding of what the community wanted to see. A lack of images that portrayed the diversity of women was a clear problem area in advertising in general.

> Women are consistently represented by a stereotype which ignores the fact that we are not all white, able-bodied, heterosexual, thin, affluent and under thirty-five (cited in *Portrayal of Women in Outdoor Advertising Report,* see Note 78).

Comments like this illustrate the perception that advertising lacks diversity. They were supported by research data that showed that only "17% of male and 17% of female respondents agreed that outdoor advertisements represent people from ethnic minority groups, and only 17% of females and 35% of males agreed that enough examples of women of different shapes and sizes are used in outdoor advertising."[58] But by far the most problematic images were those that portrayed women as sexual objects, and "there was a clear indication that these types of images caused most concern in the community."[59]

It was strongly suggested to the committee that advertising perpetuates and reinforces stereotypes, encourages negative views of women's status in society, and fosters attitudes about women and sex that are less than positive. The impact of these stereotypical portrayals was clearly evident in the research with "over one third of the responses to the Committee's discussion paper suggesting that women are pressured to try and achieve unrealistic goals in relation to their appearance, particularly their weight. Feelings of inadequacy, anxiety and poor self-esteem in women being reinforced by certain advertising images were also identified, and it was suggested that eating disorders, particularly in young women and girls, were related to the prevalence of unrealistic images of women in advertising."

The report led to the creation and adoption of guidelines, which have become known as the *Victorian Government Gender Portrayal Guidelines for Outdoor Advertising,* and were developed for the purpose of assisting the advertising industry to produce positive portrayals of women and men in advertising. Two key clauses in the guidelines highlight the generic problems of negative or stereotypical portrayal of women in the media:

> Clause 3: Advertising should portray women and men as equally competent in a wide range of activities both inside and outside the home including the workplace.

> Clause 4: Advertising should portray both women and men in the full spectrum of diversity, including age, appearance, and background.

The report was released in April 2002, and two months later the Victorian government adopted the guidelines along with a number of other initiatives such as awards and commendations for outstanding advertising that responsibly portrayed women, as well as a number of education initiatives.

A critical adoption was to ensure that the Gender Portrayal Advertising Guidelines be instituted as a basis for advertising, media, and public relations campaigns for all government departments, statutory authorities, and agencies. Agencies that wanted to pitch for government accounts would have to adhere to the guidelines.

The process was an acknowledgment that self-regulation had not been successful in enforcing a responsible attitude to gender portrayal in outdoor advertising and that government had a clear role to play in upholding community standards through gender portrayals in advertising communication.

CASE STUDY 5B   Ethnic Minorities Feel "Boxed In"[60]

Stereotypes are merely caricatures representing key personal traits in types of people and are willfully accepted by consumers. Is that really the case? With the abundance of stereotypes portrayed in ads, acceptance would appear to be the standard. But as a result of significant complaints about a broad range of stereotyping in advertisements, the Independent Television Commission (ITC), the regulatory body for television in the United Kingdom, set out to determine when a stereotype actually stops being harmless and approaches something more offensive.

The ITC 2001 report, which was titled *Boxed In: Offence from Negative Stereotyping in Television Advertising,* utilized a series of focus groups and interviews with people from ethnic minorities and other stereotyped groups, establishing a number of insights into consumer responses to stereotypic images in advertising. While being accepted as part of the advertising experience, people from ethnic minorities felt particularly strongly that advertising did not reflect the cultural diversity of the United Kingdom but that it created a potential to instill racist attitudes in the community.

An outstanding example was an advertisement for *Reed Employment,* which sets up the scenario of a casually dressed black youth with dreadlocks who spots a smartly dressed white man in a crowded street and who appears to deliberately bump into the white man. The white man immediately suspects that he has been robbed, and a flashback confirms that the black man has indeed picked his pocket skillfully. But there is a twist in the tail. Instead of stealing anything, the black man has placed a note in the white man's wallet advising him about a job opportunity.

To most respondents, this advertisement was seen as an overt example of a potentially damaging racist stereotypic. The scenario links with "the stereotype of young, African Caribbean men—that they are 'naturally' criminally inclined. African Caribbean respondents, in particular, felt the advertisement had the potential to increase racial tensions."[61]

Advertising was regarded by many respondents as a medium via which racism could be either reinforced or challenged, for example, by the presence or absence of ethnic minority participants and by the ways in which they were portrayed on the TV screen. Many respondents also believed in the cumulative effect of advertising, along with other societal influences, that could gradually and subtly build and reinforce stereotypes, with the report referring to the "slow drip potential for harm."

CASE STUDY 5C   Accessory to a Handbag

The woman is young and beautiful. Leisurely resting on her elbows in a half-reclining position with her head slightly tilted back, her long auburn hair cascading over her half-bare shoulders, she looks wistfully past the camera and across to the people waiting for the train on platform one. Her white skirt falls halfway down her flawless, slender legs to mid-thigh. She is clutching a white-and-beige handbag to the side of her reclining torso. The woman's pose is strikingly sensual and erotic. The caption at the top of the billboard reads, "Condura Accessories."

CASE STUDY 5D   What a Drag It Is Getting Old[62]

A gray-haired woman shuffles along munching on chips, oblivious to the runway steamroller barreling down on her. Chevy Chase climbs a wrecking ball to rescue the chips. The woman is plowed into wet cement. However, this is a story about a commercial for Doritos chips written by Kevin Goldman, the adverting columnist for the *Wall Street Journal* back in 1993. Goldman's description of the commercial[63] captures powerfully the problem of stereotyping people, in this particular case, people of a certain age group.

CASE STUDY 5E   Would the Real Cultural Icon Please Stand Up[64]

A young Asian Indian man eyes his ageing car, and then he proceeds to smash the front and rear of the car into a wall; next, an elephant sits on the hood; finally, he takes a hammer and bashes the car into a very beaten-up replica of the Peugeot 206. Proud of his new creation, he takes to the streets in the car, looking for the "eyes of the ladies." This commercial for the Peugeot 206, called *The Sculpteur,* uses the ethnic stereotype of the culture of India as being underdeveloped and unsophisticated to set up a humorous situation in which to frame Peugeot's proposition. Such creative devices seem commonplace in the media and advertising environments, and audiences accept them with little thought of their ethical significance or consequences.

In the Australian TV commercial for Fuji/Hanimex titled *Born Photographer,* a Japanese woman is in the act of giving birth, and then the child is presented to the family of onlookers. The baby is holding a camera and captures their surprised faces with a beautifully composed shot. This is a humorous spot that perpetuates the ethnic stereotyping of the Japanese as a technology-obsessed race and as habitual serial photographers.

An Australian TV spot for Email/Simpson, called *Sari About,* that shows a group of Asian Indians washing their clothes in the river when they are exposed to the new Simpson washing machine. They prod it, look puzzled by its controls, and eventually use it as a beating pole for drying the clothes (demonstrating the strength and stability of the machine). The portrayal of the Indian culture as technology-inept and underdeveloped becomes the convenient setting for demonstrating the benefits of the product at the expense of that culture.

When fast-food retailers introduce a Mexican variety of food to their menu, we invariably see the unshaven, sombrero-wearing, gun-slinging characters riding through a cactus-inhabited desert. Similarly, an Indian variety of food will generally feature a character riding an elephant, and Asian varieties are associated with scenes of martial arts confrontations. Although the signifiers are clearly identifiable, their moral justification is arguable.

In Australia, Nescafé advertised their espresso brand through the portrayal of a young Italian man, with his shirt open and exposing a chest covered in gold jewelry, with slicked-back hair shining with grease, in a pose that would not look out of place in *Saturday Night Fever.* A pasta brand is given similar Italian authenticity by showing the typical Italian mealtime. The large, apron-wearing mama is shown placing the huge bowl of pasta onto a long table that is covered with a checked table cloth; the men, who are sitting around waiting for the meal to arrive, are surrounded by children and grandchildren chasing each other around the table. This scene stereotypes the Italian evening meal and family orientation. Which image has the right to authenticate Italian culture? The suave (or some might think sleazy) and cosmopolitan young man, or the conservative and family-orientated unit?

In the United Kingdom, Reed Employment (in the previously cited case) was criticized for its advertising, which shows a black Rasta man putting his hand in the pocket of a white man. The viewer's initial assumption is that the Rasta man's intention is to steal the white man's wallet, when in fact the intention is to leave him a card offering him an exciting job opportunity. The dreadlocked image of the Rasta man was used with creative effect to place a twist in the story, implying at first that the Rasta man must be up to no good.

Viewers of these so-called culturally representative images have indicated that most appear to be acceptable, with just a few perceived to be harmful.[65]

The balancing act for the advertising industry is to determine at what point the semiotics applied to the communication become harmful by their reinforcement of undesirable or nonrepresentative cultural traits and at what point industry-regulatory bodies should intervene.

PROFESSIONAL PRACTICE

Hey! I'm Joe

> Hey! I'm Joe a 25 yr old property consultant, I live with my girlfriend in a city studio apartment, it's close to the action. By action I mean bars, cafes, clubs and late night shopping centers. The only problem with being close to the action is that I tend to spend way more than I can afford. Right now I'm paying off my last vacation, Bahamas, Wow. Then there's my other obsession, music. My CD collection is my real pride and joy, I go to enormous lengths to find an obscure piece of music . . . Nu Jazz that's what I'm really into. I deal with the daily stresses of life in the gym, on my cycle and on the dance floor. My real measurement for how much fun I'm having is my credit card. I'm young, I work hard and I love to have fun, credit let's me be who I want to be.

A description of a consumer, a description vivid enough to visualize the person behind it, but the description is merely a composite or a construction, a device that allows the architects of advertising communication to focus on whom their communication is destined for and on what it must say, do, and feel like, to break through. This process is how advertisers create a target or target image that merely represents a collection of characteristics that together build a "pseudo-person," a stereotype.

Effective communication is receiver-centered, or consumer-centered. This outside-in approach to advertising has paved the way for growth in planning departments or strategy departments in agencies, in particular in the role of account planners. These people in the agency are supposed to represent the consumer or to be the voice of the consumer within the agency. Their role is to understand consumers as people and look for some insight that will lead to more relevant (and therefore more effective) communication. Research is their key tool for discovering this insight. Generalized descriptions highlighting key consumer attributes and attitudes (like the one at the beginning of this section) are a means of articulating their consumer understanding. In essence, advertising talks both internally and externally in stereotypes.

Divide and Conquer—Basic Marketing Practice

A basic strategy of marketers or marketing communicators is to divide the market into types of people or consumers, on the basis of some identifiable and common attributes. This process of segmentation allows for an understanding of people, their habits, and their personalities and characteristics, and assists in the creation of relevant messages for those segments or target audiences.

This practice then becomes the foundation for the communication created for each of these types of consumers. The message strategy and indeed the strategic focus of campaigns are based on targeted characteristics, which are embellished through the communication to "dramatize the benefit" against those characteristics or needs (discussed in Chapter 6). This process inevitably leads to the creation of materials that appeal to "collected" characteristics or needs, that is, they are dramatized to appeal to a particular stereotype. In essence, advertisers partition consumers with a view to speaking to them in different ways. Although stereotypes are an inevitable byproduct of advertising construction, the power and ubiquity of advertising communication can produce negative consequences for groups in society that are stereotyped.

What Is Stereotyping, and How Does It Fit into Advertising?

Stereotypes are a character shortcut, or a form of shorthand, that groups a number of shared characteristics under one label—mother, wife, Mexican, homosexual. Although they are not necessarily negative and are in fact generally accepted as part of the advertising genre, they are potentially damaging or negative through their limiting effect, that is, to propose that these particular characteristics are in fact shared by all of those who carry the label and that they are connected to some social reality rather than really being a convenient construct for communication objectives.

Because advertising is delivered to its targets via some form of media, it is important to recognize the role of mediation in the advertising process. Communication is mediated and therefore has a standpoint or context that in turn offers meaning to the representations made within that media. The media is a system of representation whereby messages and images are represented to their intended receivers. We know and understand the world through language and representations: all our learning about the world is mediated. This reality adds fuel to the debate about whether the media mirrors or makes society. Either way, advertising has a responsibility to avoid the creation of negative stereotypes and the perpetuation of existing negative stereotypes.

Industry Regulation

This responsibility has been taken up by a number of industry bodies. The United Kingdom's Independent Television Commission's (ITC) Advertising Standards Code[66] specifically deals with the issue of stereotyping under Section 6, Harm and Offence, where rules are intended to prevent advertising leading to harm. Observe in particular Section 6.6, Harmful or Negative Stereotypes:

> Advertisements must not prejudice respect for human dignity or humiliate, stigmatize or undermine the standing of identifiable groups of people.[67]

In its notes for the section, the ITC succinctly puts the role of stereotyping in advertising into perspective:

> The ITC recognises that the use of stereotypes is an inevitable part of establishing characters within the brief span of a TV commercial. But some stereotypes can be harmful or deeply insulting to the groups in question and care is needed that they do not condone or feed prejudice or perpetuate damaging misconceptions.[68]

These damaging misconceptions are the negative byproducts of advertising practice and have come under criticism for their part in negatively stereotyping gender roles (particularly the portrayal of women), ethnicity, and minority groups.

The Canadian standards body, Advertising Standards Canada (ASC), set the criteria for acceptable advertising using their *Canadian Code of Advertising Standards,*[69] which serves as the principle tool for self-regulation. The codes are embellished by the *Gender Portrayal Guidelines,*[70] which cross-reference gender portrayal with the general ethical standards expected of the industry. The *Guidelines* were designed by and for the advertising industry to help advertisers develop positive images of women and men through commercial messages. Key principles advocated in the guidelines include equal representation of women and men in roles of authority and as single decision-makers; avoidance of exploitative sexuality of both men and women; portrayal in the full spectrum of diversity; and the avoidance of language that misrepresents, offends, or excludes either gender.

Similarly, in Australia the Victorian state government commissioned its Portrayal of Women Advisory Committee to establish a set of *Gender Portrayal Advertising Guidelines,* which it uses as criteria to judge the responsibility of advertising in Victoria. (see Case Study 5a).

The *British Codes of Advertising and Sales Promotion* contain specific rules about taste and decency in advertisements. When people complain to the ASA about the portrayal of women and men, their complaint is generally considered under Clause (5.1):

> Advertisements should contain nothing that is likely to cause serious or widespread offence. Particular care should be taken to avoid causing offence on the grounds of race, religion, sex, sexual orientation or disability. Compliance with the Codes will be judged on the context, medium, audience, product and prevailing standards of decency.[71]

In Australia, the Association of National Advertisers (AANA) deals with issues of portrayal under Section 2 of its Advertiser Code of Ethics:[72]

> (2.1) Advertisements shall not portray people or depict material in a way which discriminates against or vilifies a person or section of the community on account of race, ethnicity, nationality, sex, age, sexual preference, religion, disability or political beliefs.

The industry's agency body, the Advertising Federation of Australia (AFA), highlights the issue to its constituency under section 4 of its code of ethics:[73]

> (4) Respect all people. No stereotypes please. Individuals should be understood, not portrayed in a way that could bring disrespect. Use humour, but avoid cheap shots.

In the United States, the American Advertising Federation (AAF) promotes diversity through its mission to "Promote diversity in advertising by encouraging the recruitment of people of diverse cultures"[74] and through the adoption of AAF Advertising Principles of American Business, which contribute the definition of standards for truthful and responsible advertising. In particular, here is Section 8, "Taste and Decency":[75]

> Advertising shall be free of statements, illustrations or implications which are offensive to good taste or public decency.

The key issues of portrayal of diversity, authority, and offense remain relevant across a broad range of stereotypes and are considered generic principles for adjudicating responsible advertising.

Problematic Stereotyping

Gender

As suggested throughout this chapter, the stereotyping of gender and gender roles—the particular stereotype on which we have chosen to primarily focus our attention—is a critical issue across a broad number of advertising communities with the portrayal of women as the most prevalent concern. The key issues center on their portrayal as the "sexual woman," the "domestic woman," and the "ideal woman."

The Sexual Woman

Sophie Dahl's sexually suggestive image for YSL's Opium (see Case Study 7b, Chapter 7), which became the most-complained-about piece of advertising in the United Kingdom in half a decade, challenged regulators in most markets. The advertisements presented the model suggestively reclining naked on a bed except for a pair of high heels and a diamond necklace—the pose was strikingly erotic.

Objections clearly directed at the poster campaign complained that the image was offensive and degrading to women, perpetuating the role of women as sex objects. This campaign, while gaining much attention and notoriety, epitomizes the problem of objectifying women, which in turn offers the potential for communities to adopt the beliefs perpetuated in the communication. Research seems to support this view:

> Ads depicting scantily clad women posing as decorative objects may activate the beliefs that women are seductive and frivolous sex objects, whereas ads depicting women as homemakers may activate the beliefs that women are nurturing, communal, and domestically-minded.[76]

The Thin Ideal

The Sophie Dahl Opium campaign, while perpetuating a potentially harmful stereotype, did, however, receive some support for the fact that it did not portray women in the "thin ideal,"

that is to say, it did not use "stick-insect" role modeling.

The use of thin and perfect-skinned models in advertising has been greatly criticized for its impact on women's (particularly young women) self-image. The use of such models achieves the advertiser's objectives of gaining attention, appealing to aspirations, and dramatizing the benefits of products. The side effects are the creation of potentially harmful stereotypes.

People's perception's of their size, shape, and appearance, that is, their body image, has been closely linked with a number of societal problems such as eating disorders, again particularly in young women. The constant exposure to oversexualized and underfed images in media is believed to contribute to body-image and other emotional problems.

A study conducted in 1997 found that one of advertising's unintended effects is the impact that models have on female preadolescents and adolescents. It found that girls compare their physical appearance with that of the models, and thus their self-esteem may be affected, depending on the motive for comparison. Other studies have shown that this stereotypical portrayal, which often goes unnoticed by women, may contribute to eating disorders. This study also seems to support that the "thin ideal" is often overlooked or accepted as a sociocultural norm by female college students.[77]

The potential consequences of these stereotypes were evident in the comments made by respondents to the ITC's research:

> Some women and young girls were particularly alert to sexist stereotypes such as the use of "perfect skinny bodies" to sell products. Although there was widespread acceptance that advertising of this kind was reflecting a wider cultural bias, some felt advertising reinforced such bias in society.[78]

This bias was clearly not reflecting the diversity of people of different shapes and sizes in society and was placing pressure on conformity to some thin ideal.

The Domestic Woman

We have seen in recent times a move away from the historic depiction of women as domestic housewives and the portrayal of women in more professional roles. This trend is indicative of the increasing number of women in the workforce and in executive positions, particularly in the advertising industry. This evolution of the professional woman has prompted more thoughtful portrayals of women. Since there is an obvious need for advertising to appeal to the market rather than to offend, sympathetic and more representative portrayals are now more commonplace. Regulatory bodies around the world have established guidelines for the portrayal of women (see Case 5a) in an endeavor to ensure that they are not perceived as being the experts on washing-machine operation, or dimwits about car mechanics, or specialists in child-rearing. Again, the issue of diversity of people's interests, skills, and expertise comes to the fore to ensure that women are not overrepresented in domestic settings and underrepresented in out-of-the-home occupations, and also not portrayed as dependent, unintelligent consumers of products. Similarly, men have questioned their portrayal as sex objects or as beer-drinking, domestically incompetent, sports-obsessive caricatures.

Ethnic and Racial Stereotyping

In Australia, as mentioned earlier, a campaign for Simpson washing machines placed the product in India on the side of the Ganges River, with the women using traditional methods of washing, wringing, and bashing on the rocks. The Simpson appears, the Indian people are confused about its operation, and ultimately the women use it to bash their clothing clean and dry. Essentially this is an advertisement that portrays the Indian ethnicity as technologically ignorant and economically depressed. This portrayal of Indian culture uses a part of that culture to dramatize a benefit of the product, its sturdiness, a strategic vehicle no doubt seen as appropriate for creative purposes. But at what and at whose expense? The creative device in this scenario, which is characteristic of ethnic stereotyping, takes one aspect of the culture and dramatizes it, ignoring the diversity within that culture. As demonstrated in Case Study 5b, the constant usage and reinforcement of specific ethnic characteristics can contribute to the potentially harmful "slow-drip" effect.

Through the ITC's research into negative stereotyping,[79] advertising was regarded by many respondents as a medium via which racism could be either reinforced or challenged, for example, by the presence or absence of ethnic minority participants and by the ways in which they were portrayed on the TV screen.

Omission and Underrepresentation of Ethnic Groups

The tendency in Western culture has been for media representations to be produced by whites, and thus most representations epitomize a white view of the world and of other ethnic groups. Also, the domination of whites in Western advertising agencies is a contributor to this white view in advertising communication.

In both television programming and commercials, studies show that less than 10 percent of human appearance time includes any nonwhites, and most of these are African Americans, leaving Latinos and Asian Americans almost invisible.[80] The consequence of this lack of portrayal is not only an inaccurate portrayal of the diversity of society but also a clear case of inequality. As Michael O'Shaughnessy[81] writes,

Afro-Americans like Australian Aborigines have consistently been denied their own images, stories, representations, histories, social customs, and rituals, and until it is redressed this lack will continue to contribute to ethnic and racial inequality.

This deficiency in representations of ethnic groups in the media affects the way that these groups see and understand themselves; a dominant hegemonic view pervades, and stereotypes survive.

ETHICAL ANALYSIS

Stereotyping in advertising involves presenting a group of people in an unvarying pattern that lacks individuality. It often reflects popular misconceptions and involves a misrepresentation of the group of people stereotyped. Types of stereotyping can involve gender, race, ethnicity, age, religion, class, demographics, sexual orientation, and other kinds of stereotypes.

So what is wrong with stereotyping? There is nothing inherently wrong with stereotyping as such. On the contrary, stereotyping is a necessary means for providing cognitive and semantic representational models of the world for our mutual understanding. Our minds are designed to apprehend and comprehend the world around us, by categorizing it into relevant stereotypes. We do so all the time. It is an effective shorthand way of classifying the world of *particular* things into categories of *types* of things through generalizing particular things that have or appear to have certain similar characteristics in common. Pasta consists of many different particular varieties of different shapes, sizes, colors, length, and thickness that require different cooking times, but we all recognize all those different particular varieties as belonging to the type "pasta," even when we are presented with a new particular variety that we have not encountered before. Even under the general type of "pasta," we might be able to further discern and categorize pasta into additional subtypes of pasta and

so on, since there can be many layers of type classification.

ARTHUR: "What type is he?"
MARTHA: "Funny you should ask: he is quiet, reserved, and intense, but after his third martini, boy, you can't hold him back—he suddenly becomes amicable, animated, and expansive."
ARTHUR: "He sounds like a typical Scorpio!"

Well, we probably all know someone like that or at least recognize the type in this imaginary dialogue when we come across one (even if he is not a Scorpio!). We are all born stereotypers. Scientists too make observations of particular things, whether asteroids, ants, or atoms, and then generalize and classify those particulars under generalized types of similar particulars. Scientific theories in general try to explain and predict the pattern of behavior not of particulars as such (which would be an endless task, since each particular varies in some respects from other similar particulars, and there are zillions of different particular things in the world) but of types.

In advertising, stereotyping is an essential effective and efficient communication of visual, audio, or semantic messages about products to consumers through *typical* images that consumers easily and readily recognize and relate to, either directly or indirectly, through association with, for example, values, aspirations, emotions, or lifestyles, which the association with the stereotypes evokes.

The ethical problem with stereotyping in advertising, however, arises either because insofar as stereotyping is a misrepresentation of reality, it is a form of deception, and deception is morally wrong (unless it is used out of sheer necessity for the avoidance of a greater evil that cannot be avoided otherwise), or because the use of stereotypes in advertising harms the people who are being stereotyped, and that act is also morally wrong.

Usually the two wrongs go hand in hand. That is, the stereotyping of a certain group of people can harm the people in that group by misrepresenting them, and through misrepresenting them, can diminish them in some way and make them seem less than what they are. In other words, stereotyping in advertising that misrepresents people can *belittle* them and by so doing harm them as persons. The systematic presentation of women in ads as merely housewives or sex objects, for example, or aged people as doddering and helpless figures of ridicule or pity, diminishes and belittles women and aged people through misrepresenting their fullness as persons.

There may, of course, be some women and some aged people who may predominantly exemplify the characteristics of being a housewife or a doddering old person. But in an attempt to stereotype all women and all aged people as typical groups by applying to them those very restrictive particular characteristics, advertising misrepresents those groups of people by underrepresentation. In so doing, it diminishes their full typicality as persons, which they share as members of particular complex typical groups of people.

This tendency points to an interesting and ethically problematic inherent paradox: on the one hand, stereotyping in advertising seeks to establish some *typical* characteristics that various groups of people have in common by virtue of belonging to the same complex group types, so as to convert them into stereotypes that purport to represent those groups of people as realistic *types* in advertisements. On the other hand, however, because the stereotypes used in advertising are at best only partial, since they comprise a very small and restricted number of particular characteristics that may apply to some individuals in a group type but not to all, advertising misleadingly constructs and applies partial stereotypes to complex group types of people that fail to represent them in their full complexity as realistic *types* and succeeds only in underrepresenting them as unrealistic *stereotypes*.

By being restricted to a few simplistic particular characteristics that may describe, if at all, some one-dimensional individuals (if such exist), advertising stereotypes underrepresent and thus misrepresent the groups of people that it seeks to treat as types. In fact, groups of people, just as individuals, are complex entities that cannot be adequately represented by just a few restricted characteristics that may apply, if at all, to some individuals within the stereotyped group but cannot, because of the essential complexity of any typical group, apply to all the members of the group collectively. Hence, stereotyping in advertising involves an inherent misrepresentation of reality simply because advertising stereotypes are not typical enough; and by not being typical enough, they are not real enough and thus fail to adequately represent the complexity of the typical groups that advertising stereotypes. Through their inherent restricted and oversimplified particularity, stereotypes in advertising are too partial and thus are unable to do justice to the complexity of the typical groups that it seeks to stereotype. In failing to do so, advertising misrepresents the groups of people that it stereotypes through underrepresentation and thus diminishes them as people both collectively and individually.

Misrepresentation through underrepresentation occurs not just by commission but also by omission when some racial or ethnic groups are underrepresented in advertising and rendered almost invisible by stereotyped omission. As we saw earlier, less than 10 percent of nonwhites are represented in TV commercials in the United States. In Australia, the situation is similar, with "ethnic" Australians of European, Asian, and African origin hardly being featured in TV ads and with indigenous Australians being conspicuous by their absence. Even when "ethnic" Australians are featured in ads, they are heavily stereotyped. For example, when Italians are featured in commercials about pasta and pasta sauces, they are invariably depicted talking

English in quaint Italian accents, accompanied with stereotypical overemphatic and enthusiastic use of their hands.

The effect of this ethnic and racial underrepresentation and near-omission of representation, as in the case of indigenous Australians in both print and TV advertisements, is to further marginalize these ethnic and racial groups through undue reduction or omission of representation in advertising, rendering them mere appendages to the overrepresented Anglo mainstream cultural group in Australia. If a non-Australian who had no other sources of information about Australia had to determine the ethnic and racial mix of Australia merely on the basis of advertisements that appear in the Australian media, he or she would draw the mistaken conclusion that Australia was composed almost exclusively of people of a white Anglo background; and contrary to the reality, the rich multicultural mix that Australia is composed of today would remain invisible to him or her behind the veil of a constructed advertising stereotype of a white Anglo nation.

Insofar as advertising purports to reflect society and not to construct it, the underrepresentation of ethnic and racial groups in advertising has the effect of undermining that objective. Instead of reflecting society realistically, the underrepresentation and near-omission of certain ethnic and racial groups in advertising, especially in multicultural nations such as the United States and Australia, have the effect of depicting society as an unrealistic grand stereotype that not only does not reflect society but also misrepresents it by stereotyping it through reduction and exclusion.

Insofar as this is the case, then not only does advertising misrepresent piecemeal by *commission* through the inclusion of particular social groups that it misrepresents through stereotyping, but it also misrepresents society overall by *omission* by constructing society into a grand stereotype that underrepresents and nearly excludes certain ethnic and racial groups from that unrealistic societal stereotype.

This situation presents advertising with yet another paradox: on the one hand, if advertising increases the representation of ethnic and racial groups in advertisements, it risks stereotyping those groups and thus misrepresenting them though underrepresentation, not by omission but by commission through piecemeal stereotyping. If on the other hand, it underrepresents them or excludes them from advertising, it omits the piecemeal misrepresentation of those groups by specific stereotyping but risks the overall misrepresentation of society by constructing a grand stereotype of society that misrepresents it through the underrepresentation or exclusion of those groups.

The solution to this paradox, of course, is to offer a greater representation of ethnic and racial groups in advertisements commensurate with their presence in society, which advertising after all purports to reflect, but at the same time to avoid misrepresenting those groups as well as all other social groups by avoiding the misrepresentation of those groups though simplistic and misleading partial piecemeal stereotyping. If this goal could be achieved, then both piecemeal stereotyping by commission and grand societal stereotyping by omission could be reduced, if not entirely eliminated. This, however, may prove a difficult task, given that because of time and financial constrains, the problem of partial and misrepresentative stereotyping in advertising is inherent.

So far we have discussed the ethical problems of stereotyping as problems of misrepresentation. And as problems of misrepresentation, they are also problems of deception. And as deception is generally morally wrong, so is misrepresentation of social reality through misleading stereotyping. Whereas a number of advertising strategies that employ fiction, fantasy, and metaphor to relate consumers to products require the suspension of disbelief (see Chapter 4), stereotyping, by contrast, because of its inherent tendency to misrepresent social reality, should alert consumers to a suspension of belief. That is, if belief is a necessary condition for knowledge (see Chapter 4), it is certainly not warranted in most forms of stereotyping used in advertising.

However, although misrepresentation through stereotyping renders stereotyping ethically problematic for advertising generally, it still does not explain how a particular individual person or a particular individual group can be harmed through stereotyping, even if stereotyping does, in the ways just discussed, misrepresent the societal groups that it stereotypes. After all, as we have seen, misrepresentation through stereotyping in advertising is inherently problematic by virtue of the nature of advertising itself. That is, given that advertising has to communicate information on radio and TV in 30-second bytes or less, it is not surprising that stereotyping in advertising is by necessity partial and incomplete and can thus misrepresent the richness of detail and variety of particularity of any of the societal groups that it stereotypes. But that might just be one of the instrumental professional costs that advertising has to wear. So long as this is a *theoretical* ethical problem for advertising that does no actual harm to any specific individual or group of individuals that are stereotyped by advertising, then there is no moral wrong done to anyone in particular, and therefore stereotyping does not raise any *practical* ethical problems since no one is actually harmed by it.

In order to answer this quite reasonable objection to the moral wrongness of stereotyping, we will now examine what might be *practically* morally wrong with stereotyping by investigating the actual and potential harmful consequences that stereotyping can have on the individuals and groups of individuals stereotyped by advertising.

Stereotyping is ethically problematic not only theoretically but also practically because of its tendency to convert real individual persons into artificial constructs that function as objects for the promotion of consumer products. As the subtitle of this chapter suggests, people's identities, both as individuals and collectively as members of different societal groups, are commodified through stereotyping into *artificial* objects that are intended to function merely as means in the promotion of consumer products. These are products that advertising invests with a *real* branded identity, seemingly more real than the *artificial* identity that advertising invests in human stereotypes. In Case Study 5c, the anonymous young woman's personal and gender identity as a person is commodified into an artificial stereotyped accessory merely as a means in the promotion of a handbag and its branded identity, "Condura."

According to Immanuel Kant's Categorical Imperative, which we encountered in Chapter 1, people are *ends* in themselves who are inherently worthy of respect and moral consideration in their own right and thus should never be treated merely as a *means* for the sake of the ends of someone else. By converting people into artificial constructs through stereotyping, advertising treats people whom those stereotypes purport to represent but actually misrepresent, as mere means for the end of promoting products for the sake of advertisers and their clients.

This practice is morally wrong on two counts. First, because in converting people, even symbolically, into artificial objects through stereotyping, advertising treats the people whom it commodifies as objects, with disrespect, both with regard to their personal identity as well as with regard to their particular cultural identity that they are invested with as members of the particular societal group to which they belong. Second, because advertising treats the people it commodifies as mere means for the commercial end of promoting consumer products for the benefit of the advertisers and their clients, advertising treats the people whom it stereotypes with a lack of moral consideration. Thus, stereotyping is morally wrong for both rendering people artificial by commodifying their identity and for turning people into objects that are then used merely as a means for the end of promoting products. Thus, in the case of the Simpson washing machine ad, the Indian people in the ad are rendered, symbolically at least, artificial constructs that misrepresent them as real full persons; moreover, the people are treated as a mere means for the end of promoting the Simpson washing machine for the benefit of the advertiser.

But how does the mere symbolic misrepresentation of a particular group of people through stereotyping that converts them into an artificial construct and uses it as a mere means for the end of promoting consumer products cause harm to actual real people? After all, how can mere images and words used in advertising harm an individual, real person of Indian descent, as in the case of the Simpson washing machine ad? The answer to that question is quite simply that the ad degrades and demeans a person of Indian origin by presenting Indian people, on the whole, as unsophisticated and technologically inept peasants who mistake the simple function of a washing machine for that of a rock by the river on which to beat dirty laundry clean in the "traditional Indian way." The ad that would in all probability appear to an Indian person to have been conceived from a "superior Western perspective" is offensively condescending; and even if it is humorous, which it might be for some people, the joke is at somebody else's expense, in this case, that of the Indian people.

Our individual identity as persons is partly constituted by our societal group identity, including ethnic, racial, religious, gender, sexual orientation, age, and other relevant components, any one or more of which indirectly contributes to who we are as individual persons. Hence, the degradation of a societal group to which we as individual persons may belong, degrades us personally by degrading the societal identity that partially, at least, constitutes our own personal identity. For that reason, calling a person a

"nigger" or a "wog"[82] can offend that person by offending the societal group to which he or she belongs. Words can break as many bones as can sticks and stones—and perhaps more bones—through depriving people of the respect they rightfully and inherently deserve as human beings.

A woman would *justifiably* take offense from the Condura Accessories ad (Case study 5c) just because the ad is degrading to women by depicting them collectively as mere accessories and sex-objects, which are by semantic extrapolation "sex accessories to men for their pleasure"—at least that would be a reasonable interpretation of the ad that any woman could make and would justifiably find offensive.

The operative word for the purpose of determining from an ethical perspective what a particular societal group may find degrading and offensive in advertising stereotypes is "justifiable." That is to say, what may justifiably count as degrading or offensive in stereotyping is what any person from the relevant stereotyped group may reasonably find degrading and offensive from his or her own individual personal perspective, as well as vicariously, from his or her group's collective perspective. On the basis of this qualification, both the Simpson washing machine ad as well as the Condura Accessories ad can justifiably be interpreted as degrading and offensive to Indians and women respectively, just because any ordinary Indian person and any ordinary woman could reasonably find those ads degrading and thus offensive.

The test of what might count as degrading and offensive in advertising stereotypes is to imagine that one is a member of the relevant societal group being stereotyped and to put oneself in the shoes of that imaginary person, and then to determine from that person's perspective, and not from one's own actual perspective, which is irrelevant for the test, as honestly and objectively as one can, whether he or she, as a hypothetical member of the stereotyped group, would justifiably feel degraded and offended by the stereotype in the relevant ad. If the answer to this question is yes, then one can assume with some epistemological confidence that an actual person from the stereotyped group would, or at least could, find the stereotype in the relevant ad degrading and offensive. And insofar as the stereotype in the relevant ad appears to be justifiably degrading and offensive to the relevant group stereotyped, then that ad is not only morally objectionable but also unethical, irrespective of any other instrumental merits it may have.

In conclusion, stereotyping in advertising that degrades people as individuals by degrading the societal group to which they belong is morally wrong because degrading and demeaning people is morally wrong simply because people are inherently worthy of moral respect. Apart from Kant's principle of the Categorical Imperative that supports the view that persons are inherently worthy of moral respect and consideration simply by virtue of being persons, Alan Gewirth's Principle of Generic Consistency (PGC) also supports the inviolable moral respect that people deserve by virtue of being persons.

It will be recalled that the Principle of Generic Consistency supports and justifies the possession of rights to freedom to well-being by all individuals on the basis that all persons need freedom and well-being in order to pursue and fulfill their individual particular purposes. It is by virtue of their common human purposiveness that all persons have universal rights to freedom and well-being.

Human beings, however, not only have prima facie rights to freedom and well-being so as to enable them to act in pursuit of their individual chosen purposes, but they also have rights to freedom and well-being because some minimal freedom and well-being is needed for the protection and preservation of their personal dignity, as individuals and as members of a particular societal group.

It is a common observation throughout history that human beings would fight for their freedom and their well-being for the sake of their dignity and would choose to die rather than live as slaves or near-slaves under a tyrannical regime that degrades them as persons. Various national wars of independence and civil rights movements throughout the world, including the American War of Independence and the civil rights movements in the United States, Ireland, and South Africa, are just a few examples that attest to the common observation that freedom and well-being are essential conditions for people's dignity, which they will protect with their own lives because of the realization that life is worth living only if it can be lived with human dignity, which essentially requires freedom and well-being.

People may sometimes choose to end their lives though voluntary euthanasia when suffering from an incurable terminal illness once they arrive at the realization that they can no longer live the rest of their lives with dignity. Hence, people must have rights to freedom and well-being not only to enable them to act in the pursuit and fulfillment of their individual purposes but also in order to enable them to protect and preserve their personal dignity, rights that are universal simply because the need for personal dignity is a universal need that all human beings have in common. Therefore, insofar as stereotyping in advertising degrades people as persons and harms their personal dignity by degrading the societal group to which they belong, stereotyping violates people's rights to freedom and well-being and hence is unethical.

A SUMMARY OF INSTRUMENTAL AND ETHICAL CONSEQUENCES

Desirable

1. Stereotyping in advertising is an effective and efficient communication of visual, audio, or semantic messages about products to consumers

though *typical* images that consumers easily and readily recognize and relate to, either directly or indirectly through association with, for example, values, aspirations, emotions, or lifestyles, which the association with the stereotypes evokes. As an effective and indeed essential communication advertising strategy, stereotyping is instrumentally highly desirable, and it is difficult to imagine how advertising could operate without some form of ethically acceptable stereotyping.

Undesirable

Though essential to advertising, stereotyping, as we saw earlier, suffers from a number of ethical shortcomings of various degrees of ethical concern. The following is a summary of those shortcomings:

1. Insofar as stereotyping misrepresents or under-represents the people it stereotypes, it is deceptive and thus ethically undesirable, as all unjustified deception is unethical.

2. Paradoxically, stereotyping commodifies the collective group identity of people that it stereotypes and personifies the commodities that it advertises. This inversion, first recognized by Karl Marx as the "fetishism of commodities," has the tendency to treat people, at least symbolically, as a mere means to the advertising and marketing end of promoting consumer commodities. Deontologically this treatment is ethically undesirable, even if instrumentally desirable, since it violates Kant's Categorical Imperative (see Chapter 1). As Case Study 5c illustrates, the woman in the ad, and symbolically by extension all women as well, is portrayed as a mere accessory to a handbag, a paradoxical inversion of a handbag personified through the commodification of the woman's personality.

3. Consequentially, it is the stereotyping that degrades people by treating them with disrespect, as Case Studies 5a through 5e illustrate, which presents the biggest ethical concern. In fact, stereotyping that seeks to promote consumer products by degrading people through portraying them collectively through pejoratively demeaning images that injure[83] can cause harm to these people through insult and ridicule.

In conclusion, stereotyping, though essential to advertising, is inherently ethically problematic, and all efforts should be taken to ensure that stereotyping when employed should be used with great ethical care so that people's dignity is not compromised for the sake of the mere promotion of consumer commodities; and of equal importance, people should not be insulted, ridiculed, or in other ways demeaned by stereotyping images that injure and that treat them with lack of moral consideration.

chapter six

Endorsements and Testimonials: It Is All about Credibility!

INTRODUCTION

This chapter will examine specific issues concerning the advertising of products through endorsements and testimonials. What constitutes credible endorsements and testimonials, and what distinguishes credible from noncredible endorsements and testimonials? To answer this question, the chapter will take a short detour into the theory of knowledge in order to determine what constitutes credible testimony. If independence is a necessary condition of credible testimony, can testimonials in advertising that lack independence ever be credible? The chapter will address the issue of credibility in at least four different ways: The credibility of the endorser's character, the credibility of the endorser's alleged expertise, the credibility of the endorsement with regard to its relevance to the product endorsed, and finally, the credibility of the endorsement with regard to the reality of the endorser—is the endorser a real person, an actor pretending to be a real person, or merely a constructed fictional character? The chapter will conclude by examining whether testimonials are another form of advertorials and thus are inherently ethically problematic.

CASE STUDIES

Case Study 6a Carl Lewis—"The Athlete with an Old Man's Bones"

Once the fastest man alive, Carl Lewis now faces the rest of his life in a wheelchair. Crippled by a punishing, lifelong training schedule that helped him earn a record nine Olympic gold medals, Lewis has been told by doctors that he has degenerative arthritis and the spine of a 60-year-old man.[84]

The preceding extract from an article that appeared in the English newspaper *Sunday Times* on June 27, 1999, announced starkly that one of the most famous athletes in the world had degenerative arthritis. Nicole Veash of the London *Observer* reported[85] that Carl Lewis, in an effort to raise awareness of the disease, had disclosed that he had degenerative arthritis. Veash also reported that Carl Lewis had found relief from taking a Dutch herbal remedy, Zenaxin. According to the report, Lewis had claimed that by taking Zenaxin tablets for a year, which contain extract of ginger that apparently is known to be good for joints, the pain from his arthritis had definitely improved.

However, a few days after the media reports of Carl Lewis's arthritis condition surfaced, his agent, Joe Douglas, categorically denied that Lewis was suffering or had ever suffered from acute arthritis. Douglas also said that the media reports that made those claims were completely inaccurate and that there was no truth in the alleged arthritis claims and no truth that Lewis was confined to a wheelchair. In addition, Douglas went on to explain that the basis of the false rumors could have been Lewis's endorsement of the drug Zenaxin used for the relief of arthritis pain but emphasized that Lewis did not have or ever had arthritis. Lewis, when he later spoke to the media of his Zenaxin endorsement, denied the report of his alleged arthritis disease.[86]

The upshot of this story was that Carl Lewis was endorsing Zenaxin, a drug used in the treatment for arthritis, though he himself had never suffered from arthritis; moreover, according to both Lewis and his agent Joe Douglas, the media reports that had claimed that he was suffering from degenerative arthritis, on the basis of his endorsement of Zenaxin, were totally untrue. Is this perhaps a case of an advertising endorsement involved in a head-on collision with Lewis's public relations machinery that did not want Lewis to appear as someone suffering from arthritis, irrespective of whether the media reports that had claimed that he had arthritis were true or false? After all, a world-famous Olympic athlete with the bones of an old man is not a winning public image for a successful athlete, especially a commercially successful athlete!

CASE STUDY 6B Sony Pictures Entertainment[87]

(In)credible Views: Sony Plays "Patriot" Games with Consumers

In June 2001, Sony Pictures Entertainment found itself embroiled in a controversy that would not only harm the credibility of the organization but also place question marks on an advertising strategy that had flourished for decades—the practice of using testimonials or endorsements.

Sony took the authenticity and credibility-building strategy of using "typical-person" testimonials and applied it to a television campaign for the Mel Gibson film *The Patriot.* These typical persons were supposedly ordinary moviegoers who agreed to give on-the-street interviews praising the film. The only problem was that two of those "typical persons," who had just emerged from seeing the film, happened to be employees of Sony Pictures Entertainment who were deliberately posing as ordinary moviegoers. The execution of this tactic had overtly deceived viewers of the television commercial into believing that they were witnessing the unbiased views of authentic moviegoers. It was, in fact, a staged presentation of message content designed to give these views credibility and relevance to the consumers.

A spokesperson for Sony Pictures defended this deceptive practice by declaring that "using actors, real people or employees as spokespeople is not unique to the entertainment business, is not specific to Sony Pictures Entertainment and is not something that is practiced only by me." This is a defense that opens the curtains to an advertising strategy that has long been questioned by consumers, particularly young consumers. While many in the industry would acknowledge that the use of actors as endorsers is a typical strategy, they would undoubtedly draw the line at using their own employees in that role.

This tactic by Sony clearly raises the concern about the role of endorsements and testimonials in advertising. It is an effective strategy for breaking through the skepticism of consumers, but it is just as scripted and structured a communication strategy as the devices that consumers are rejecting and questioning. But the key issue at the heart of the Sony tactics is the deception that is the result of the scattering of "fake" real people throughout the testimonial commercial. This tactic not only misleads the consumer but also builds mistrust for this advertising device.

Consequently, industry bodies have produced guidelines and principles to protect both the consumer and the industry. In the United States, the Federal Trade Commission guidelines governing testimonial advertising stipulate that the testimonials "must reflect the experience of the endorser, must be truthful, must reflect what other consumers can expect to experience and must be obtained in a manner that does not bias the opinion."[88]

Sony Pictures's response was to suspend the marketing executives responsible for the commercial and build new internal guidelines that would enable the verification of the accuracy and authenticity of testimonial views.

CASE STUDY 6c   Apple Computers[89]

When Thinking Different Is "Real" Thinking

Think Different has been the decree of Apple Computers, Inc., since 1998, a declaration that has been backed by iconoclastic images of some of the world's greatest thinkers and innovators, such as Bob Dylan, Albert Einstein, Pablo Picasso, John Lennon and Yoko Ono, Edison, Muhammad Ali, Alfred Hitchcock, Miles Davis, Amelia Earhart, Jim Henson, Frank Lloyd Wright, and Jerry Seinfeld. The images in this award-winning campaign made the connection between the brand attributes of Apple MacIntosh and the targeted consumers. In effect, they work as endorsers for innovative thinking and by association serve as indirect endorsers of the attributes of the brand. The campaign pays tribute to the thinking and creativity of these icons, these people who have challenged conventional thinking. This practice is really a covert form of testimonial.

But four years down the track, this strategy of brand-attribute recognition by association has been replaced by a more overt form of testimonial, the "voice of the consumer" strategy that focuses on real people who have switched from a Windows operating environment to Apple Macs. Titled "Real People," the campaign featured folks with likely mass-market appeal: a public relations consultant, a radio DJ, a quilt designer, who have opted to switch to Apple Macs and tell the story, in their own words, of how they felt after moving away from Windows. "It was a horrid little machine," sneers writer Sarah Whistler. "I work all day with Windows and then I go home to the Mac that works," says Aaron Adams, a network administrator who works with a Windows-based network. The statements are informal and personal, and they represent a credible word-of-mouth form of communication that adds to the believability of the message and the situation that the message is placed within. But just how ordinary are these newfound converts?

There was speculation that the twelve enlistees who appear in the television and print advertisements had links with Apple computers, with *US News and World Report*'s investigations connecting DJ Liza Richardson and publisher David Carey with Apple. In its defense, Apple's cofounder and chief executive, Steven P. Jobs, said that the company had selected the people in the ads from more than 10,000 e-mail messages it had received in the form of unsolicited testimonials.[90]

Thus, even though speculation regarding the veracity and credibility of the Apple testimonial may be unfounded, it does raise questions concerning the ethical justification of testimonials as a communication strategy. Insofar as they are designed to create credibility, their execution potentially leaves the brand open to discredit if the testimonials proves noncredible or false.

PROFESSIONAL PRACTICE

Endorsers and the Human Billboard Syndrome

Jamie Oliver, the globally recognized celebrity chef, fills his shopping cart full of trusted products from the Sainsbury's chain of supermarkets, golfer Tiger Woods sweetly times the perfect drive using a Titleist golf ball, basketball player Michael Jordan performs seemingly impossible on-court acrobatics in Nike Air gym shoes, and even actor Pierce Brosnan as James Bond 007 is rescued by a piece of flat plastic with Visa imprinted on it. Today's celebrities are the perfect vehicle for contemporary branding. When we watch them in action, are we watching human endeavor and achievement or just another set of brand attributes? Advertisers see audience numbers, audience types, and branding opportunities. Today's celebrities have become human billboards.

Barely a day goes by without a personality, or an expert, or a "typical person," being placed in front of you as a spokesperson for a product or service. This person is considered to be a credible deliverer of a message, adding to its persuasiveness and appeal, as well as providing a tangible connection with a brand; a connection that means an emotional link for the consumer and big business for the endorser.

Michael Jordan's link with Nike has been well documented to the point where it is estimated his association with the brand has been valued at more than \$10 billion.[91] Tiger Woods's endorsement contracts with companies such as Nike, Buick, Titleist, and Walt Disney Corporation are worth a reported \$50 million a year.[92] At the height of their success in 1997, the Spice Girls employed their own specialist management group to control their merchandising and endorsements, which included brands such as Pepsi and Sony; even U.K. supermarket chain ASDA introduced more than 40 Spice Girl products. Michael Jackson's eminence placed him in Pepsi territory, and former world number one tennis player Pat Rafter had his "Mr. nice guy" attributes transferred to Lays Potato Chips. The objective of these endorsements is to instill recognizable brand attributes and to break through the clutter that is the contemporary advertising environment.

Today's advertising environment is a complex animal constructed by an increasing number of competing brands, a proliferation of media options, and a more communication-savvy consumer. In order to survive in this environment and to live successfully in a consumer's mind, thoughtfully designed and strategically placed brand messages are imperative. The use of testimonials and endorsements is a tried-and-true strategy that has survived the evolution of advertising, through reinvention and reengineering, to remain one of the most potent of branding devices.

So What Is a Testimonial or an Endorsement?

Word of mouth is an extremely powerful and convincing form of communication. It consists of words and opinions propagated from the mouths of trusted and reliable sources. In essence, this is an endorsement: an opinion or a message offered by a reliable and credible source.

The U.S. Federal Trade Commission (FTC) has its own formal view on what constitutes a testimonial or an endorsement. Section 255(b) of its Advertising Guidelines states the following:

> An endorsement means any advertising message (including verbal statements, demonstrations, or depictions of the name, signature, likeness or other identifying personal characteristics of an individual or the name or seal of an organization) which consumers are likely to believe reflects the opinions, beliefs, findings, or experience of a party other than the sponsoring advertiser.[93]

This definition clearly identifies the element of independence of the endorser as a third party, and this independence becomes a critical component in evaluation of the authenticity of endorsements and testimonials.

The FTC's point of clarification is whether or not a spokesperson is clearly identified as speaking, by word or by action, what is believed to be an independent opinion. For example, a film critic or racing car driver is considered an expert in his or her field and may offer an independent view on the quality of a particular film or type of car tire. Even if an expert makes no verbal statement but is simply seen using a particular brand, then the person is perceived to be an endorser by association.

A critical differentiation is considered to be the spokesperson's familiarity with consumers;

for example, a pair of housewives discussing the pros and cons of a brand of laundry detergent or a man dressed in a white coat voicing the advantages of a particular brand of cough syrup would not be considered as endorsements unless they are substantiated with a statement of endorser authenticity. Actual consumers' views should be delivered by actual consumers to be genuine testimonials or endorsements. Without this qualification, the statements are seen purely as statements from the advertiser.

Types of Endorsements and Testimonials

In a bid to allow a brand to infiltrate a consumer's consideration set, it must have relevance; it must break through the clutter and make a connection with a target; and that connection, in turn, is strengthened when the brand possesses some rational or emotional credibility. An endorser provides both rational and emotional credibility sources dependent upon the type of endorser.

A variety of endorser labels exist that include references to celebrities, experts, consumers, satisfied customers, spokes-characters, and typical persons. In this treatment, we will refer to four types of endorsers: the authority figure, the celebrity, the typical person, and the artificial endorser.

Authority Figure

The authority figure is the expert endorser who has a voice of authority on a topic, issue, or product. It is expected that this person possesses some qualification or expertise in respect to the claim being made in the message, and this qualification is made evident in the message environment. It is this person's experience of the product environment that brings credibility to the message. An example is a dentist who speaks of the virtues of using a particular type of toothbrush.

It is not expected that anyone would challenge Tiger Woods's opinion on which is the best golf ball in the market.

Celebrity

This authority figure is generally a high-profile actor, athlete, or entertainer, known to the public for achievements or attributes outside of the endorsed product's environment. In this case, consumers' feelings toward a celebrity and/or the meaning the consumer associates with the celebrity are expected to transfer to the endorsed brand through their recurring association. The figure's role is to make the emotional link between the brand and the consumer (for example, a model and a hair shampoo brand). It is typical, however, that the celebrity endorser has some rational connection with the brand's product environment. For example, Michael Jordan's long association with Nike footwear is a case in which the endorser acts as an authority figure and celebrity endorser. Tiger Woods's authority on Disney products or Spice Girls' authority on bath towels is a little more questionable.

The use of the celebrity endorser is the most overt of endorsement strategies and the one that is subject to most skepticism because of the celebrity's lack of authority and the proliferation of celebrity-endorsed brands. It is estimated that in the United States, close to one in four of all advertisements use the strategy of celebrity endorsements.[94] The celebrity endorser's attractiveness (physical) is a key factor in the effectiveness of his or her endorsement, and his or her likability will determine the degree of believability that is transferred to the endorsed brand.

The celebrity's high profile provides "cut through" as well as the opportunity to present a global image, and his or her well-known attributes provide a tangible link to a brand. It is no wonder that they command such high prices for their fame.

Typical Person

Generally portrayed as a satisfied user, a "typical person" is an actual consumer or a typical person having had experience with the brand or attribute proposed in the advertising message. These are regular people using the product and acknowledging its benefits. For the typical person endorser his or her credibility is paramount. Convincing consumers that the endorser is an actual consumer like themselves is a key to the testimonial's effectiveness. And similarly, regulators are charged with the responsibility to ensure that the endorser is just that (see Case Study 6b).

Artificial Endorser

The artificial endorser is a constructed character. Like the celebrity endorser, the endorser could be likable or credible for attributes attained outside the product environment. The most common artificial endorser is the animated character. Animated characters have proliferated in parallel with the development of digital technologies, from the basic cartoon characters such as Mickey Mouse, the Road Runner, and Scooby Doo (who have been used to sell an enormous range of products) to the more sophisticated animations such as Lara Croft. All of these characters contain attributes (one of which is enormous fan bases) that are utilized in both the branding process and the selling process. One of the unique attributes of these endorsers is that their image is not likely to be scarred by negative publicity, and their longevity is a little more guaranteed.

Another constructed character is the actor "framed" as the credible source who delivers the message with conviction or the character who endorses a brand by attribute association. An example is discussed in Case Study 6c, Apple Macintosh's use of "great thinkers" actually transfers the innovative attributes of the characters across to the brand, just as celebrity endorsers so frequently do.

We also previously referred to the white-coated lab assistant who talks about the virtues of a particular ingredient that is a gum-disease-prevention agent. The realistic portrayal and recurrence of these characters do, in fact, make them spokespersons and brand ambassadors. It is debatable as to whether or not they are any less believable than the animations or celebrities that act as credible sources for products. In Australia, Pizza Hut created the character Dougie, the pizza delivery boy, who became a regular spokesperson for the brand. His personality traits transferred across to the brand with great success. Unfortunately, the actor who portrayed Dougie fell afoul of the law, and the character was written out of future campaigns. Consumer research revealed that consumers actually missed Dougie, so he was resurrected, with a different actor, of course.

Regulatory Issues with Endorsements and Testimonials

In applying some regulation, or consumer protection, to endorsements, regulators consider two key factors: honesty and substantiation. For example, the U.S. FTC in its Advertising Guidelines makes the consideration that

> Endorsements must always reflect the honest opinions, findings, beliefs, or experience of the endorser. Furthermore, they may not contain any representations which would be deceptive, or could not be substantiated if made directly by the advertiser (Code 255.1 a.).[95]

Substantiation or proof of endorser opinion is the key to identifying misleading or deceptive practice. This is the main concern reflected in the ASA's British Codes of Advertising and Sales Promotion.[96] Code 14.1 states that

> Advertisers should hold signed and dated proof, including a contact address, for any testimonial

they use. Unless they are genuine opinions taken from a published source, testimonials should be used only with the written permission of those giving them.

Code 14.4 reinforces the honesty directive:

> Fictitious testimonials should not be presented as though they are genuine.

British Sky Broadcasting Example

In April 2000, British Sky Broadcasting came under the scrutiny of the Advertising Standards Authority through objections to a national press advertisement and a mailing for a sky satellite channel. The advertisement showed two elderly ladies sitting on a park bench. One had a speech bubble above her head, which stated, "These days, young people have no-one to set them an example. They need some guidance." The lady featured in the advertisement objected that the picture had been taken and used in the advertisement without her permission and that the sentiment expressed was not hers. The authority upheld the complaint, reminding the advertisers that the codes (14.1) urged advertisers to get written permission if they portray or refer to individuals in an advertisement and that a review of the advertisers' procedures in this regard be undertaken.[97]

Not the Final Say

Much has been written about what makes an effective endorsement, whether it's the attractiveness of the source, the credibility of the source, and the relevance of the source to the product endorsed. To debate this is not the purpose of this book. What we have established is the use of endorsements and testimonials as an advertising message and branding strategy, a strategy that has been proven to be effective. Their use provides a tangible link between a brand and a set of attributes; provides an effective element for brand recall and recognition; and provides a message with credibility, believability, and likability. But like most advertising strategies discussed in this book, the use of endorsements also harbors ethical problems and consequences.

ETHICAL ANALYSIS

A critical factor in the use of endorsements and testimonials is their *credibility.* The credibility of the endorsements (for convenience of reference we will henceforth use the term "endorsements" to refer to both endorsements and testimonials unless otherwise specified) primarily depends on the *reliability* and *independence* of the *source* of the endorsement. More specifically, it depends, like knowledge claims, which we examined in Chapter 4, on three conditions: belief, justification, and truth:

1. The endorser *believes,* to the best of his or her knowledge, that the claim that he or she is making is true.
2. The endorser can provide or is capable of providing independent corroborating evidence to substantiate and *justify* the endorsement. For this to happen, it is necessary, in turn, that:

   a. The endorser possesses *knowledge, expertise, or experience* that is directly or at least indirectly *relevant* to the product or service that he or she is endorsing. For example, Tiger Woods's knowledge, expertise, and experience would be directly relevant to his endorsements of golf balls or other golf equipment. Equally but to a lesser extent, his knowledge, expertise, or experience would be less relevant but still indirectly relevant to his endorsements of running shoes if, as a matter of fact, he runs to stay fit for playing golf. Similarly, Michael Jordan's knowledge and experience would be directly relevant to his endorsements of basketball shoes or other

basketball products but only indirectly relevant to his endorsements of running shoes if, as an athlete, it is highly probable that he used to run to stay fit for playing basketball. By contrast, Michael Jackson's endorsement of basketball or golf products would lack credibility because it would lack the authority of knowledge or experience of the endorser relevant to the products endorsed. Michael Jackson's knowledge, expertise, or experience in music, singing, and dancing would not be directly or indirectly relevant to golf or basketball products.

   b. The endorsement reflects the honest opinions and beliefs of the endorser either directly through his or her own statements or claims or by association of his or her person to the product endorsed. In other words, the endorsement should primarily reflect the honest opinions and beliefs of the endorser and not those of the advertiser. Hence, the endorser's statements or claims about the product endorsed should be *independent* of those of the advertiser. Notice how the *condition of independence* tracks the *condition of belief,* described before in section 1. That is to say, the endorser's beliefs of the statements or claims he or she is making in the endorsement of a product, either directly by his or her own statements or indirectly through the association of his or her person to the product endorsed, reflect the endorser's own honest beliefs of the product endorsed, independently of those of the advertiser.

The condition of independence refers primarily to the *epistemological status* of the endorser's opinions or beliefs about the products of his or her endorsements and not to the financial arrangements with the advertiser concerning the financial payments to the endorsers by the advertisers for making those endorsements. Insofar as all endorsers are paid for their endorsements by advertisers—and paid handsomely—the endorsements cannot be strictly independent in the sense that they are freely initiated by the endorsers without any financial inducement or reward.

However, financial payment to the endorsers by the advertisers renders those endorsements to *appear* less independent and ultimately *less credible* than they would otherwise be without the financial payments to the endorsers. It is of course possible that the endorsers' opinions and beliefs about the products that they endorse truly reflect the honest opinions and beliefs of the endorsers, notwithstanding that they have been paid by the advertisers for making those endorsements. Nevertheless, payment to an endorser for an endorsement makes the endorsement less credible because the testimony of the endorser concerning the product endorsed *appears* to a consumer less independent and therefore less reliable, since the endorser has been paid by the advertiser to endorse a particular product. This is especially the case with regard to the *authority* and *typical person* types of endorsements discussed earlier when the veracity of the testimony of the endorser is critical, since the endorsements purport to be those of "authority figures" or "real persons" who have relevant knowledge through their expertise or experience of the products endorsed. As such, that knowledge by definition needs to be either true or at least, to the best of the endorser's knowledge, believed to be true.

However, being paid to make the endorsement undercuts the veracity and, by extension, the epistemological credibility of the endorser's claims about a product. By contrast, in the case of endorsements of products by *celebrities* or artificial *endorsers,* the endorsement works by *status association,* roughly in a similar way in which the association of a consumer product with an aspirational value, such as happiness, is designed to raise the status of the product advertised to the status of the aspirational value that the product is associated with. For example, in the advertisement "Happiness Is Hyundai," the advertisement is designed to raise the status of the brand "Hyundai" in consumer consciousness to that of the aspirational value "happiness."

Similarly, celebrity and artificial endorsements work metaphorically and do not purport to be the informed opinions of knowledgeable expert endorsers who have relevant knowledge about the products endorsed. Therefore, the Spice Girls' endorsement of bath towels or Michael Jackson's endorsement of Pepsi or Einstein's "endorsement" of Apple computers in the "Think Different" advertising campaign do not purport to ascribe relevant and honestly held opinions to the endorsers about the products endorsed. The endorsements are intended to work by metaphorical association in the sense that the celebrity status or intelligence status of the endorsers will be transferred in the minds of the consumers to the products endorsed. The consumers in these types of endorsements care more for the endorser's celebrity status as a pop idol or famous scientist than the reliable and credible knowledge that the endorser has about the products endorsed. To consumers influenced by these types of endorsements, that credibility is irrelevant. Not so, however, when the endorser is being presented as a credible witness either in the form of an authority figure or a "real" typical person who has relevant expertise and experience of the products endorsed. Then the epistemological reliability and credibility of the endorser concerning the products endorsed by him or her is not only relevant but also critical for the consumer.

The perceived financial dependence of an endorser's claims about the products he or she endorses raises a problem concerning an inherent *conflict of interest* at the heart of endorsements, specifically, in the case of the "authority figure" and "typical person" types of endorsements. Before we can examine why endorsements constitute a conflict of interest, we need to get a clear idea of what a conflict of interest is. According to the "standard view,"[98]

A conflict of interest is a situation in which some person *P* (whether an individual or corporate body) has a conflict of interest. *P* has a conflict of interest if and only if (1) *P* is in a relationship with another requiring *P* to exercise judgement in the other's behalf and (2) *P* has a (special) interest tending to interfere with the proper exercise of judgement in that relationship. The crucial terms in this definition are "relationship," "judgement," "interest" and "proper exercise."

The "relationship" required must be fiduciary, that is, it must involve one person trusting (or at least be entitled to trust) another, to exercise judgment in his or her service. "Judgment" is the ability to make certain kinds of decisions that require knowledge or skill, correctly and reliably. "Interest" is any influence, loyalty, concern, emotion, or other feature of a situation tending to make *P*'s judgment (in that situation) less reliable than it would normally be. "Proper exercise" of judgment is normally a question of social fact and includes what people ordinarily expect, what *P*, or the group *P* belongs to, invites others to expect, and what various laws, professional codes, or other regulations require.[99]

What is generally wrong with a conflict of interest is that it renders one's judgment less reliable than what it normally should be and results in a failure or an abuse of a fiduciary duty. Let it be understood that "fiduciary duty" as used with regard to endorsements, especially the "authority figure" and "typical person" types, is applied in a much more general and wider sense than normally intended when strictly used in its quasi-legalistic sense. Significantly for our present purposes, what the term as used here is intended to convey is a relationship of trust that involves one person (the consumer) trusting (or at least be entitled to trust) another (the endorser as the "authority figure" or "typical person" type) to exercise reliable and trustworthy judgment in his or her service. Thus when someone like Carl Lewis, who is perceived as an authority on physical fitness and by extension an authority on matters of health, claims that a particular drug is effective in alleviating the pain of arthritis, a

consumer is entitled to take Lewis's testimony as trustworthy and reliable. In that sense, Carl Lewis owes the consumer a fiduciary duty of trust that requires him not to deceive or mislead consumers by his testimony regarding the important matter concerning the treatment of arthritis.

By contrast, in the case of the type of endorsements that work mainly by association, a fiduciary duty of trust would not be present or expected because it would not be relevant in that context. Thus, Michael Jackson would not be expected to owe a fiduciary duty of trust to Pepsi drinkers simply because Jackson is not perceived, within that context, to be an "authority" on soda. Thus, it would be unreasonable for a consumer to expect Jackson's endorsement of Pepsi to be a credible and reliable testimony, as in the case of Carl Lewis's endorsement of Zenaxin. Generally, endorsements that work by association would not be as ethically problematic as those of the "authority figure" and "typical person" types, because it is only the latter but not the former that contains the implicit condition of a fiduciary duty understood in the wider sense.

Endorsements of the "authority figure" and "typical person" type involve an inherent conflict of interest that is both real and perceived. Insofar as the endorser has an interest, in this case financial, that has a tendency to interfere with the proper exercise of his or her judgment about the endorsed product regarding the reliability and credibility of the information communicated in the endorsement to the consumers, who are ordinarily deemed, and in fact expected, to rely on the credibility and veracity of the endorser's opinions and claims about the products endorsed by him (otherwise the endorsement would have no effect in influencing the targeted consumers about the products endorsed), then the endorser is involved in a conflict of interest. Moreover, the conflict is not only apparent but also real, since the financial interest that the endorser receives from the advertiser has a tendency to interfere with, and potentially at least, to undermine the reliability and credibility of the endorser's judgment about the products that he or she endorses.

However, even if we acknowledge that endorsements constitute a conflict of interest, as it seems that we must, given the standard view of what constitutes conflict of interest, what is wrong with a conflict of interest? There are at least three reasons why a conflict of interest may be considered morally wrong:[100]

1. A person (*P*) involved in a conflict of interest may be negligent in allowing himself or herself to get involved in a conflict of interest and also may be negligent in not responding to the conflict of interest. That is, insofar as *P* is unaware of the conflict of interest in which he or she is involved, he or she has failed to exercise proper duty of care and judgment for the benefit of those to whom he or she owes a fiduciary duty, and thus he or she has acted negligently, an action that is morally wrong. For our present concern, if the endorser was, through lack of reflection, unaware that his or her paid endorsements involved him or her in a conflict of interest and has, as a result, failed to exercise proper duty of care and judgment for the benefit of those to whom he or she owes a fiduciary duty, namely the consumers who relied on his or her endorsements, then he or she has acted negligently toward those consumers, and that action is ethically wrong.

2. If those to whom *P* owes a fiduciary duty are unaware of a conflict of interest in which *P* is involved and if *P* knows that those to whom he or she owes the fiduciary duty are unaware—or at least *P* should know that they are unaware—and does not reveal the conflict to them, then he or she has acted deceptively, and deception for one's self-gain at the expense of others is morally wrong. For our present concern, most consumers would probably be unaware of what a conflict of interest is and why endorsements constitute a conflict of interest. Hence, they would, in all probability, be unaware that an endorser is inherently involved in a conflict of interest. Insofar as an endorser knows that he or she is involved in a conflict of interest and, moreover, knows that the

consumers who are relying on the credibility and veracity of his or her endorsements are unaware that he or she is involved in a conflict of interest, he or she has acted deceptively toward those consumers and has therefore acted unethically. Deception, especially toward those to whom one has a fiduciary duty to tell the truth, is unethical behavior.

3. Notwithstanding that *P* has disclosed his or her conflict of interest, the conflict of interest still remains, if not as a moral problem, at least as a technical problem that can still remain ethically problematic if it harms the reputation of *P*'s profession or institution. This outcome goes to show that the best remedy for resolving a conflict of interest is to avoid it in the first place whenever possible.

Apart from anything else, the fundamental ethical problem with endorsements in advertising is that they constitute an inherent conflict of interest, one that involves the endorsers not only in an apparent but also in a real conflict of interest, at least potentially. The source of this inherent conflict of interest is the inherent conflict between the two potentially opposing principles at play in advertising that we discussed earlier, namely, *the principle of information* and *the principle of persuasion.*

In their intent to appear as credible information, endorsements embody the *principle of information,* which requires information as a form of knowledge to be both true and justified through independent corroboration and verification. On the other hand, as a form of paid-for advertisements, endorsements embody the *principle of persuasion,* which does not necessarily require the information communicated to be either true or justified.

Of course, information that is both true and justified can be, and often is, persuasive. However, persuasion need not necessarily be achieved through information that meets the conditions of knowledge, since misinformation, half-truths, and lies can just as easily be persuasive if presented in the right format. As a form of misinformation, persuasion can be very persuasive, yet it does not qualify as information since it does not meet any of the conditions of knowledge of belief, justification, and truth. Like advertorials, the hybrid nature of endorsements as being at once intended as credible and reliable information provided by expert and experienced witnesses who are purported to possess relevant knowledge about the products endorsed, and as being a persuasion strategy in the form of a paid advertisement that undercuts the endorsement's credibility and reliability as a source of information, which is understood as knowledge, renders endorsements ethically problematic with regard both to the endorsers and to the advertisers. Insofar as endorsements are known to be deceptive or misleading by both the endorsers and the advertisers, they amount to a complicity of deception that is morally objectionable.

Although difficult to determine with any degree of certainty, the Carl Lewis endorsement of Zenaxin as a product that relieves the pain of arthritis (Case Study 6a) raises the question of complicity between Carl Lewis as the endorser and the manufacturer of Zenaxin as the advertiser to deceive the consumers. In the absence of any clear evidence that there was an intention to deceive consumers about the use of Zenaxin by Carl Lewis as an alleged sufferer from arthritis, such complicity of deception remains speculative and inconclusive.

However, the way that consumers may have been led to believe that Carl Lewis's endorsement of the product was based on his own experience of Zenaxin as a successful treatment of arthritis, raises a question of negligence on the part of both Lewis as the endorser and the manufacturer of Zenaxin as the advertiser. That is, if Lewis and the advertiser of Zenaxin were aware, or at least should have been aware, that consumers might have reasonably been led to believe from Lewis's endorsement of Zenaxin that Lewis himself had used Zenaxin for treatment of

his own alleged arthritis, then steps should have been taken to dispel that ambiguity and confusion in the minds of consumers by clearly communicating to the consumers the fact that although Lewis was endorsing Zenaxin, Lewis himself had at no time been a sufferer of arthritis and hence had not had any personal experience of its alleged therapeutic or pain relief merits.

Such a statement would have removed Lewis's endorsement from the "authority figure" category of endorsements that requires the endorsement to be based on reliable and credible experience or expertise of the endorser relevant to the product endorsed, and would have placed it instead in the celebrity category of "celebrity" endorsements, which do not require such reliable and credible experience or expertise relevant to the product endorsed.

In sum, Lewis as the endorser and the manufacturer of Zenaxin as the advertiser acted either deceptively or at least negligently in allowing consumers to form the reasonable opinion or belief that Lewis's endorsement of Zenaxin was based on Lewis's own knowledge and experience of the drug in the treatment of arthritis as a sufferer of arthritis himself, especially if, as it is reasonable to assume, the endorsement was intended as an "authority figure" type endorsement. This assumption is in keeping with the U.S. Federal Trade Commission's Advertising Guidelines section 255(b), as mentioned earlier. Hence, as a form of negligence, Carl Lewis's endorsement of Zenaxin was morally irresponsible; and as a form of deception, if the intention to deceive was in fact the case or at least the intention was to create an ambiguity in the meaning of the communication of the endorsement that was likely to deceive the consumers, then the endorsement was morally objectionable.

By parity of argument, the same rationale applies to the Apple computers case (Case Study 6c), in which the ambiguity of whether the endorsers were genuine and real "typical persons" offering their own honest opinions of the merits of

Apple computers and not merely expressing the opinions of the advertiser as hired guns. The ambiguity could have been avoided if the endorsements were accompanied by a clear and unequivocal statement that none of the "typical persons" endorsers were in any way professionally or organizationally associated with Apple. To the extent that it allowed the ambiguity to occur without correction, Apple was negligent and thus ethically irresponsible, and to the extent that Apple deceived the consumers about the independence of the endorsers as real "typical persons," Apple acted deceptively and thus acted unethically.

In a more straightforward case, Sony (see Case Study 6b) acted unethically in presenting fake "real" typical persons as endorsers, since clearly the intention was to deceive the consumers into thinking that the opinions expressed by the endorsers for the film *The Patriot* were the honestly held opinions of the "real" typical persons making those endorsements and not simply the opinions of Sony, which the fake endorsers were paid to repeat.

Because the conflict of interest with regard to the "authority figure" type of endorsements is an inherent conflict of interest that lies at the heart of these types of endorsements, the ethical problems associated with this type of conflict, which were discussed before, constitute a *systemic* ethical problem for advertising. The ethical problem is systemic because it arises as a result of the conception and design of this type of endorsement as an advertising strategy that, as we saw earlier, combines two potentially opposing principles, that of information and that of persuasion, two principles that are constitutive of advertising itself and that render the communicative methodology of the *advertising system* as a whole, ethically inherently problematic.

As a systemic problem that characterizes the whole of advertising, this is an *intractable* problem that, being systemic, can only be addressed piecemeal by trying to minimize any actual and potential harmful ethical consequences of specific advertising strategies. In the case of endorsements, the ethical problems with the misleading "authority figure" type of endorsements, as the ones discussed before, can be by ameliorated reducing, as far as possible, any ambiguity regarding the reliability and credibility of those types of endorsements and by informing the consumers clearly and unequivocally that "authority figure" endorsements are a form of paid advertisements. The latter solution would have the same effect of *disclosing* a conflict of interest. Though the proposed solution does not eliminate the conflict of interest, it does, however, alert the consumers to its presence, something which consumers may, unreflectively, not be aware of. Alternatively, the conflict of interest can be *avoided* by using only "celebrity" and "artificial endorser" types of endorsements, which as we saw, do not involve a conflict of interest, as do only the "authority figure" and "typical person" types of endorsements.

A SUMMARY OF INSTRUMENTAL AND ETHICAL CONSEQUENCES

Desirable

1. As an effective advertising strategy, endorsements and testimonials (for convenience we will refer to both as "endorsements" henceforth) are highly instrumentally desirable, especially when the endorsement takes the form of the "authority figure" and "typical person" discussed earlier. This is the case because the endorsement of an authority figure of a product that he or she has expert knowledge about, such as, for example, Michael Jordan's endorsement of basketball products, lends the endorsement maximal credibility in the mind of the consumer. Equally, the endorsement of a real "typical person" also has credibility because it is perceived by the consumer as being the honest, independent, and true opinion of the endorser about the product endorsed. Word of mouth can be an effective marketing promotion for any product

or service precisely because it is perceived by its recipients as being the honest, independent, and true opinion of the endorser. Every time we recommend a film to an acquaintance, we are in effect acting as a real "typical person" endorser.

Undesirable

1. The effectiveness of the "celebrity" and "artificial endorser" types of endorsements is achieved not because of the perceived veracity and credibility of such endorsements, which as we saw is ultimately irrelevant with regard to these type of endorsements, but through the establishment of a positive emotional association or bond between the product and the celebrity or the artificial endorser. Thus advertisers hope the positive emotions of the admirer for Michael Jackson's music and dancing are transferred in the mind of the admirer to Pepsi, for example, simply because of the association between Michael Jackson with that product. By contrast, however, veracity and thus credibility play a crucial role in the case of the "authority figure" and "typical person" types of endorsements, which, unlike the "celebrity and "artificial endorser" types of endorsements, do rely on the veracity of the endorsement, which in turn is dependent on the veracity and credibility of its source, namely the endorser.

   The ethical problem that arises with the "authority figure" and "artificial endorser" types of endorsements is, as Case Studies 6a, 6b, and 6c illustrate, deception. Whether intentional deception, as in Case Study 6b, or borderline deception between what may be intentional deception or simply accidental deception through negligence or ambiguity, as in Case Studies 6a and 6c, these case studies demonstrate how endorsements of this type can deceive and mislead consumers either intentionally by design or accidentally though negligence or ambiguity in the way that the endorsement is communicated to the consumers. Because deception is generally unethical, "authority figure" and "typical person" types of endorsements that are misleading or deceptive are ethically undesirable, whether the deception is intentional or accidental.

2. The general ethical problem with "the authority figure" and "typical person" type of endorsements is that they involve an inherent conflict of interest that is based in turn on the potential inherent conflict between the dual function of persuasion and information that characterizes the nature of advertising. The conflict of interest involves, as we saw, the tendency of the financial interests that the endorsers receive for their endorsements to interfere and undercut the independence and veracity of those endorsements, which in turn undermines their credibility.

   Because conflicts of interest are generally ethically undesirable and remain, for the most part, ethically problematic even when disclosed (for their disclosure does not eliminate the conflict of interest but merely communicates its presence to the stakeholders, whose informed judgment is reliant upon it, namely, the consumers in this case), endorsements of the "authority figure" and "typical person" types, though instrumentally desirable from a professional perspective as an effective advertising strategy, remain ethically problematic because of their inherent conflict of interest. At the very least, consumers should be informed by the advertisers of the financial interest that an endorser has in the endorsements that he or she makes. This step would not eliminate the conflict of interest with regard to a particular endorsement but would alert the consumers of the presence of the conflict of interest explicitly and would thus allow the consumers the opportunity to put up their epistemological guard regarding the veracity and hence the credibility of the relevant endorsement.

In conclusion, though instrumentally desirable, endorsements of the "authority figure" and "typical person" are ethically problematic and potentially at least ethically undesirable when they result in deceiving or misleading consumers, either intentionally or accidentally. Moreover, the conflict of interest inherent in them should be disclosed to the consumers, since conflicts of interest are generally ethically problematic because of their tendency to mislead, and thus their nondisclosure is ethically undesirable.

chapter seven

Target Advertising and the Ethics of Time and Space

INTRODUCTION

A lot of advertising these days targets specific groups of individuals in order to sell particular products. For example, a sexist ad about a product targeted to young men may appear only in a men's magazine. Similarly, an ad aimed at a mature audience may be screened on television late at night to ensure that children don't watch it. Some forms of advertising targeting may reduce or eliminate potential ethical problems in the case of certain ads. However, some ethical problems with stereotyping, for example, a sexist ad that is demeaning to women, does not cease to be ethically problematic because it is targeted at

a group of men who may not find it in the least ethically problematic or offensive.

Generally, the specific medium of an ad will raise ethical problems and issues particular to that medium. For example, because of its wide exposure, billboard advertising raises specific ethical issues that cannot be minimized or eliminated through target advertising. In some cases, instead of eliminating or minimizing an ethical problem, target advertising may in fact create an ethical problem: for example, the targeting of children, who are not capable of making informed purchasing decisions, or the targeting of young women, who may be adversely influenced in becoming anorexic in attempting to emulate the appearance of thin-looking models in the targeted advertisements.

Some of the key ethical issues that concern targeting have already been addressed in Chapter 3 and Chapter 5. This chapter will examine some other, more pervasive current trends in advertising targeting. One such trend is ambience and 360-degree advertising strategies that attempt to permeate all aspects of the consumer's life. Lately there has been a proliferation of ambient and out-of-home mediums of advertising: billboards, bus shelters, kiosks, train tickets, escalators, massive video screens on train platforms, toilet doors, telephone on-hold advertising, SMS (Short Message Service) messages, viral advertising in bars and other entertainment venues, and the skies above, to mention just a few. The invasion of one's personal and private space, as well as our shared communal public spaces, and the lack of consent in being subjected to these forms of advertising, raise several ethical issues that will be addressed in this chapter.

CASE STUDIES

CASE STUDY 7A   Fictomercial Requires a Read between the Lines[101]

"I want that necklace," hisses Doris Dubois, eyeing a rare, colorful Bulgari piece in red, gold and steel, bright porcelain, and deep ruby. This is not the headline, tagline, or slogan from the latest TV commercial or print campaign but the words of the protagonist in a story of greed and glamour penned by British author Fay Weldon. The twist in the scenario is that the story is actually part of an advertising campaign masterminded by Francesco Trapani, chief executive of the Italian jewelry company Bulgari.

Trapani told *The Times of London*[102] that "It was my idea. If you want to shorten the distance between yourselves and the largest company you have to be more creative. You have to find a different way of communication. We started talking to Fay and she was intrigued with the idea." Weldon was intrigued so much that she agreed not only to mention the brand name throughout the novel but also to base the plot around it and, bonus of bonuses, to use the name in the title.

The Bulgari Connection started out as a promotional piece commissioned by Bulgari for a gala that it held for its clients but ended up as the latest offering from the British author. Fay Weldon, a former advertising writer, was paid an undisclosed sum to mention Bulgari in the book at least twelve times, but she went further, deciding to revolve the novel around Bulgari jewelry and the Italian company's store in London.

In a communication environment where messages and brands are placed on gas pumps, at automatic tellers, in elevators, on taxi seat-backs, on sporting celebrity's attire, in the sky, in films and TV series, in camouflaged editorial content, it requires a creative strategy to stand out in this omnipresent clutter. But when is a point of contact with consumers appropriate, and when have advertisers overstepped the mark?

In the view of the literati, Fay Weldon has done just that. In a review of *The Bulgari Connection*,[103] *New York Times* writer Sylvia Brownrigg credits Weldon with "pioneering this form of fictomercial." She observes: "As the novel's title suggests, Weldon has not hesitated to put Bulgari's elegant Sloane Street store front and centre . . . Bulgari figures as the fulcrum on which her plot can balance." The Bulgari strategy to appeal to an aspirational consumer, to connect with an existing fan base, and to have the brand cut through the communication clutter is clear. But critics of the strategy are adamant that because Weldon was paid by Bulgari to write the novel, it should be called exactly what it is—advertising.

There is an argument that the commercialization of books is not a new strategy, that Shakespeare's sonnets were written for hire, that Ian Fleming's James Bond novels mentioned brand names of cars, that characters are often described by the clothing brands that they wear and the brands of soft drink they that prefer. Writers argue that these signifiers become the thumbprint for characterization, just as they become an advertiser's means of describing a target audience. Who, then, does decide whether or not *The Bulgari Connection* is a bona fide piece of literature or a clever piece of marketing? The answer becomes more difficult when there is a continual blurring of the line between advertising and content in an environment where competition is fierce to develop the next and most innovative media strategy.

This example shows the covert nature of persuasive communication in today's competitive media environment, with increasing amounts of advertising content competing for space in the consumer's mind and for space in the consumer's surrounds. Within this environment, Bulgari has gained a competitive advantage by camouflaging its communication as well as effectively targeting communication to a lucrative and relevant target group or segment.

CASE STUDY 7B   The Sting—The Song Remains the Same?[104]

Pop star Sting sits back as his chauffeur-driven vehicle guides him through a picturesque desert landscape, his latest song "Desert Rose" providing the soundscape. So this must be the latest video from Sting, and I must be watching MTV? Wrong . . . it is actually a commercial for Jaguar— a selling strategy with a double edge.

In 2000, the music of Sting wasn't really considered cutting-edge material. The lack of radio airplay and subsequent lackluster sales supported this status. Enter manager Miles Copeland, whose ingenuity contrived a winning promotional strategy. In making the video for the new song "Desert Rose," for the album *Brand New Day,* Copeland included shots of Sting being chauffeured through

the desert in a car that caught the singer's fancy: the Jaguar S-type sedan. The visuals were the result of a deal with advertising agency Ogilvy and Mather that would give Sting strong brand association and a new audience, while giving Jaguar an added emotional connection to the brand as well as the free brand exposure from video plays on MTV. This is a wonderful example of cross-branding and covert communication.

Barbara Lippert wrote the following in *Adweek* on May 22, 2000:

> Talk about strategic nirvana! Sting is an international luxury brand. So is Jaguar! Sting is on a journey. So is Jaguar! Sting offers an emotional, sensual experience. So does Jaguar! An added bonus: At 47, Sting could break through to the younger, kipper types Jaguar's entry-level car wants to reach.

Jaguar, spending around $19 million on airtime, played a major part in hyping the single's album, *Brand New Day,* in the TV spot. Subsequently, as a result of the commercial's airing, album sales soared. Similarly, Jaguar was introduced to a new range of customers.

Not to let a good strategy go to waste, Sting followed up the campaign with a series of commercials for Compaq, supporters of his national Brand New Day tour. "To sing for me is the greatest freedom," he says in his voiceover for the Compaq commercial. Since we learn in the commercial that Compaq powers and sponsors his tour, we experience a natural affiliation between the artist and the brand, not just another paid testimonial.

CASE STUDY 7C   Not the Opium for the Masses[105]

Creating impact is a key objective of most advertising campaigns, but the byproduct of "widespread offense" is often not within the brief . . . or is it? This is the question raised by Yves St. Laurent's Opium advertising campaign featuring British model Sophie Dahl. The advertisements present the model suggestively reclining naked on a bed except for a pair of high heels and a diamond necklace—the pose, strikingly erotic. The advertisement has become the most-complained-about British advertisement in the past five years, accounting for one-third of all complaints about billboard advertisements in 2000.

Objections were clearly directed at the poster campaign, with complainants stating that the image was offensive, degrading to women, and unsuitable in a public place. The image of the pale, naked woman (model Sophie Dahl) set against a dark blue background, lying on her back with her knees raised, head reclined and lips parted, left hand covering her left breast and right breast exposed, was considered by the United Kingdom's Advertising Standards Authority to be sexually suggestive and likely to cause serious or widespread offense.

In response, the advertiser, Yves St. Laurent, claimed that the image was designed as a work of art to reflect the spirit of Opium and that they believed the image was sensual and aesthetic.

The image was originally placed in glossy magazines; in this environment, the image was deemed acceptable because it was targeted at a specific group and elicited only three complaints. A statement from the Advertising Standards Authority claimed that "It was acceptable in that case because it mainly appeared in women's magazines and was seen by a target audience . . . whereas when the posters went up nationwide the complaints flooded in." The poster accounted for 2,168 of the 12,000 complaints received by the ASA in 2000, its prevalence and prominent placement too much for the British public.[106]

In Australia, the Advertising Standards Board supported this notion that placement rather than image is what offends people when it dismissed complaints against the YSL advertising for Opium. The board determined that the ad did not objectify or demean women because it had been exclusively placed in magazines targeting an adult female readership.

It appears that the image is considered "high art" when it appears in women's fashion and lifestyle magazines but is considered offensive and indecent on the street.

CASE STUDY 7D　The Name Is Brand, James Brand[107]

The James Bond series of films is a franchise that has been entrenched in the minds of consumers for forty years, and apart from the memorable array of stunts, gadgets, and glamorous "Bond women," there has been a parade of brands adorning the sets, scenes, and actors. The series represents product placement at its most potent, since James Bond has come to represent the best things in life. His association with advertised brands means an instant jolt of class, sophistication, and product credibility for those brands.

The franchise's 2002 offering, *Die Another Day,* attracted 45 million pounds of U.K. currency from companies lining up to have their products given the Bond endorsement. The 2002 Bond uses a Phillips shaver, drinks Bollinger champagne and Finlandia vodka, drives an Aston Martin Vanquish, flies British Airways, and wears an Omega Seamaster watch to complement his Brioni suits. This is a departure from the previous Bond, who was a BMW driver, wore a Rolex watch, drank Smirnoff vodka, and flew Olympic Airways. The new revelation about Bond's character is that he is obviously a brand switcher, but the bottom line is that the placement of brands in films is big business and is not a new strategy.

A brief history, not of time but of brand placements in films, reveals that in 1955 when James Dean used an Ace comb in the film *Rebel Without a Cause,* the comb sold out. Coca Cola began its association with the medium in the 1963 film *It's a Mad Mad Mad Mad World* (the brand's continued presence in the medium is estimated at $740 million annually). In the 1964 film *Goldfinger,* James Bond became an Aston Martin driver (only to change his preference to a BMW in 1995). The Hershey confectionary company's Reese's Pieces became a prominent brand through its presence in the 1982 block-buster movie *E.T.* (sales increased 66 percent in the first three months after the film's release). Heineken beer features in *Austin Powers 2: The Spy Who Shagged Me* (1999). FedEx is prominent in 2000's *Castaway.* The 2003 sequel to *The Matrix* sees stars Keanu Reeves and Hugo Weaving fighting in front of a background of $5 million worth of high-tech television screens supplied by LG (LG Electronics) (a separate scene is being reshot in front of Zenith televisions for the U.S. market). And although the 2002 futurist film *Minority Report* satirized product placement, it also had no problem attracting around $25 million from companies wanting to put their brands on the big screen.

Norm Marshall & Associates is a product placement company devoting most of its efforts to securing deals for big movies for its clients. It understands the global branding value of the medium along with the breakthrough that the tactic achieves. So too does the marketing industry, which has honored the work of the company by bestowing awards for its product placement strategies (most notably launching the BMW Z3 in the 1995 Bond film *Golden Eye*).

In a marketing environment in which the consumer is media savvy and is resentful of the intrusion of advertising into their lives, product placement serves as another covert form of "invisible advertising" that provides both brand exposure and brand credibility.

PROFESSIONAL PRACTICE

But why has this covert communication strategy become so critical and seemingly palatable?

Average consumers today are bombarded with more communication than they can handle. Advertising messages are everywhere and on everything, creating a media environment that is cluttered and unpredictable. Advertisers consider the world simply as an artist's palate for advertising messages. Estimations on the amount of advertising that the average person is subjected to range between 1,000 and 3,000 exposures daily. This degree of clutter, which is created by the sheer volume of advertising, is a barrier to effective communication and is what drives advertisers to look for that breakthrough opportunity. In order to stay competitive in this cluttered media landscape, the architects of advertising need to be creating advertising that doesn't look, feel, smell, or taste like the generic advertising that the new media-savvy and sophisticated consumers have become used to.

Traditionally, the media sell themselves on their ability to attract attention and to attract large

numbers of particular types of consumers. This reach dictates the price that the advertiser will pay and is a benchmark for forecasting the potential effectiveness of the advertising. But this advertising paradigm is reinventing itself out of the necessity to pierce the protective armor of the guarded and knowledgeable consumer.

In the past, advertising media were seen predominantly as traditional "channels of communication" that could carry advertising messages to consumers, using such channels as newspapers, magazines, television, radio, and outdoor posters. But these traditional media have been challenged as effective channels of communication on the grounds that they are too cluttered, too fragmented, too expensive, and just too obvious.

If you consider that the number of media options and spaces available to advertisers is proliferating at an increasing rate, it is no wonder that consumers have become more selective in the media and the messages that they will attend to. Media audiences have fragmented into subaudiences that have developed alternatives to the traditional sources of information and entertainment. From the traditional channels of TV, radio, magazines, newspapers, and outdoor posters have emerged competitors for advertising dollars. These challengers have grown out of the adoption of technology—the Internet, digital media such as iTV (Interactive TV), SMS (Short Message Service), and WAP (Wireless Application Protocol), and innovative media extensions such as the use of outdoor furniture and public private space, transport, cultural events, utilities, and personalities.

With this armory of communication weapons, the advertiser is fully equipped for a full-scale assault on its target. Advertisers now have their warfare templates clearly established and labeled as "integrated communication" strategies—a discipline that forces the advertiser to communicate to consumers with synergy and repetition. Also, 360-degree strategies are being developed that prompt the advertiser to surround the target, using a fully researched and planned combination of media options. Such sophisticated methodologies give the consumer little chance but to raise their hands and surrender. Consumers are so well-researched and targeted that they can be covertly seduced by a strategy that surrounds them and that infiltrates their physical and mental space, often without their realization. To the advertiser, this is an effective strategy.

Consider this scenario: Take the time poor, urban, young professional, let us call him Arthur, who is concerned for his health but has not had the time to do something about it. A case in point is breakfast. Brand K has a solution—the "eat on the go" breakfast bar. While this may seem like a solution, is it really? Does it contain the nutrients that will really keep the consumer on the go and feeling healthy? Regardless, the advertiser can surround this consumer with the communication that positions this questionable solution as a viable proposition.

The consumer's lifestyle and habits have been tracked, their mindset has been calculated, and their esteem needs and self-doubts have been identified. It is time to set the trap. Using a carefully planned mix of media, the target will be surrounded with communication. Knowing that train travel is a key transport option for the target, this "experience" is being used to create a pathway to the consumer's mindset. He waits for his train at platform A, all the time staring at a poster that tells him that K-Bar is "good food for people on the go." His train arrives, he is seated and looks up to see an interior poster that reminds him that he has probably not eaten healthily this morning and that K-Bar is "good food for people on the go." He toys with his train ticket, twisting it over and over, only to realize that the ticket back reinforces the now familiar message. He alights at his usual destination to be greeted once again by a station billboard that reminds him that K-Bar is "good food for people on the go." He takes the nearest stairs to exit the platform, only to be distracted by a series of stair risers that tell him that K-Bar is "good food for people on the go." He makes it to the top, where the station hall is a blaze of corporate color reinforcing the K-Bar packaging on floor mats, wall posters, and mobiles, all adorning the message that K-Bar is "good food for people on the go." Finally, he is greeted by a healthy specimen of a female costumed in those familiar brand colors, who smiles and offers a free taste of the wonder product K-Bar. He has been seductively ambushed, and the trip to work will never be the same again. He will look for those familiar colors, and they will be the messages that remind him of how healthy he is now that he consumes a K-Bar on route to work. His commuting habit now consists of the ritual visit to the K-Bar vending machine.

Using this strategy, the target (as he is a target in every sense of the word) has not volunteered to receive any of the advertising that he has been subjected to. He has not switched on a TV or radio, nor has he opened a newspaper or magazine with the mindset that this habit comes at a price—advertising. No, he has been seduced by effective, targeted, integrated, and cleverly constructed covert communication.

This strategy has been effective for the advertiser and ingested by the consumer without question. There have been no complaints to an advertising standards bureau, since no standards appear to have been infringed. The acceptance and effectiveness of such strategies have only fueled the creativity of the advertising architects, who continue to invent new channels for communicating. This search for innovation has seen the development and growth of tools such as product placement (pushed to the limit by Bulgari); branding of cultural events and personalities; corporate ownership of public spaces; and the emergence of the new media badge "ambient media," which is loosely defined as the range of alternative, innovative, covert, and maverick media ideas that generally cannot be pigeonholed into an easily recognized class of media. This collection of ambushing tools is the new weaponry in the war against the sophisticated and savvy consumer who not only accepts but appreciates the surprise invasion and who often rewards the creativity with his or her undivided attention. Mission accomplished, says the advertiser.

ETHICAL ANALYSIS

We can now begin to explore why the forms of advertising just described are, or are not, ethically problematic. After all, if advertising is in the business of trying to persuade consumers to be favorably disposed toward certain products, then the dual strategies of saturation and target advertising would appear to be effective in their design in meeting that objective and thus would appear to be in congruence with the role morality of advertising. However, as we saw earlier (Chapter 1), professional role morality must give way to universal public morality when the two come into a mutually exclusive conflict. Do

saturation and target advertising undermine in any way the public morality? To determine whether they do or not, let us consider the following arguments.

The Privacy Argument

Our right to privacy is a right based on our generic rights to freedom and well-being (see Chapter 1). For inasmuch as we need some private time and space to ourselves to pursue our chosen legitimate goals and activities without interference or hindrance from others—goals and activities that generally contribute to our overall freedom and well-being—then we have a right to our own private space and time. We therefore have, as individuals, a right to privacy, a right that can be only infringed by another conflicting right that justifiably takes precedence. For example, a politician's right to privacy may justifiably be infringed by the media when public exposure of an illicit activity that she pursued in private is a matter of public interest. The politician's illicit activity becomes a matter of public interest when the illicit activity that the politician is engaged in can reasonably be perceived to impact on her ability to properly dispense with her duties and responsibilities as a politician.

Because our right to privacy is based on our right to freedom, the right to privacy is closely related to our right to freedom of choice. With some forms of advertising, we can choose to switch our television or radio sets off when unwelcome ads come intruding into our private space, and to switch the sets on again when the ads have finished. In those circumstances, we are able to exercise the choice not to view or hear the unwelcome ads. In general, we can exercise the choice not to watch or listen to commercial media channels or to view ads in newspapers or magazines. We also have a choice to hang up on unwelcome and unsolicited marketing offers or ads that come over the telephone.

In Australia, people can also place a sign indicating that they do not want unsolicited advertising material placed in their mailbox.

Sometimes, such as when we go to the movies, we choose, at least notionally and implicitly by default, to waive our collective right to freedom of choice with regard to the screening of premovie ads. We may justify the waiving of the right of choice with regard to premovie ads on the basis that a ticket to the movies would cost a lot more if movie screenings were ad free. Similarly, in the case of free-to-air TV and radio, we may tolerate the ads because we get the broadcast programs free, at least financially free. In sum, there are a lot of forms of advertising over which we can exercise our freedom of choice or waive that right, to view, read or listen, to ads.

However, there are forms of advertising that take that choice away and render us unable to choose whether or not to view, listen, or read unwelcome and unsolicited ads. Billboard ads placed in public places are one example. Pedestrians may divert their gaze from the unwelcome ads, but that choice may not be available to car drivers who may not be able to avert their eyes from the unwelcome billboard ads on the chance of causing a traffic accident. Still, pedestrians and drivers may accept waiving their right of choice to being involuntarily exposed to billboard ads, at least implicitly, in the belief that a fraction of revenue generated from billboard ads is somehow spent by the government on the improvement of roads and pavements.

In general, we may reasonably assume that consumers are willing to accept the curtailment of their freedom of choice as whether or not to view, listen, watch, or read free-to-air TV, radio, and billboard ads, as well as ads in other forms of media that pervade our private and public spaces, on the understanding that these forms of advertising are cost-reducing against other benefits and services provided by those forms of media. Let us refer to this argument as the "The Suspension of Discontent" argument.

The Suspension of Discontent Argument

Simply put, the suspension of discontent argument claims that consumers may be willing to waive their right to freely choose whether or not to be exposed to advertising, at least notionally, when advertising leads to some cost reduction in products or services, for example, in the case of free-to-air TV and radio programs, or free Internet and e-mail services. Cost reduction advertising would appear to be a win-win situation for consumers, advertisers, and product and service providers alike. It seems that everyone is a winner, at least financially.

More generally, consumers may be willing to suspend their discontent at being exposed to unsolicited ads without their consent if there is some kind of trade-off. Moreover, the financial trade-off in terms of cost reduction in products or services could take the form of other nonfinancial gains, such as entertainment provided by clever or humorous ads. Clever and humorous ads have a tendency to lighten up our collective and communal mood.

Thus, according to the suspension of discontent argument, consumers may be willing to accept the infringement of their rights to privacy and consent by their involuntary exposure to unsolicited ads if it results in some benefit, either in the form of cost reductions in consumer products and services, or in nonfinancial benefits in the form of entertainment provided by clever and humorous ads.

The Time-Out Argument

Imagine lying on the golden sand of your favorite beach on a beautiful summer day, looking up at a cloudless blue sky. Suddenly a plane appears and starts skywriting some advertising message for a consumer product or service. How would you feel? Chances are that like most people, you may feel slightly annoyed that your tranquil reverie has been disturbed by the unwelcome and unsolicited ad overhead. After all, we expect that certain spaces like the skies should be kept free of advertising.

An argument for thinking so may run as follows: There are certain cultural, natural, and spiritual spaces, such as beaches, forests, botanic gardens, public parks, art galleries, museums, and temples that have been set aside for our quiet collective enjoyment, relaxation, and edification. These are places to which we can periodically retreat when we wish to escape briefly from the hassle and bustle of a busy life.

As a society, we expect such places to be free from the invasive practices of advertising, and generally speaking, they are. Perhaps such places of retreat are deemed essential for our collective well-being. They are places where we can briefly take time out from the hectic activities of commercial enterprise, including the relentless onslaught of advertising. It is not much to ask, considering that every nook and cranny of every conceivable space in any city, town, or village, including the endless miles of highways, have been branded with some form of advertising. We need these spaces where we can be ourselves and be by ourselves without being told by advertising messages what to desire or what to eat, drink, drive, wear, or otherwise consume, or aspire to acquire. Moreover, because such places are deemed priceless to us, their value is intrinsically part of the core of our common humanity. No payoff or trade-off can compensate us enough for implicitly agreeing to suspend our collective discontent at having these spaces open to advertising. It is reasonable, therefore, to assume that most people will not be willing to waive their collective consent in allowing the invasion of these spaces by advertising. We can conclude that advertising in those spaces could prove so unpopular that its primary purpose of generating a pro-attitude in consumers with regard to the advertised products or services would become self-defeating and therefore instrumentally and pragmatically pointless.

The Preservation of Aesthetic Space Argument

Like forests, parks, temples, and beaches, art that is in the form of literature, music, sculpture, and painting provides a cultural retreat where people can seek enjoyment in the freedom of their imagination, comfort, relaxation, and edification. As in the case of the natural spaces, it is reasonable to assume that people expect these aesthetic spaces to be free of the commercial tentacles of advertising. That assumption might explain why people may feel unease when they discover that their favorite piece of music is being used to advertise a car or an aftershave lotion.

In Case Study 7a, an elaborate advertisement for the Italian jewelry company Bulgari was presented in the form of a novel, *The Bulgari Connection,* by the British writer Fay Weldon. Insofar as *The Bulgari Connection* can be described as a "fictomercial," then it is similar in kind to advertorials, which, as we saw earlier, are commercial ads masquerading as editorial comment. As a fictomercial, the book faces the same ethical problem that all advertorials face. It is deceptive. Any person who read Weldon's fictomercial and thought that he or she was merely reading a novel and not an elaborate advertisement for Bulgari jewelry would have been deceived. And deception is, as discussed earlier, unethical.

Moreover, the invasion of the aesthetic space of the novel by advertising is also ethically problematic because such spaces are normally expected by readers of literature to be free of the invasive practices of commercial advertising. Similarly, in Case Study 7b, the cross-branding of Sting's song "Desert Rose" with the ad for Jaguar's luxury S-type sedan seems to overstep the line that separates the space of art and culture generally from that of advertising (see, for example, Case Study 7d, which clearly illustrates the different covert ways in which culture has become commodified through multibranding).

The commercial nature of the cross-branding of Sting's music and the S-type Jaguar is not itself the ethical problem; commercial interest is one of the main, if not primary, considerations in the production of music and one that may in fact justify, at least instrumentally, this type of cross-branding. Rather, it is the invasion of the artistic domain of music by advertising and its associated aspirational values that music generally, and Sting's music in particular, is perceived to evoke. Unlike an advertorial and Weldon's fictomercial, however, its real purpose, although ambiguous, is not concealed from its intended audience and therefore escapes the ethical charge of deception. Nevertheless, by invading the aesthetic space of music, a space that it seems reasonable to assume that we as a community would prefer to keep, like other sacred spaces, free of advertising, cross-branding advertising as in the cases of Weldon's novel and Sting's music, remains ethically problematic.

As was discussed in Chapter 3, the advertising industry has a collective ethical responsibility not just to its clients but equally to society at large, namely, the responsibility for contributing to the preservation and protection of the collective aspirational values that we share as a community. This responsibility includes the preservation and protection of the natural, cultural, and aesthetic spaces in which those values can find true expression free of the commercial concerns and constraints of marketing and advertising. As we saw earlier, the time-out argument ethically requires the advertising industry to stay out of these spaces. For ease of reference, let us henceforth refer to these spaces as our collective "sacred spaces."

The Overload Argument

If, as Aristotle claimed, one swallow does not make a summer, likewise, one individual ad that might periodically invade any of our collective and communal sacred spaces does not spell an ethical catastrophe, and in the greater scheme of things, it is not such a big deal. Rather, the problem lies in the onslaught of saturation branding of these sacred spaces by advertising. Soon, if the trend continues, there might not be any sacred spaces left empty of advertising, and this outcome could lead to the emptiness of any sort of cultural meaning in society other than the meaning of brands. Do we as a society desire such a scenario? We believe not. Even the people who work in the advertising industry must prefer to keep their own favorite sacred spaces of retreat free from advertising. This assumed preference might well take the form of Kant's Categorical Imperative (see Chapter 1), namely, that one could not consistently will that the invasion of all our sacred spaces by advertising should become a Universal Law.

If the wholesale invasion of our sacred spaces by advertising is not our preferred option as a community, then the advertising industry must as a body take measures of moral self-regulation to ensure that our communal sacred spaces, including town squares, parks, forests, beaches, temples, the skies, art galleries, and museums, as well as the aesthetic spaces of music, literature, and other forms of art and culture, are kept free of advertising. However, advertisers are faced with the problem of collective action. On the one hand, it may well be that all advertisers prefer and deem it desirable that our shared sacred spaces are kept free of any form of invasive advertising. On the other hand, if they are faced with a situation in which other advertisers start to exploit such spaces, they may feel that they will lose out on such commercial opportunities unless they follow suit. This outcome would inevitably lead to an escalation resulting in the gross invasion and degradation of sacred spaces by advertising. To overcome the problem of collective action, what is required is *collective regulation* instigated by the advertising industry as a whole. Such collective regulation was successfully implemented in the case of tobacco advertising, and it is hoped that similar collective regulation can equally be instigated with regard to declaring sacred spaces, as the ones just described, as advertising-free zones.

This undertaking may involve some cross-regulation with relevant government and community groups to ensure the effective protection and preservation of our communal sacred spaces as in the case of cross-regulation with regard to other forms of pollution. In other words, the systematic gobbling up of our communal spaces by advertising (thankfully the majority of our sacred spaces are still relatively safe) is a form of brand pollution that needs to be controlled like other forms of environmental pollution.

The overload argument derives its ethical justification indirectly from the argument for the Principle of Generic Consistency that provides justification to both individual and collective communal rights to freedom and well-being (see Chapter 1). If sacred spaces are important and essential to our collective well-being as a society, and we have argued that they are, then our collective rights to freedom and well-being require that those spaces be kept free of advertising. Moreover, the same collective rights require that the advertising industry act responsibly in controlling and, in some acute cases, reducing the overload effect of advertising on our communal spaces that are increasingly becoming branded by a proliferation of new advertising techniques.

A SUMMARY OF INSTRUMENTAL AND ETHICAL CONSEQUENCES

Desirable

1. In an attempt to penetrate the clutter and noise of so many advertisements that seek the consumer's divided and fragmented attention, advertisers are increasingly developing innovative new techniques and strategies to reach the ever jaded but savvy consumer. These techniques and strategies aim primarily to go under the radar-detection threshold of the consumer in a surprise attack on his or her communication receptive channels.

To the extent that these techniques and strategies work, they can be seen as an instrumentally rational and effective way of reaching consumer markets that otherwise might remain immune to traditional channels of advertising communication. From a rationally instrumental perspective, these innovative techniques and strategies are therefore desirable within the context of advertising and the commercial activities to which they give rise.

Undesirable

In the order of the arguments adduced before, we can outline a number of reasons why these otherwise instrumentally rational and effective advertising techniques and strategies might be considered, if not unethical, at least ethically problematic:

1. Some of these forms of advertising have the capacity and potential to violate people's rights to privacy. Such violations to privacy are always ethically undesirable unless they can be justified on the basis of the principles of public interest or of the public good (see Chapter 1).

However, as we saw from the "argument from the suspension of discontent," this *violation* can nevertheless be reduced to an acceptable *infringement* if it results in an overall comparative benefit to the individual consumer or the community of consumers generally. Under those circumstances, it is reasonable to assume that consumers, both individually and collectively, will choose, at least implicitly, to suspend their discontent in having their rights to privacy and informed consent infringed by advertising. Thus in cases in which advertising in private and public spaces can be shown to result in some overall net benefit to the consumers, either individually or collectively, then that advertising can be tolerated, even if considered undesirable, on the basis that an infringement of our rights to privacy and consent in being exposed to unsolicited ads can be considered, implicitly at least, waived.

2. On the other hand, however, as the overload argument has shown, the invasion by advertising of our private and public spaces must be tempered and controlled within acceptable limits negotiated among the advertising industry, consumer groups, and the government, according to a suitable cross-regulation policy. This process is in keeping with other general antipollution policies that are designed and introduced to protect the environment from degradation. We have argued that the overload of advertising in our communal spaces is a form of pollution, since it degrades, if left uncontrolled, our communally cultural and natural spaces that define, as a society, our collective social identity. Not everything is for sale or for hire.

3. Moreover, certain sacred spaces such as forests, beaches, temples, art galleries, and museums, our common skies, and the aesthetic spaces of art where our imagination can roam free and where we can periodically take time out to retreat and seek relaxation, comfort, and edification, should, according to the time-out argument and the preservation of aesthetic space argument, be kept free of advertising.

The gradual invasion of advertising in these sacred spaces and the blurring of the lines between art and advertising, especially in cases in which advertising masquerades misleadingly as art, is therefore ethically undesirable for society as a whole. Both individually and collectively, we need sacred spaces to which we can periodically retreat and escape, at least momentarily, the hurly-burly of the world of commerce and the shadows that advertising casts over our more robust human reality. We must not become like the denizens in Plato's "Allegory of the Cave," who are led by the manipulating puppeteers to mistake the shadows on the cave walls for reality.

chapter eight

The Digital Explosion

INTRODUCTION

In Stephen Spielberg's futuristic vision *Minority Report,* moviegoers were challenged by the proposition of a future in which advertising billboards would address pedestrians by name, conjuring a hi-tech version of the type of interactive devices used by advertisers today. But just how far away are we from this dark vision? And what real benefit to society is a technology-driven imperative to information transfer?

From the earliest of times, technology has driven our development of communication from Gutenberg and the printing press to the electronic file-sharing of Napster. Technology still continues to change the way we interact. Technology is inextricably linked to information, a currency of immense value to us today, and this explosion of information-technology has created an information supermarket that reduces communication to mere data transfer.

Our means of accessing knowledge and entertainment, our ways of seeing the world, our ways of interacting with each other, and our patterns of behavior have all been affected by the revolution in communications—the computer chip, satellite and cable communications, digital television, computers, video games, virtual reality, interactive technologies, and the Internet, all impacting on change. And riding on the winds of this change is advertising.

The continuous development of information technology makes the information environment extremely fluid with significant implications for the advertising process. The proliferation of information continues to rise exponentially, and consumers everywhere are beginning to tune out the "noise" (unwanted communication) and to look for ways to focus on what's important. For advertisers, the task is to find out what is important to consumers. Consumer-focused, or "outside-in," strategies are essential for advertisers (enter technology yet again) to provide tools for consumer-focused and interactive platforms for communication.

The focus of this chapter is both an exploration of the development of digital and interactive technologies that have shaped the advertising strategies that have succeeded in the current environment, and the projection of where they will take advertisers in the foreseeable future, as well as the ethical implications of those developments.

CASE STUDIES

CASE STUDY 8A Neopia— The Virtual Reality[108]

For most of the "generation Y"[109] population, pet chores are a real drag, daily feeding, grooming, and training all part of the humdrum of domesticated existence. But for the 32 million strong community of Gen-Y'ers who are pet owners in the virtual world of Neopia, nothing could be further from the truth. NeoPets.com is a virtual community created for teen members who explore Neopia and look after their pets, endure an ever-changing series of games and grueling competitions with other pets to earn the currency of NeoPoints, which they spend on feeding and nurturing their pet of choice. Members create their NeoPet, select its name, color, and traits, such as personality, intelligence, and special abilities.

The site is a constantly evolving alternative world with a complex ecosystem, a currency whose fluctuations are tied to the Neopian stock market (the Neodaq), its own newspaper (*Neopian Times*), a bank, a hospital, an art center, a place where pets can buy their own pets, and hundreds of user-supported NeoPet guilds.

Neopets was created in 1999 by two university students who thought that they might set up an Internet game they could play with friends, but its popularity drew the attention of a marketing executive (Doug Dohring), who could see much more potential in the concept.

The potential was profit—which was achieved within three months of relaunch—generated from

integrating advertisers' products and messages into the activities and adventures of the site. Users at NeoPets.com interact directly with sponsors' products, characters, and messages for extended periods of time, ensuring lasting impressions. The site appeals to a wide range of ages: 39 percent of members are 12 or under, 40 percent are 13 to 17, and 21 percent are over 18, spending an average of five hours a week at the site.

The seamless integration of advertising into the content of the site creates a unique blend of NeoPet culture and e-commerce that Doug Dohring refers to as "immersive advertising," a concept not too dissimilar to product placement in films. Products and brand names—from branded items available in food shops to specially developed games and activities—are imbedded into the site's content. This blurring of content and advertising combined with the interactivity of the site forces the users to focus and engage with the products and brands, building an emotional bond with the brand, which is becoming far more difficult in the off-line world.

Advertisers testify to the effectiveness of the engagement. To promote the film *Spy Kids* for Miramax, NeoPets created a cinema in which users could watch a trailer and click through to the *Spy Kids* site. On the first day, the sheer volume of response crashed the servers. When Kraft decided to advertise its drink Capri Sun at the site, research found 35.8 percent of NeoPets users had tried the drink, but after six weeks on the site, that number jumped to nearly 43 percent.

Despite compliance with the Children's Online Privacy Protection Act, the site has its critics who claim that the method of "immersive advertising" is manipulative and underhanded in that the users can't tell the difference between ad and non-ad content.

With a line of merchandise, CD-ROMs, books, and foreign language versions of the site, Neopia is well and truly a virtual reality in the consumer marketplace.

CASE STUDY 8B TiVo's PVR Puts the Consumer in Control[110]

You would think that if consumers were given the opportunity to watch what they want to watch when they want to watch it, that it would mean that advertising would be out of the picture, but that's not necessarily the case.

That new technologies are pushing the weight of power across to consumers is evident with the emergence of the Personal Video Recorder (PVR). PVRs allow consumers to seamlessly record television programming, pause live TV, create channels personalized to their interests, and eliminate commercials. Research by CNW Marketing Research[111] conducted in July 2002 found that users of PVRs skip commercials 72.3 percent of the time. Such ad-skipping technology is forcing advertisers to rethink their TV advertising strategies.

It is estimated that commercial-zapping technology could be in half of U.S. households by 2007, with Forrester Research forecasting revenues collected by PVR services (such as TiVo) to hit $1.2 billion by 2007. These figures suggest accelerated adoption of the technology in the ensuing years and the fast-tracking of the development of advertising forms to meet the opportunities.

PVR service, TiVo, responded by offering advertisers the ability to create content packages that go well beyond the 30-second TV spot. Their aim is to get viewers to actually choose to view ad content by making it as compelling as the programming. TiVo's "advertainment" concept is a creative strategy designed to get their subscribers to opt-in to advertising content.

In May 2002, TiVo teamed up with mass entertainment retailer Best Buy to test its advertainment capabilities. Best Buy's content was tied into the company's "Go Mobile" campaign, whereby TiVo subscribers watching a 30-second spot on MTV would be offered a link to enhanced content starring Sheryl Crow and vignettes of varying length that feature products from the consumer electronics chain. TiVo subscribers would be able to return to their programs where they left off after watching the Best Buy's content.

The advertainment content featured an exclusively filmed behind-the-scenes jam session with artist Sheryl Crow, interview material, two new songs from the artist, product vignettes and a CD giveaway.

The technology allowed advertisers to judge the return on advertising almost immediately with metrics that show what percentage of people watch and how much of the content they watched.

The Best Buy's campaign was shortly followed up by an advertainment campaign with Geffen A&M records, giving TiVo subscribers regular enhanced content and preview material of forthcoming releases. TiVo sees these campaigns as not only a new form of advertising but also an extension of their content available only to their subscribers, who have the option of turning it on, turning it off, or repeating it.

CASE STUDY 8C VOD Means ROA?[112]

The $53 billion[113] plus TV advertising market is about to be changed forever with the rise in popularity of Video-on-demand (VOD) technology that allows consumers to choose programs to suit their own schedule. This ability to choose content whenever it's needed should forever change advertising as we know it.

Television has traditionally been a mass market medium, attracting the bulk of advertising budgets with the rationale that it achieves broad reach and a large share of voice—two important ingredients for heavyweight branding. But target advertising may well be the television strategy of the future.

A VOD viewer who has a specially enabled set-top box can, with a remote control, select and access movies listed on a VOD channel. Thus when a viewer chooses a movie, the service provider's servers stream video into that specific digital cable box. But it's the interactive nature of the service that has advertisers excited. The potential to create a two-way stream of information between the consumer and the advertiser allows for communication and advertising to be customized for the consumer. Advertisers are now developing software that recognizes household level demographics and user habits and preference in order to target their communication. These new marketing tactics will provide advertisers with finely tuned consumer data that could be customized for households and individuals. Simple strategies such as combining ZIP code data with user patterns could determine the type of suitable ads for a household. Add the merger of third-party data, and highly personalized customization could occur. An unmarried woman could receive communication about a singles' resort special, and a family could receive an offer of discount specials for kids at hotels. VOD users could even let the service provider know that they are in the market for a new car and thus receive automobile ads via their TV.

In this way, VOD operates within the direct mail tradition with the VOD server acting as their mailbox that collects the delivered customized messages. With predictions that the number of VOD-capable U.S. households will be around 14.4 million in 2004,[114] the market size as well as the pure targetability and measurability of the medium will force a paradigm shift in TV advertising.

PROFESSIONAL PRACTICE

Integrated Communication

The saturated and overcommunicated consumer environment that exists today has opened the door for consumer-focused strategies such as Integrated Marketing Communications (IMC) to take a hold on advertising thinking. This strategy is based on the notion of synergy and consumer knowledge. Synergy exists among all elements of the communication such as the central message and peripheral cues that support the message. The nature of the messages and the media used to deliver are based on consumer knowledge collected and stored in a database and adapted with each interaction with the consumer. The development of database technology and proliferation of media options has fueled growth in this strategic approach to advertising/marketing communication. This approach to advertising planning starts with the consumer or prospect to determine communication methods and points of contact that best serves the customer profile. It then proceeds to build a relationship and an enduring link between the brand and the customer via a "conversation." This conversation is regular, meaningful communication between the brand and the consumer. The digital explosion has made this conversation more attainable for advertisers to achieve.

Advertising Media

As mediated communication, advertising effectiveness relies on the mechanism used to deliver the message to its intended target. The proliferation of media options (as discussed in Chapter 7) has made this a complex decision-making process. The development of digital media has opened up more opportunities to interact with intended targets. Mediums such as the Internet, iTV, CDROM, and mobile communications have become critical elements of integrated communication strategies.

Internet

The Internet has undoubtedly changed the way that people everywhere receive and process information. The number of Americans using the Internet has grown exponentially from fewer than 5 million users in 1993 to approximately 110 million in 1999, according to the Department of Commerce.[115] As of September 2002, the "Nua.com, How Many Online?" survey estimated that there are as many as 605.60 million people on-line worldwide.[116]

The level of global adoption as well as the nature of the technology itself makes the Internet an attractive medium for advertisers. Server-based technologies enable advertisers to display advertising (predominantly banner advertising) according to user profiles and interests in a way that was not previously possible. Banner ads, pop-ups, and interstitials can now include graphics, text, and streaming audio and video. Java and Shockwave technologies can be used to deliver highly dynamic and interactive ads. Interactivity and personalization technologies have made the Internet a creatively dynamic and an effective medium as well as a highly accountable medium.

As demonstrated in Case Study 8a, the virtual reality capacity and global adoption of the Internet have made it a vital medium for interacting with consumers—creating relationship building, and consumer relevant environments for communicating a message. It is an environment where users can be so engaged in it that an advertising message can be immersed into the content so as not to be identified as overt persuasive communication. The Internet provides advertisers with an interactive medium, a virtual shopfront, a data-gathering device, and a direct route to the consumer twenty-four hours a day, seven days a week.

Is It a TV? Is It a PC? No, It's iTV

Television made mass marketing possible, delivering mass audiences to advertisers who in turn could gain high ROI from single exposures. This one-way stream of information has worked for advertisers to a point, but in today's ad environment of media proliferation, audience fragmentation, the rising expenses of television advertising, and the adoption of consumer-focused brand-building strategies, interactivity has become a critical element. . . . . Enter interactive TV (iTV).

The consumer familiarity with the television medium has made it the most promising interactive medium for advertisers. Agencies and advertisers already understand TV better than the Web, and consumers are already comfortable with it.

In an ad break (if they still exist), a viewer can enter a contest, play a game, or buy something with a flick of the remote control. Advertising on iTV services can vary from something as simple as customers being able to request a sample to downloadable short films and games. In the United Kingdom, there is a Jaguar ad that is a short film allowing consumer download and then the ordering of a test drive. The technology will enable targeting via demographics and user information at a very powerful level.[117]

A critical device in the iTV environment is the personal video recorder (PVR), which allows consumers to control their television viewing by seamlessly recording programming, pausing live TV, creating channels personalized to their interests, and eliminating commercials (see Case Study 8c). This technology has sent shivers down the spine of advertisers who have had to rethink their TV advertising strategies. The result is a shift to more immersive advertising that blurs the boundaries between content and advertising, as well as the creation of more customized and enhanced content that consumers opt-in or choose to view.

Adoption of these interactive services is growing. Jupiter Research predicts that by 2007, more than half of European households will have digital television, with 91 percent using interactive services such as video-on-demand (VOD) and personal video recorders. U.S. researchers predict around 15 million PVR users (14 percent of households) by 2006.[118]

This technology that allows consumers to dictate the type of programming they view, when they view, to shop, to e-mail, and to personalize their viewing preferences has significant implications for advertisers. They will have to treat TV as a targeted communication, they will have to personalize communication, and they will have to meet the interactive demands of consumers. To do all this, a clear understanding of the consumers will be imperative (see Case Study 8c) to customize communication in the way that direct marketers have for decades.

Ready Aim Fire! The Direct Marketing Paradigm

The foundations of direct marketing communication involve the list, the offer, and the response, that is, the list of possible targets, the offer that is just right for those targets, and the measurement of the response that the offer generated. This process produces a targetable and measurable communication process that has proven to be attractive to advertisers in the "age of accountability." This process can be visualized via the three stages of *Collection, Construction,* and *Conversation.*

Collection involves the process of gathering data on consumers, demographics, behavioral traits, personality, and buying behavior. These data are stored on a database for manipulation. The construction phase turns this consumer information into a profile that is interrogated to construct the right offer to propose to the consumer via the right combination of media. The final phase involves communicating the offer to the target and addressing the response. This two-way stream of communication is a vital phase, since it records the target's response to the offer,

which in turn feeds into the collection process for regeneration.

The main objective of direct marketing communication is to establish a relationship with a customer (via collected profile data) in order to initiate conversation that is immediate and that has measurable responses. The interactive nature of this process is obvious, and it is also obvious why it operates so effectively via interactive media such as the Internet and iTV. The previous three case studies all demonstrate the role of digital, interactive technology in creating an environment where advertisers can generate information about customers in order to enhance the relationship among the stakeholders.

It is the major advances in computer technology and database management that have made it possible for organizations to accrue and maintain huge databases containing millions of prospects and customers. This sophisticated technology and database capacity continues to improve the efficiency and targetability of direct strategies.

The Direct Marketing Association (DMA) in the United States reported an increase in direct marketing and interactive marketing expenditures in 2000 of 3.6 percent to be worth $196.8 billion, with a prediction that spending on direct advertising will rise at an annual rate of 6.5 percent until 2006. In a weak economic environment that has forced down traditional ad spending, the prediction is a testament to the effectiveness and industry adoption of the DM and interactive paradigm that is consumer-focused and truly interactive.[119]

Convergence

Imagine the power of combining media and information technology to enhance communication. Digital technology has reinvented the telephone, the television, the radio, mail systems, and entertainment options.

So what is convergence? Early explanations reflected the merging of Internet and TV into one environment, but with the spread of digital platforms and interactivity across a wider range of devices, the meaning of convergence has been stretched. With a broad range of content becoming a passenger on digital streams, the content can be packaged for consumption in multiple forms—the variety of new media used to carry the content is brought together by that content.

A digital stream of content can engage with consumers via a wide range of contact points—home PC, mobile laptop, palm pilot, digital TV, digital radio, mobile phone, SMS and WAP, and electronic gaming. By effectively combining these contact points, advertising can be sure to reach a specifically targeted consumer at the right time. The message can be adapted to fit the digital environment carrying it.

It Is All about Interaction

Technology has had the effect of isolating members of society and has created a loss of sense of community. Interaction restores this loss of contact. Neopia (Case Study 8a) is a clear example of community construction on-line. Consumers will demand interaction through communication, and interactive elements of advertising campaigns will become more important. The signs are already strong that people want to interact. Mindshare UK managing director Nigel Sheldon, considered a pioneer of iTV advertising, revealed that in the United Kingdom, a third of *Big Brother* votes were cast through iDTV, and more than four million viewers selected the interactive facility to view different (sporting) matches.[120] Interactive games have become popular content on iTV services with an "advergame" being built around a brand that is accessed via an iTV games channel. Interactive games offer enormous opportunities for advertisers and are beginning to make their

mark in the United Kingdom, where Open TV records pools of between 400,000 and 500,000 players per week, each averaging 13 minutes at a time on a game.[121] This interactive technology represents a huge opportunity for advertisers to connect with users by building games around a brand experience, using brand characters, and connecting brands with consumers through product placements within games and sponsorship of games.

This highly interactive engagement has the added value to advertisers of also being highly measurable, which makes the targeting of audiences/players and the matching of games with viewer habits a key element of strategies. Family-oriented games, trivia games for trivia buffs, and sports-oriented games for sports enthusiasts can be created and targeted by consulting the viewing habits recorded through the iTV medium.

In the current environment, interaction with advertising communication will be expected. Imagine these scenarios:

- You are walking through a suburban shopping mall, your mobile phone vibrates, and you check to see that you have received a text message telling you that there is a sale on athletic shoes at the retailer that you just happen to be standing outside. Convergence of technologies makes this a reasonable scenario.

- You are watching a local drama and notice the vase on the table. Then you think how it would suit your living room, so you pick up your remote and click on the vase on the screen. The drama stops, and you are transported to an on-line shopping site with the vase for sale. Interactive technology makes this a reasonable scenario.

The digital explosion has prompted an enormous rethink on how advertisers use interactive media and has led to the creation of customized campaigns that build a conversation and a hoped-for enduring relationship with consumers.

Some of the devices are invisible or covert in nature, and they test the ethical boundaries of persuasive communication.

ETHICAL ANALYSIS

We have seen in the preceding chapter, how the proliferation and pervasiveness of advertising raises ethical issues regarding the invasiveness of advertising in all aspects of our private and public lives. On the whole, this invasiveness, especially in public places, takes place without our individual and collective consent. Whether on public transport, in public spaces such as streets, squares, parks, buildings, the skies and the beach, we are constantly bombarded with advertising messages that we do not elicit or give our consent to. We are passive recipients of an advertising onslaught of a one-sided communication over which we have no control. Most of us, though free citizens, at least in principle, are nevertheless captive consumers, the only escape being the privacy of our homes. But think again! The saying that "an Englishman's home is his castle" may have been true in days gone by, but no longer. The moat that separated one's home from the outside world has been bridged through the digital explosion that leaves no place on the planet, this planet at least, out of its omnipresent gaze and reach. Some desert landscapes may still offer some retreat, but with the advent of satellite communication technology, that retreat may soon also be a thing of the past—there is a message on your mobile phone advertising the latest camping gear as you traverse the sands of the Sahara.

The digital explosion in new modes of media communication explored in this chapter gives further cause for concern regarding the expansion of advertising and its increasing pervasiveness through electronic communication that can target consumers in their homes or even when out and about taking a stroll, through their mobile phones. It seems that consumers have become caught by an unstoppable advertising tsunami.

There are at least four interrelated ethical problems that concern the digital explosion with regard to advertising, and these involve informed consent, privacy, manipulation of consent through inducement, and the problem of "immersive advertising," which like its cousin the advertorial, blurs the distinction between information content and advertising.

Informed Consent and Privacy

The basic unit of ethical consideration is the autonomous individual person. It is on that unit that all democratic institutions, including the political, social, legal, economic, educational, religious, and media institutions of the contemporary state are based. Nothing of importance happens in a modern democratic state, at least in principle, without the informed consent and autonomous decision of the individual citizen. So why is so little consideration given to informed consent when it comes to advertising? There is, to be sure, some degree of implied informed consent as we saw in Chapter 7, but that is often limited and does not extend sufficiently in the commodification and branding of the public and social environment through advertising, as we saw in Chapters 3 and 7. Of course, reaching a consensus of what and how much advertising should citizens be exposed to in public spaces, that are commonly shared by all citizens, might be a practical problem; one that might best be left to local governments to administer with sufficient consultation with the citizenry in keeping with ethically responsible advertising that should be responsive to the views and wishes of the community at large, an issue that will be explored in more detail in Chapter 9.

Although difficult in practice to obtain consensual informed consent from all individual citizens of what and how much advertising should be allowed in public places, the issue of informed consent is much more straightforward when it comes to advertising that is conducted through individually used media channels of communications, including TV, iTV, the Internet, cellular or mobile phones, and other digital modes of communication that target individual consumers. Paradoxically, the retreat into the virtual reality of cyberspace by individuals has increased the ways in which advertising can reach those individuals through systematic and well-planned targeting. The last remaining frontier has, like its predecessors, fallen prey to the ever prying eye and far-reaching wired tentacles of marketing and advertising. So long as digital advertising reaches its targeted audiences with their freely given informed consent, there is no problem. Freedom of information is fine and essential to a democratic way of life if it's delivered only to those who have given their prior informed consent, either explicitly or implicitly, to receive it, but not otherwise. However, if it's delivered without the recipient's informed consent, then like junk mail it is unwelcome and ethically unjustified and undesirable.

Being contacted by advertisers and marketers through your mobile phone to communicate some unsolicited message about a certain consumer product is an invasion of privacy if it occurs without your prior informed consent. Similarly, the development of new software that recognizes household level demographics and user habits and preferences that may potentially allow advertisers and marketers to collect data on one's purchasing trends (see Case Study 8c) would also constitute an invasion of privacy if it occurs without one's informed consent. Likewise, advertising soliciting through banner ads and pop-ups that accost the unwary Internet user is an invasion of privacy and equally ethically unjustified unless one has given his or her prior informed consent, explicitly or implicitly, in allowing oneself to be exposed to such type of advertising.

Although most people may perhaps not mind this type of advertising, or if they do mind, they simply just ignore it even when they have not given their consent to it, in principle this type of unsolicited advertising is still ethically unjustified just in the same way that being hustled by solicitous doormen of restaurants or clubs to visit their premises as you leisurely walk by is ethically unjustified and undesirable. It is ethically unjustified simply because you have not either explicitly or implicitly given to it your consent, a necessary condition for any transactional interaction between people, including communication. Restraining orders under the law even when violence is not an issue testifies to the importance of consent in relationships between people. If advertisers want to build "relationships" between their products and their targeted consumers, those relationships must be two-dimensional and based on the informed consent of the relevant parties. One-way unsolicited communications from advertisers to consumers, especially when they are conducted without the consumers' consent, are not "interactive" and not "conversations" even if the advertisers mislabel them as such.[122] And insofar as they invade the consumers' privacy they are ethically unjustified.

The collection of data on consumers by software technology that allows advertisers and marketers to do that, raises serious concerns about the invasion of privacy of ordinary citizens whose personal information about themselves, their families, and employment could be used without their knowledge and consent to target various individuals or group of individuals with advertising messages that purport to meet their needs. The problem with the strategy of "collection, construction, and conversation" is that the collection of data in the initial process might involve the unauthorized collection of people's data without their informed consent, and that is ethically unacceptable. Insofar as this strategy involves the unauthorized collection of data of people without their informed consent, then the whole strategy is ethically unjustified. Moreover, informed consent *cannot* be obtained from potential consumers *after* the data have been collected, constructed, and targeted as "conversations" at the point of contact with the consumers, since these consumers may not have wanted to be contacted or targeted in the first place and thus may reject the unwelcome "conversation" and withdraw their consent for further communication from the advertiser. On the contrary, informed consent *must* be elicited and *obtained* from the consumers *prior* to any collection of their personal data. Insofar as the collection and storage of the consumers' personal data is conducted without their informed consent, then the collection of such data is ethically unjustified and unwarranted, and such a practice, if it exits, is morally objectionable and should be avoided.

Manipulation of Consent through Inducement

Like the Pied Piper who entices the children out of their homes and with his alluring sweet tunes gets them to voluntarily follow him wherever he leads them, the creators and producers of Neopia in collusion with the advertisers, similarly lead children into the site so that they can introduce the children and entice them into buying consumer products. Although this may not have been the original intention of the two university students who created Neopia, it is reasonable to assume, judging from the way Neopia has been turned into a large virtual shopping mall, that the intention of the current producers of Neopia is to operate the site for the primary objective of promoting the sale of a cornucopia of consumer products to kids through "immersive advertising."

Of course, the kids who enter Neopia and participate in its various operations do so voluntarily. However, just because the kids' entry and

participation is voluntary, it is not necessarily undertaken under conditions that generally characterize informed and free consent. In fact, consent, can be induced through various means, including coercion or the promise of a reward, which may not have been readily forthcoming without the coercion or the inducement of a reward. A teenager, for example, may be coerced or induced into giving her "consent" to having sex with an adult out of a concern of not disappointing the adult for whom she may harbor some infatuation, or the promise of a reward, but her "consent," because coerced or induced, would not qualify unconditionally as free and informed consent. The teenager's consent may not qualify as informed, since the teenager may not, because of her young age and inexperience, be capable of making informed decisions about all relevant aspects of her actions. Her "consent," though in some sense voluntarily given, would certainly not be unconditionally free, because she would probably not have agreed to have sex with the adult if her "consent" was not coerced or induced in some manner.

Similarly, the kids' "consent" in entering and participating in Neopia may be considered, in some sense, as voluntary, but such consent is not unconditionally informed and free for the reasons adduced in the preceding analogous example. The kids' "consent" to enter Neopia is not free because it has been induced through the promise and expectation of a reward in the form of free games and prizes. If these rewards were not offered to the kids, would they still enter and participate in Neopia to the same degree as they do with the rewards? Insofar as the kids would not under normal circumstances enter and participate in Neopian activities to the same degree without the rewards, then it is fair to say that the kids' "consent" is not unconditionally free and thus does not qualify as proper informed consent, a consent that one offers unconditionally without fear or favor. Hence, the kids' induced entry and participation in Neopian activities for the primary objective of enticing them to purchase the products advertised in Neopia is a form of manipulation and thus ethically unjustified and objectionable.

Immersive Advertising: An Immense Deception?

The blurring of content and advertising material amounts to deception and is thus ethically unacceptable. Similarly, the "immersing" of advertising material into content, as in the case of Neopia, is potentially deceptive if the distinction between content and advertising is deliberately made opaque so that consumers cannot tell the difference between the two. As in the case of advertorials, "immersive advertising" that "seamlessly" blends advertising material with content obfuscates the vital distinction between communication whose primary function is *persuasion* and communication whose primary function is *information*. As argued previously, information by definition must meet the necessary conditions of knowledge (justified true belief) that persuasion, as half-truths and lies as attested by successful propaganda, need not be true, justified, and objective, nor believed by those who engage in it. Thus the blurring of these two potentially conflicting modes of communication in the strategy of "immersive advertising" is ethically problematic, since it can deceive or at least mislead consumers into thinking that advertising material presented to them as "content" has the characteristics of information that a reasonable person expects from content but not necessarily from advertising.

The interesting question is why advertisers resort to this gimmick. One plausible answer is that by blurring or "immersing"[123] content with advertising material, advertisers hope that the blurring of content, which has a much higher epistemological rating and more robust credibility than most advertising material can ever command, will be transferred by association of the "seamless" blending of the two to advertising and imbue it with the same robust credibility of information content. Insofar as this is a reasonable and plausible supposition, then "immersive advertising" and advertainment, like advertorials, are potentially deceptive or at least misleading and hence ethically unacceptable.

In conclusion, advertisers are more likely to avoid unethical conduct if they just stick to advertising through fictional and metaphorical modes of communication that do not require truth or justification and thus can elicit the consumers' consent through *suspension of disbelief*, rather than run the moral risk of misleading or deceiving consumers through modes of communication that purport, like wolves in sheep's clothing, to seem other than they are, which are more likely to elicit the consumers' withdrawal of consent in the communication process through *suspension of belief*.

A SUMMARY OF INSTRUMENTAL AND ETHICAL CONSEQUENCES

Desirable

1. If the ultimate objective of advertising is to persuade consumers to feel predisposed toward certain products, services, or messages, then persuading as many consumers as possible to feel predisposed toward the advertised products, services, or messages is instrumentally desirable, since it maximizes the desired goal of advertising. Insofar as the digital explosion and other similar strategies in advertising have the effect of maximizing the number of consumers targeted, then such an explosion is instrumentally desirable, at least from an operative perspective.

Undesirable

1. The digital explosion in advertising, and other types of advertising proliferation that were examined in Chapter 7, can constitute an invasion

of privacy and a violation of people's right not to receive unsolicited advertising material without their informed consent. Invasive advertising that infiltrates people's private and public spaces without their explicit consent, or at least implicit consent in situations in which it is reasonable to presume implied consent, is ethically undesirable and should be avoided.

2. Consent, even when given, can be induced consent engendered through manipulation that exploits the vulnerability of teenagers and young people as illustrated by Case Study 8a. Since the manipulation and the exploitation of the vulnerability of others primarily for one's self-interest is ethically objectionable, the exploitation and manipulation of teenagers and other vulnerable groups by advertisers through digital or other forms of targeting is ethically undesirable and should thus be avoided.

In conclusion, the digital explosion in advertising and its proliferation through other pervasive strategies examined in Chapter 7 is highly instrumentally desirable from an operative perspective as it maximally promotes the ultimate goal of advertising. It is nonetheless ethically undesirable when it results in the unjustified invasion of people's privacy without their consent or the exploitation of impressionable and vulnerable groups of people such as teenagers through the manipulation of their consent through commercial inducements. Though the instrumental consequences of such advertising strategies may be desirable, at least from a strictly operative perspective, and may be perceived as supported from the advertising industry's own role morality, those consequences are nevertheless ethically undesirable and should thus be avoided. As we saw in Chapter 1, when a profession's Role Morality comes into conflict with Universal Public Morality, which precludes the violation of people's right to privacy and the exploitation of vulnerable groups of people such as teenagers, the latter should always take precedence over the former. Thus advertising strategies that can potentially result in the invasion of people's privacy or the exploitation of people by manipulation of their informed consent through commercial inducements are ethically precluded by Universal Public Morality and should thus be avoided.

chapter nine

Ethical Advertising

INTRODUCTION

This chapter looks at current trends in advertising that appear to reflect ethical awareness. For example, are advertisements that employ the honest and direct approach in presenting consumer products merely a smokescreen or a step in the right direction? The chapter will examine the different ways in which advertising can be made more ethical. Perhaps honesty may not be the best policy in advertising, but it may be the most ethically responsible. In a world that is increasingly becoming more ethically aware, ethical advertising may in fact make good business sense. The chapter will conclude by demonstrating why personal and professional integrity, including integrity in advertising, is important and desirable. If integrity is at once a form of internal consistency and harmony

(personal character) and also an external social consistency and harmony (professional, social, political, and institutional), then advertising must not only recognize and fulfill the ethical commitments that flow from its institutional role but must also recognize and fulfill those ethical commitments that emanate from its social character in accordance with the ethical requirements of universal public morality (see Chapter 1).

The chapter will conclude by revisiting the issue of self-regulation raised in Chapter 1 and examine what measures must be taken to improve self-regulation in the advertising industry. Also, the chapter will conclude by demonstrating the close relationship between self-regulation and integrity. Underlying both is a strong commitment to leading an ethical life that is consistent with a comprehensive moral worldview.

CASE STUDIES

CASE STUDY 9A Sport and Religion

The print ad shows the Pope kissing the ground, having just stepped off the plane and onto the airport tarmac on his last visit to Australia. Superimposed just in front of the Pope's prostrated white-clad body is a rugby ball. The caption on the ad reads, "One of the Great Religions is coming to Foxtel."[124]

CASE STUDY 9B Shock Tactics Set the Tone for Social Change[125]

An Australian tactic of using shocking and hard-hitting advertisements has changed forever the social and cultural habits of adults. Such advertisements have depicted, in most graphic fashion, children and adults being hit and dragged under cars; a mother cradling a son killed on a crosswalk by a speeding car; and a youth with a broken neck, crying for a brother whom he killed in a drunk-driving crash.

The tough advertising campaign helped give the Australian state of Victoria what it says is the lowest highway fatality rate in the world—sinking the rate to a 44-year low and giving the shock-tactic approach to advertising a new authority with safety agencies around the world. The in-your-face campaigns, first created by Grey Advertising for the Victorian Transport Accident Commission (TAC) in 1989, have had a dramatic effect on Victoria's road toll, seeing road fatalities reduced by 50 percent in the first five years. Despite their shocking nature, the ads have won public respect.

Research by the TAC indicated that a significant number of respondents (87 percent) believed that the campaign had been successful and effective. There is a high level of recall for many of the advertisements used in the campaign, with 99 percent of people agreeing that the ads disturbed them—but wanted them to remain on the air.

The TAC says that, after ten years, the public expects it to produce shocking ads and that although they are largely perceived as being successful, it is also becoming harder to portray a handful of road safety themes in different ways. The ads have been bought or replicated by several other state and international governments and have won numerous international and local advertising awards.

In 2001, U.K. agency Abbott Mead Vickers BBDO employed the tactic with their Think! Slow Down campaign, offering a graphic depiction of a child being hit by a car. The campaign was supposed to shock and get a reaction, and it sought justification for the tactic with a reduction in the number of road deaths.

The result of the strategy is that the public has come to accept, even expect, that noncommercial advertising must use shock tactics to make sure that its message cuts through. The flip side is that it is nearly impossible to shock an audience that is expecting to be shocked. But the results show that social change is the positive byproduct.

CASE STUDY 9C Automobile Advertisers Put on the Brakes[126]

A Ford XR Ute successfully drags off a rocket-powered car, a Holden Ute is shown going through the rigors of "circle work," creating a picture of dust and power; meanwhile, another commercial depicts a scene in which a male driver of a Holden Series 2 Commodore is about to enter a home driveway when he sees it strewn with toys. Watched by a young boy from an upstairs window, the man repositions the toys in a zigzag slalom formation, and then he drives the car through the obstacles and into the garage, where he checks a stopwatch.

These three Australian car commercials demonstrate effectively the power and handling ability of the cars but will no longer be seen on Australian televisions, since the automotive industry, after receiving pressure from government and motoring bodies, adopted a seven-point code that promotes road safety and safe driving practices. The new code of conduct governing vehicle advertising, outlaws the portrayal of reckless and menacing driving, speeding on public roads, unsafe driving practices, the use of drugs and alcohol, people driving while fatigued, and motorcyclists' not wearing helmets.

The Advertising Federation of Australia supported the code, reflecting the view that "the advertising needs to show that it is in touch with community sentiments and therefore a code is a sensible way forward."[127] The Australian regulatory body, the Advertising Standards Bureau, administers the code as part of its review of advertising practices, and the guidelines have been agreed to by car, commercial vehicle, and motorcycle distributors.

Similar codes have been established in New Zealand, which state that car advertising that glorifies excessive speed and/or unsafe driving practices is unacccptable. In the United Kingdom, a similar detailed set of codes also exists. The British Codes of Advertising and Sales Promotion, administered by the Advertising Standards Authority (ASA), contains a special section on motoring to reflect society's concerns about dangerous driving practices and to ensure that automobile advertisements do not promote irresponsible behavior. Some of the main requirements are that advertisements should not

- make speed or acceleration claims the predominant message;
- portray speed in a way that might encourage motorists to drive irresponsibly or to break the law;
- give the impression that vehicles in normal driving circumstances on public roads are exceeding the U.K. speed limit; and
- portray or refer to practices that encourage antisocial behavior.[128]

The establishment of these codes and guidelines in each of these markets is a strong example of the communication industry stakeholders' recognition of the problem of road safety and recognition of the need to support policies that encourage social responsibility and, as such, to support the regulation of its advertising.

CASE STUDY 9D   "Think Before You Drive"— Kia Sells Walking Over Driving[129]

In 2001, Korean automobile manufacturer Kia adopted the radical strategy of launching a campaign to encourage people to drive less. Its multifaceted campaign, called "Think Before You Drive," represented a landmark, because it was the first time an automobile company had undertaken such an initiative.

In an environment of substantial road deaths and casualties, increasing victims of road rage, frustrating traffic congestion, and unhealthy CO_2 emissions, Kia's across-the-board ethical policy, encapsulated by their "Think Before You Drive" strapline (advertising term for "Slogan"), marked a significant approach to socially responsible advertising and corporate communication. Kia implemented thc strategy through an integrated campaign with four key elements, each with a specific message and role to perform. The Sedona (a Kia model) people mover was sold with a free mountain bike for shorter journeys, to combat the one-driver, large-vehicle syndrome. An RAC Risk Awareness Course was given away, with its Carens (a Kia model) model to raise awareness of the hazards of driving. Kia also sponsored the British Heart Foundation's "Walking the Way to Health" program to encourage people to consider walking as a viable, and valuable, alternative to automobile travel.

In partnership with the London newspaper the *Daily Express* and the United Kingdom's Pedestrians Association, Kia launched the concept of "The Walking Bus"—a series of supervised walking routes for children to take to school to encourage exercise and reduce exposure to traffic fumes. It also contributed to a reduction in road congestion with the adoption of more than 100 of these "Walking Bus" routes.

Kia's innovative strategy targeted a number of automobile-created problems in society while also endearing itself to a community unfamiliar with such socially responsible brand communication.

Case Study 9E Corporate Social Responsibility—Actions Speak Louder than Buzz![130]

It is standard knowledge that a company that does not react to customer demand generally suffers in the marketplace: one emerging customer demand is for companies that feature the added value of social responsibility to their brand offering. There is also the added bonus that when companies apply their marketing expertise to a social cause or problem, they contribute not only to the betterment of society but also often to their own profitability.

The modern consumer is a far more complex proposition, with one eye on a brand's offering and another on the social consequences of the offering. Nike's and Gap's public battles over their "sweatshop" manufacturing policies is a case in point. To appease this socially aware consumer, modern brands often include a socially responsible tactic in their communication strategy. French hypermarket retailer E. Leclerc responded to the issue of environmentalism with a campaign that featured their discarded plastic shopping bags in beautifully shot natural environments. These visuals were augmented with these headlines: "No. Leclerc does not really want to be seen everywhere," "There are some places we don't want to see our name," and "Some advertising we'll pass up willingly."

A corporation with a genuine sense of social responsibility will adopt a true corporate social marketing program. Such a program is defined by Bloom, Hussein and Szykman[131] as "an initiative in which marketing personnel who work for a corporation or one of its agents devote significant amounts of time and effort toward persuading people to engage in a socially beneficial behavior." In their article "Benefiting Society and the Bottom Line" (1995), they cite the example of a 1980s Kellogg's All-Bran campaign to "encourage the eating of a high-fiber, low-fat diet as a means of reducing the risks of some types of cancer." An integrated campaign of print ads, television spots, mailings to health professionals, and public speaking engagements was used to deliver the basic message. The toll-free telephone number of the National Cancer Institute's Information Service was placed on the back panel of the All-Bran box.[132]

Post-campaign studies confirmed that the Kellogg campaign had significant impact on consumers' knowledge, attitudes, and practices regarding the consumption of fiber.[133] The results achieved by this campaign are generally recognized to be something that could not have been achieved by the National Cancer Institute or any other nonprofit group acting alone. The funding and knowhow provided by Kellogg's marketing people, coupled with the credibility of the National Cancer Institute, created positive outcomes for both Kellogg and society.[134]

Although campaigns like this clearly benefit society, their value to the advertiser is difficult to measure at the cash register, although research does hint that consumers do prefer to be aligned with "good corporate citizens."[135]

Case Study 9F CCA—Concerned Children's Advertisers[136]

Concerned Children's Advertisers is a nonprofit Canadian industry group including 24 Canadian companies (Mattel, Kellogg, and McDonald's are among its membership) that market and advertise to children and their families. CCA's mandate centers on utilizing the shared resources and influence of each member company to keep pace with the media and social issues in children's lives (www.cca-canada.com).

Over the past 10 years, CCA has produced a child-directed television series of more than 35 high-quality commercials that address issues of substance and child-abuse prevention, self-esteem, healthy life-coping skills, and media literacy. Voluntarily broadcast daily across Canada to youth aged 3 through 17, CCA's messages air in prime children's programming (www.cca-canada.com).

By airing positive messages, CCA members hope to be seen as socially responsible marketers who do actually care for children. Their 2002 campaign deals with the pervasive and serious issue of bullying, which has grown to become a problem affecting one in four kids, according to an Ontario study.[137] The campaign is being created pro bono by Publicis Toronto (an advertising agency), with major TV networks donating commercial time during children and family programming.

The CCA's most famous campaign was the 1999 Golden Marble Award winner (Best PSA) "I louse Hippo." The commercial was an inventive spot featuring a miniaturised hippopotamus designed to remind children that not everything on television is real. It encouraged children to think about what they see on TV and to ask questions.

CCA's mission is to be the credible, caring, and authoritative voice of responsible children's advertising and communications. CCA actively works in partnership with government, educators, parents, and issue experts to identify issues of concern in children's lives and deliver solutions to help children.

CASE STUDY 9G   Ethical Shops Open for "Good" Business[138]

Socially responsible marketing is a growth industry. Its customer base appears to be expanding as more media savvy and socially conscious consumers begin to support their citizenship with their money. One agency to identify with this is the Generative Company, formed in 2002 by St. Luke's founder John Grant, which intends to tap into this growing area of ethical and socially responsible marketing.

But the intentions of the founders of The Generative Company go beyond the profit margin. The company aims to "help clients create a lasting legacy of good rather than just offering slogans." According to Grant, "business has reached an ethical and environmental watershed. Marketing and communications have to adapt to work in this new context."

The founders are keen to stress that it is not simply about "doing good" now. A generative company is one that also benefits future generations.

ETHICAL ANALYSIS

Ethical Self-Regulation

You will recall that in Chapter 1, we examined and established the importance of rational justification and practical motivation for ethical compliance that leads, or is at least capable of leading, to ethical conduct and action. Our outlined model for ethical decision-making that comprises justification, motivation, and compliance,

indicated that the best form of ethical compliance is the one that is based on self-regulation, and specifically ethical self-regulation, both at the personal as well as the organizational and institutional levels. Thus our schematic model of ethical regulation for institutions in general and for the advertising institution in particular was as follows:

Justification—Motivation—Internal
Self-Regulated Compliance
(Individual + Organizational + Institutional)

This model contains the essential components of ethical reasoning and ethical decision-making and thus is capable, at least in principle, of providing a practical model for ethical conduct in both personal actions and professional practice. Moreover and crucially, our model establishes an important conceptual intrinsic connection between ethical conduct and self-regulation. Ultimately, ethical conduct is a matter of self-regulation, both individual self-regulation at the personal level and collective self-regulation at the organizational and institutional levels, as well as overall self-regulation at the social and communal level. Beginning with individual ethical self-regulation at the personal level that reflects our thinking, at least in Western liberal democracies, that the individual is the basic moral unit and thus ultimately responsible for his or her personal actions, ethical self-regulation becomes collective at the organizational, institutional, and social and political levels, and it introduces a collective ethical responsibility, one that must be shared in common by each employee, professional practitioner, and citizen.

This dual personal and collective moral responsibility is reflected in almost all contemporary ethical theories, including deontological, teleological, and consequentialist or utilitarian theories (see Chapter 1), because the individual good and the collective good are viewed by these theories as integrally interrelated, at least in Western liberal democracies, a view that goes back at least to Plato and Aristotle, who conceived the ethical good of the individual as being integrally inseparable from the good of the polis, or society. It is both conceptually and practically for this reason that individual professionals as well as their professions and institutions collectively, have ethical commitments to the community and society at large that cannot be circumscribed or overridden by their own restricted personal or professional interests, since those interests must ultimately accord and be in harmony with the overall interests, especially ethical interests, of the whole community.

As we saw in Chapter 3, advertisers sometimes err ethically by not only not acting in accord with the ethical interests of the community but also actively undermining those interests by targeting vulnerable groups like children (junk food that results in obesity), teenage girls (exaggerated and false images of beauty that result in anorexia), young people (associations of alcohol with aspirational values such as friendship, sportsmanship, and glamour that can result in alcohol abuse), and generally the commodification of communal institutions like education and sport by advertising and marketing sponsorships that have the potential effect of demeaning the traditional values of those institutions, even though they may assist those institutions operationally by much-needed financial injections of cash. Ultimately, however, we have to decide as a society whether there are certain values that are so important to our collective cultural well-being and shared communal identity as citizens that need to be protected and preserved, like species facing extinction, from degradation by commodification by advertising and marketing. The legacy that we pass on to future generations not only must require us to preserve and protect the natural environment from degradation but also must equally require us to protect the social and cultural environments from degradation, including degradation of aspirational values and social institutions, from pervasive and widespread viral commodification of those values and institutions by aggressive and ethically irresponsible advertising and marketing.

The ethical responsibility for the protection and preservation of the cultural and social environments, including the aspirational values and institutions of those environments, lies personally with every individual citizen and every professional practitioner and collectively with every organization, with every institution or profession and ultimately with the whole community and the government as political representatives of the community. As mentioned in Chapter 1, if ethical compliance that is necessary for effecting ethical professional practices in the advertising industry for the protection and preservation of the cultural and social environments cannot be achieved, at least in the short to medium term, through self-regulation at all the ethical levels—personal, organizational, institutional, and social (the preferred option)—then it is ethically incumbent upon the government, as representatives of the community, to introduce regulative measures and controls by way of rewards and penalties for ethical and unethical conduct respectively, so as to compel the advertising industry to adopt ethical practices that result effectively in ethical compliance and that reflect the norms of public and universal morality.

Integrity and Morality: The Unity of the Right and the Good

> "We study ethics not to know what goodness is, but how to become good persons."
> Aristotle, *The Nichomachean Ethics*

As we saw from our discussion in Chapter 1 and from our preceding discussion, a personal commitment to ethical conduct, though necessary for compliance with professional ethical practice, is, however, not sufficient. It is not sufficient because a moral individual working in an amoral or immoral professional environment, or at least an inadequately ethical environment that lacks any organizational or institutional commitment to ethical practice supported by appropriate ethical principles and ethical regulative controls, may not be able to act alone in ensuring compliance with ethical practice within the organization and institution in which one is placed. Such ethical principles and controls, both at the organizational and institutional levels, are ones that to be compliance-effective must incorporate appropriate rewards and penalties for ethical and unethical conduct respectively, and that incorporation requires collective effort and action at

those respective levels in inculcating an ethical cultural environment within an individual organization, as well as within the relevant professional institution within which the organization is placed. This, in turn, requires a collective commitment to ethical professional practice, not only at the personal level, but equally and importantly, at the collective organizational and institutional levels respectively. Thus professional ethical self-regulation requires a commitment to both personal and collective organizational and institutional ethical conduct that together are capable, at least in principle, of bringing about practical compliance with ethical professional practice.

In this section, we will examine the nature and crucial importance of personal and professional integrity for ethical compliance through ethical self-regulation, in both one's personal and one's professional roles. To do so, we need to take a closer look at motivation, one of the three key components in ethical reasoning and ethical decision-making, along with justification and compliance.

Motivation, as we have seen previously, is the ethical lynchpin between justification and compliance. On the one hand, its relation to justification is one of *direct proportionality,* whereas on the other hand, its relation to compliance is one of *inverse proportionality.* That is, with regard to justification, the more justification there is (provided through ethical principles supported by cogent sound arguments that are embedded in contemporary ethical theory), the greater the motivation for ethical action becomes (on the given assumption that the agent is a normal, rational person, and not a psychopath or sociopath, for example). By contrast, the more motivation there is, the less *external compliance* is required; and similarly, the more external compliance that is required, the less motivation there is. Thus since enhanced motivation through enhanced justification requires minimal external compliance, one approaching $(0) = 0\%$, $(.5) = 50\%$ and so on, with maximum motivation approaching (1) = 100%, it is very important for ethical self-regulation (the preferred ethical option) to have ethical strategies that increase ethical motivation, thus decreasing the requirement for external compliance. This is the case because motivation carries and provides its own *internal compliance*. Thus with maximal motivation approaching (1), there is, at least in principle, proportional maximal ethical internal compliance approaching (1) that renders external compliance superfluous and unnecessary. Thus with maximal motivation approaching (1), accompanied by proportional internal compliance approaching (1), the inversely proportional external compliance required is one approaching (0).

The following are some ethical strategies for increasing ethical motivation and proportionally increasing internal compliance, while simultaneously decreasing the requirement and the need for external compliance through punitive measures and controls, at the personal, organizational, and institutional levels:

Internal Practical Motivation through Principle

This type of motivation is primarily provided by rational arguments embedded in contemporary ethical theories like the ones examined in Chapter 1. For example, an argument like the argument for the Principle of Generic Consistency (PGC) demonstrates that morality is overriding and rationally binding on every individual person and its prescriptions required by practical reasons that are at once personal and impartial, by virtue of one's own internal rational train of thought. Thus the argument for the PGC can provide, from within its own internal rational and normative structure, one that emulates the internal dialectical train of rational thinking of a putative individual person, adequate ethical motivation capable of generating ethical compliance through ethical conduct.

Internal Practical Motivation through Virtue and Sentiment

Internal motivation engendered by principle, as before, can be enhanced by the inculcation of the virtues and the cultivation of the rational sentiments.

Virtues

Virtues are essentially dispositions of character that can enable one to act ethically and do the right thing in most, if not all, circumstances. Examples of virtues are courage, temperance, prudence, and justice (the cardinal virtues). Some other virtues are honesty, truthfulness, compassion, loyalty, perseverance, fortitude, generosity, kindness, and mercy. Like trained muscles and physical and mental discipline that enable the athlete or sportsperson to participate in athletic and sporting events, virtues enable a person who has inculcated the virtues in his or her character through ethical habituation to act ethically and to do the right thing in most, if not all, circumstances. Such virtues will reflect a commitment not only to public and universal morality but also to the role morality of the particular profession or institutional practice in which one is placed. Thus a journalist would need to be truthful and honest and a police officer fair and courageous in the discharging of their respective professional duties as determined by their particular role moralities.

Virtues can enable ethical conduct both by commission and by omission. Thus for example, an investigative journalist acts courageously by commission by investigating and exposing political corruption. On the other hand, a police officer acts courageously by omission by refusing the rewards and threats of his or her fellow police officers to engage in corrupt activity. Similarly, an individual in an advertising agency acts courageously by omission in refusing to participate in the unethical practices of his or her agency. Thus the virtues can be exercised both by commission in acting ethically as well as by omission in not acting unethically. A whistleblower who publicly exposes the unethical practices of his or her organization, in which he or she refuses to engage personally, acts courageously and ethically both by omission and by commission.

Moral Sentiments

Some examples of positive sentiments are consideration for others, politeness, amicability, gratitude, calmness; and some example of negative sentiments are indignation, resentment, regret, remorse, guilt.

Sentiments both the positive and the negative can motivate ethical conduct by acting as rewards and punishments respectively. Typically positive sentiments will precede, accompany, and follow ethical conduct, rendering the emotional experience of ethical conduct rewarding, one that dispositionally at least reinforces and motivates future ethical conduct. Likewise, negative sentiments like regret, remorse, and guilt, which may follow unethical conduct through scruples of conscience, can act as emotional forms of punishment to demotivate future unethical conduct.

Thus both the virtues and the moral sentiments can help boost ethical motivation for ethical conduct, making the inculcation of virtues and positive moral sentiments, especially those relevant to one's profession, and avoidance of negative sentiments, a highly desirable, if not a necessary, source of additional psychological motivation for moral conduct in both one's personal and one's professional roles. The answer to the question Why inculcate the virtues and cultivate the rational sentiments? is that it helps to additionally motivate moral conduct, and moral conduct is justified. Insofar as the inculcation of the virtues and the cultivation of the moral sentiments help to provide additional motivation for ethical conduct, then the inculcation of the virtues and cultivation of the moral

sentiments are a moral requirement in the same way that a healthy diet and regular physical exercise are a requirement for good health.

Ethical Motives and Ethical Actions

"If the choice is to be a good one, both the reasoning must be true and the desire right; and the desire must pursue the same things that the reasoning asserts."
Aristotle, *The Nichomachean Ethics*

In keeping with Aristotle, ethics generally, and Gewirth's Principle of Generic Consistency specifically, require not only good actions but also good motives that motivate those actions. That is to say, with regard to ethical conduct, both the motives and the actions that they motivate must be moral. Thus in the case of some types of stereotyping in advertising, the motives and the means that they motivate in the form of stereotyping cannot be justified by the professional perception, justified as that may be, that stereotyping is an effective means for the advertising end of successfully promoting consumer products if those means are detrimental to the people stereotyped.

Through the inculcation of the virtues and the cultivation of the moral sentiments, professional practitioners, specifically in advertising, can dispositionally acquire moral motives through habituation, which can in turn motivate them to act ethically in accordance with the theoretical and practical requirements of not only the role morality of their profession but also, and more importantly, in accordance with the requirements of public and universal morality (see Chapter 1).

Moral Integrity

Moral integrity at both the personal and the professional levels can be conceived of as a state of internal congruence, synergy, or harmony between one's motives and one's actions, a state in which the means of one's actions are as far as possible always in congruence with and track the ends of one's actions. Given that one's actions, both with regard to oneself as well as with regard to others, must always be ethical in accordance both with professional role morality and with public universal morality, personal and professional integrity requires that the motives of one's actions are likewise ethical and track one's moral actions. Similarly, personal and professional integrity requires that one's means are also ethical and always track, as far as possible, one's ethical ends as required by both role and universal moralities. Thus a lack of personal and professional integrity is a state in which one's motives are not congruent with one's actions and in which one's means are not congruent with and do not track one's ethical ends to which one is committed, if not by one's professional role morality then at least by public universal morality to whose requirements everyone is bound.

For example, in the case of advertisers and marketers using material inducements to promote products to vulnerable groups of consumers such as children, as we saw in Chapter 3, the motives of exclusive self-interest by the advertisers that do not have the interests of the targeted group of children at heart, are not congruent with their "caring and beneficent" actions of offering books, toys, or free games to the targeted children, purportedly for the "good" of the children but ultimately for the good of the advertisers themselves. Such lack of internal congruence as illustrated by this example is an instance of a lack of professional integrity because it fails the universal moral requirements of public morality with which all personal, professional, and social action is required to accord.

The Unity of the Right and the Good: A Summary Argument

1. The Principle of Generic Consistency (PGC) is at least one ethical principle that provides both rational justification and rational motivation to act morally, that is, to act with respect for the generic rights of freedom and well-being of others as well as one's own.

2. Since the virtues can enable one, through habituation, to act morally in accordance with the requirements of the PGC, it is one's moral duty to personally and professionally cultivate those virtues. This is both self-regarding in relation to oneself and other-regarding with relation to others.

3. The moral sentiments demonstrate empirically that one can be emotionally rewarded in doing the right thing by others but can suffer harm through feelings of remorse, regret, and guilt by harming others. According to the PGC, it is wrong to harm others as well as to harm oneself. Therefore, one should avoid harming oneself through harming others. Not only does self-preservation require physical and mental integrity, but also, with equal importance, it requires moral integrity. Thus self-preservation requires moral self-preservation.

4. In conclusion, we are required by our own rationality and ultimately by our own self-interest, at least long-term interest, to do what is right and to be good, since being good enables us to do what is right.

An Integrated Single Comprehensive and Consistent Worldview

The unity of the right and the good further requires the adoption of an integrated, single comprehensive and consistent worldview that is ethically good, one that accords with Universal Public Morality.

You will recall that according to Boylan (see Chapter 1), a person's worldview should be holistic and integrated, one that eschews fragmentation that can result in dissonance. On the contrary, what is recommended is consonance between one's thinking and one's motives and actions as informed by one's holistic, comprehensive, and consistent worldview. Central to this recommendation is the view that one should be critically reflective about one's life in keeping with Socrates' famous dictum that "the unexamined life is not worth living," meaning that an unexamined life is not worthy and thus not becoming of a thinking human being whose nature is at least partly defined by his or her ability to think rationally and reflectively about everything he or she does or does not do.

According to Boylan, "many people reside in several self-contained worlds that dictate how they should act in this or that situation. These worlds are often contradictory." As we saw earlier (see Chapter 1), one's Role Morality as a practitioner in a particular profession or other institutional practice may involve one in a potential conflict with Universal Public Morality by whose requirements everyone, including the professional practitioner, is required to abide. Thus when such a moral conflict arises, Universal Public Morality will always trump the narrower requirements of one's Role Morality and will require the professional practitioner to act in accordance with the requirements of Universal Public Morality over those of his or her profession's role morality. The "Instrumental and Ethical Consequences" summaries that function as ethical balance sheets at the end of the relevant chapters in this book highlight how the instrumental requirements dictated by the narrow requirements of the Role Morality of advertising get trumped and are overridden by the wider ethical requirements of Universal Public Morality, to which one is ethically obliged to conform simply by virtue of being a human agent regardless of the narrower professional or other personal or familial commitments that one might have.

The adoption of an *integrated* single comprehensive and consistent worldview that is morally good is in keeping with our earlier argument that the unity of the right and the good, a unity required by the Universal Public Morality, is an essential requirement for the preservation and maintenance of one's personal and professional *integrity*. Unlike the member of the Mafia who might be able to create an amoral, integrated

worldview that defies the demands of Universal Public Morality,[139] that option is not available to the professional or other institutional practitioner who must always abide, and be seen to abide, by the requirements of Universal Public Morality, both for ethical and instrumental reasons. That is, unethical practice is not only not good for society but ultimately also not good for business.

Ethical Advertising

The hybrid nature of advertising that combines persuasion with information creates a tendency by which information is undermined by advertising strategies that give preference to persuasion over information, for example, as in stereotyping, where stereotyped groups of people are diminished and degraded through misrepresentation, or by advertising strategies that present persuasion tactics disguised as information content that have the potential to mislead and deceive consumers, such as in advertorials. The latter strategy is particularly of ethical concern because in an attempt to get advertising "under the radar" of consumer detection, advertisers are increasingly resorting to blurring or completely obliterating the boundary between promotional advertising material and program content so as to keep the consumers tuned in to their ads.

Insofar as the consumer is deliberately misled by this strategy in mistaking advertising promotion for program content, such a strategy is a form of deception and thus unethical. Even when not deliberately deceived by the blurring between advertising promotion and program content but insofar as the consumer is not given a choice to waive or withhold his or her consent for having advertising promotions presented to him or her as program content, the consumer's freedom of choice has been violated and his or her consent merely induced through commercial manipulation, if not deception. This practice too is unethical. Of course, the media accomplice to this strategy, whether TV, radio, print, or other outlets, is equally at ethical fault as the advertiser itself.

Moreover, the paradoxical nature of advertising by which commodities are anthropomorphized (as when consumer products are invested with human values—for example, "Happiness Is Hyundai"—and people and social institutions are commodified (as when people are stereotyped for the sole purpose of drawing attention to particular consumer products) degrades both values and people by associating them pervasively with commodities that not only lack those values but also lack the essential defining human characteristics that people possess but that commodities do not. Our collective human values, such as truth, beauty, independence, romance, friendship, and happiness, need to be protected from the wholesale degradation and trivialization to which advertising and marketing subjects them through commodity branding. Values are not for sale and thus should not be promoted as if they were sale commodities. Only an exceptionally cynical person would consider important and fundamental values as items of sale. Ethically speaking, we reject such unwarranted, because unjustified, cynicism.

In addition, the all-pervasive nature of advertising that manifests itself in all areas of our human activities has a tendency not only to invade our personal privacy but also to display a tendency to invade our collective public "sacred spaces," such as the beach, the park, the bar, the child-care center, or even the rest room, places that we have traditionally designated as public and private spaces in which we can at times retreat and take time out to replenish our sometimes depleted, from over-commercialization of the natural and social environment, humanity. As human beings, we need such spatial and temporal spaces in which to reenchant our personal and social environment and to imbue it with meaning that goes to the core of our common

humanity and that is far removed from the narrow commercial concerns of the marketplace, which of course, have their place—but not in our collective "sacred spaces."

Finally, the targeting of vulnerable groups by advertising such as children, teenage girls, young people and elderly people, amongst others, can as we saw result in bad and harmful consequences not only for the individuals within those groups but for the community as a whole who are burdened with the health and social costs that this kind of advertising, potentially at least, creates.

The preceding paragraphs highlight the three main ethically problematic areas of advertising practice. The problems manifest themselves more directly when the various advertising strategies and practices that fall into any one of those ethically problematic areas result in bad and harmful consequences for individuals or groups of individuals and for the community as a whole, such as in the case of the advertising targeting of children with junk food that leads to obesity.

The three preceding types of ethical issues that arise in advertising are of concern not because they are incidences that an effective regulation compliance system can adequately monitor and control through rewards and penalties but because they constitute wholesale and systematic ethical transgressions. They are, in effect, ethically problematic precisely because they are part of a pattern of ethical misbehavior that manifests itself through the systematic use of particular advertising strategies whose very design and purpose is inherently ethically problematic.

In developing ethical advertising, the advertising industry must adopt a harm-minimization policy by which bad and harmful consequences from various advertising strategies and practices that fall into any one or more of these three main areas of ethically problematic advertising (and there may be others), should be, if not eliminated, at least minimized. To this end, appropriate ethical policies that include adequate ethical training for practitioners, codes of ethics, and adequate self-regulative ethical controls with teeth by way of rewards and penalties, should be adopted by the advertising industry institutionally as a whole; if self-regulation is to prove effective, then it must have the support of the leadership of the advertising institution as a whole.

Ethical advertising, like ethical self-regulation as described earlier, can then be devolved to the individual organizations and practitioners within each organization, thus creating a cultural environment that not only is responsive to ethical advertising but also is an environment in which each individual member and organization will be encouraged to be ethically pro-active in enhancing the ethical possibilities of advertising that meet the challenges of its hybrid and paradoxical nature. One way of accomplishing this goal is by creating new innovative strategies that are maximally ethically consistent with the inherently ethically problematic nature of advertising and that eliminate or maximally minimize advertising practices that have the tendency to result in bad and harmful consequences for people and the community as a whole. Such strategies must not only operate to eliminate harmful consequences piecemeal but must also, and more importantly, operate in a wholesale manner to eliminate the intrusive and pervasive effects of advertising that people increasingly perceive as an unwelcome and unwholesome intrusion into their personal and social times and spaces.

With the exception of Case Study 9a, the preceding case studies indicate the ways in which the advertising industry has been both responsive and pro-active in establishing ethical advertising practices that exhibit ethical social responsibility. Case Study 9c is an example of how the advertising professional institutions in Britain and Australia have been responsive to community concerns about the effects of dangerous driving practices featured in some car commercials. Case Study 9b is an example of how governments in both Britain and Australia have used radical but effective advertising tactics

to shock their respective communities into adopting safer driving practices that ultimately benefit the whole community by reducing the injuries and fatalities from unsafe driving.

The respective ethical advertising practices illustrated by Case Studies 9b and 9c are in keeping with sound deontological, teleological, and consequentialist ethical principles that support ethical action because they employ means, even if somewhat radical, for the end of safeguarding the individual as well as the collective interests of the citizens in those respective communities, and by doing so, increasing the overall good for the greatest number of people in both communities. Moreover, Case Studies 9b and 9c are indicative of the type of effective cooperation that can take place in establishing a coregulated professional environment that involves all the key stakeholders, such as the advertising industry, its representative institutional bodies, the government, and the community, working together to create a safer road traffic environment through effective ethical advertising that takes into account the interests of the whole community.

Case Studies 9d and 9e are illustrative of the way in which commercial advertisers can be pro-active by initiating ethical advertising campaigns that attempt to provide consumers with important information that serves the consumers' interests by informing consumers, as citizens, of the health disadvantages of excessive reliance on car transportation and the health benefits of walking, as in Kia's innovative advertising campaign "Think Before You Drive" (Case Study 9d), or by Kellogg's encouraging people to eat more high-fiber foods, including bran cereals, as a means of reducing some type of cancer (Case Study 9e). As in Case Studies 9b and 9c, similarly Case Studies 9d and 9e are illustrative of advertising strategies that are in keeping with sound deontological, teleological, and consequentialist principles as they are ethically concerned and take into account the individual and collective interests of the community as a whole for the overall good of the community.

Moreover, Case Studies 9b through 9e are indicative of the congruence that can be engendered between advertising as a form of *persuasion* and advertising as a form of *information* through ethical advertising. By contrast, we have seen throughout this book how unethical advertising practices can give rise to an incongruence and conflict between the persuasion and the information functions of advertising when persuasion tactics are allowed to unscrupulously undermine the essential informative content of advertising through misrepresentation or deception. These tactics, as the cases presently discussed indicate through contrast, are not only bad ethics but also bad business, since they earn the advertising organizations responsible for such unethical practices a bad reputation that not only undermines their own social capital but also tarnishes the reputation of the whole industry. On the contrary, Case Studies 9f and 9g are illustrative of the kind of pro-active and innovative socially responsible advertising that will, in our estimation, become increasingly important and dominant in an increasingly ethically aware and responsive social and cultural environment.

Case Study 9a was deliberately placed among the other case studies that, as in our discussion, illustrate ethical advertising, so as to highlight this as an example of lazy and unprofessional advertising that is likely to offend a lot of people by denigrating the Catholic religion through associating the Pope with a rugby game in what is by all accounts a disrespectful portrayal of the leader of one of the major religions in the world that commands the allegiance of hundreds of millions of people around the globe. In contrast to the other case studies discussed in this chapter, this is an instance of socially and ethically irresponsible advertising that undermines, rather than promotes, the interests of the community.

Insofar as personal and professional integrity is important, so is ethical self-regulation, since it is required by ethical integrity which in turn requires ethical consistency between one's motives and actions, one's character and conduct, as required in turn by ethical principles such as Kant's Categorical Imperative and Gewirth's Principle of Generic Consistency (see Chapter 1). And insofar as the advertising industry values personal and professional integrity, then it should adopt policies and strategies that avoid unethical practices and that promote ethical practices in keeping with the concept of ethical advertising as ethical self-regulation that requires ethical responsibility at the personal, organizational, and institutional levels, and moreover at the social and communal level.

In addition and in keeping with the necessity of having both personal and professional integrity that constitutes a unity of what is right and what is good, advertising practitioners should also adopt the Personal Worldview Imperative (see Chapter 1) that requires them as individuals to adopt and cultivate an integrated comprehensive and consistent worldview that is good and in accord with Universal Public Morality.

A Summary of Instrumental and Ethical Consequences

Throughout this book we have focused on the many different ways in which certain advertising strategies and practices can be viewed as downright unethical or at least as ethically problematic. And although we pointed out how some of those advertising strategies and practices can be instrumentally desirable from a strictly professional operative perspective, one in keeping with the fulfillment of the role and ultimate goal of advertising, we nevertheless pointed out the overall ethical undesirability of those strategies and practices.

In this chapter, by contrast, we have attempted to demonstrate the many different ways in which advertising can be both instrumentally as well as ethically desirable. We have thus hopefully demonstrated in some small measure that ethical advertising need not be an oxymoron.[140] Indeed, advertising can be conceived and conducted not merely in an ethically neutral manner (neither ethical nor unethical), a category in which a lot of advertising falls, but in a positively ethical manner.

The following is an outline of the desirable instrumental, as well as ethical, consequences and commitments of ethical advertising:

1. Insofar as being trustworthy is both good for one's professional, organisational and personal reputation, trustworthiness is not only ethically but also instrumentally desirable. Thus avoidance of advertising strategies and practices that deceive and manipulate consumers by stealth should be avoided, since they undermine trustworthiness once the deception has been discovered and exposed.

   The truth of the matter may be that most people, especially young people who have grown up with the proliferation and pervasiveness of advertising, do not mind advertising or mind being targeted by it, but they do mind the various attempts by advertising and marketing to deceive them. Thus, in-your-face advertising that does not attempt to deceive consumers by cloaking itself misleadingly and deceptively in content, information, or culture, as in the case of infomercials, advertorials, and other concealed advertising weapons such as songs, films, and books that are essentially advertising campaigns masquerading as culture, is far more desirable both instrumentally and ethically than deceptive forms of advertising.

   It is therefore highly desirable both instrumentally and ethically that advertising preserve its professional integrity by avoiding deception of all shapes and forms and by being true to itself to preserve its ethical credibility and trustworthiness.

2. As illustrated by the case studies in this chapter, advertising can result in overall good consequences for the whole community and thus can be shown to be positively ethical. Because of its persuasive power, advertising is in a prominent position to use its various strategies to bring about good consequences that are not only instrumentally viable but also ethically desirable.

   Paradoxically, by being perceived by the public to work not merely for its own operative self-interests but also ethically for the interests of the consumers and the community generally, that perception can enhance the operative self-interest of advertising organizations by benefiting their professional reputation as being ethically responsible corporate citizens, thus increasing their social and ethical capital. In a world that is increasingly becoming more ethically sensitive and aware, this is no small gain.

   Though the previous observation may appear as paradoxical, it does not really amount to paradox, because the good consequences that result from ethical advertising are in keeping with the attempt to treat consumers not merely as a means to the advertisers' ends but as ends in themselves worthy of their own moral consideration. The happy marriage between consequential and deontological reasons for professional and corporate conduct can produce optimal ethical and, indeed, instrumental results.

3. As suggested throughout this book but especially in Chapter 7, the pervasiveness and unrestricted proliferation of advertising that threatens to engulf all aspects of our private and public domains remains the biggest ethical problem in advertising. It may, however, prove very difficult for the advertising industry itself to control through self-regulation the pervasiveness of advertising so as to ensure that it does not encroach on our shared communal sacred spatiotemporal spaces. If this proves the case, the advertising industry may have to liaise and cooperate with the government as the representative of the citizenry to introduce coregulation that protects our communal sacred spaces from advertising, at least commercial advertising, by declaring that those sacred spaces be advertising-free zones from which all commercial advertising is barred. Ethical advertising that is socially responsible and thus sensitive and responsive to the community's needs, demands this protection.

Notes

1. See Alan Gewirth's *Reason and Morality* (Chicago: University of Chicago Press, 1978).

2. Ibid., pp. 104–198.

3. For the notion of justice as fairness, see John Rawls, *A Theory of Justice* (Oxford: Oxford University Press, 1972).

4. The concept of "worldview" and its ethical significance and implication are developed and discussed at length by Michael Boylan in his book *Basic Ethics* (Upper Saddle River, New Jersey: Prentice Hall, 2000), pp. 23–28, 173–182, and 186–200. The main purpose of Boylan's book is to introduce the essential concepts that guide the series of books titled *Basic Ethics in Action*.

5. Ibid., p. 27.

6. Ibid., p. 27.

7. Ibid., pp. 186–187.

8. Ibid., p. 187.

9. Ibid., p. 195.

10. Ibid., p. 181.

11. Ibid., p. 27.

12. Sources are ASB Case Report, March 17, 2000, Complaint reference number 79/00, http://www.advertisingstandardsbureau.com.au/bureau/industry/windso_smith.htm; *Self-regulation: Haven't we been there?*, B&T Weekly, August 10, 2001; *Windsor Smith Blows Off Standards Board, B&T Weekly*, March 24, 2000; *Marketer Defends Bawdy Billboard, B&T Weekly*, March 17, 2000; AANA Advertiser Code of Ethics, Section 2.1, http://www.advertisingstandardsbureau.com.au/industry/aana_code_ethics.html.

13. As cited in AANA Advertiser Code of Ethics, Section 2.1, www.advertisingstandardsbureau.com.au/industry/aana_code_ethics.html.

14. Sources are *French Connection Ads Roil Censors, The Asian Wall Street Journal*, April 6, 2001; *Fcuk Advertising Strategy, Creative Business* in *Financial Times*, April 10, 2001; *Shock Tactics Short-circuited, The Daily Telegraph*, April 10, 2001; http://www.asa.co.uk.

15. Jean J. Boddewyn (1989). *Advertising self-regulation: True purpose and limits. Journal of Advertising*, Vol. 18, No. 2, p. 20.

16. Andrew Belsey and Ruth Chadwick. *Ethical Issues in Journalism and the Media* (London and New York: Routledge, 1992).

17. The title of the case study was inspired by the title of the book *Consuming Children: Education-entertainment-advertising,* by Jane Kenway and Elizabeth Bullen (Buckingham: Open Court University Press, 2001).

18. Faith McLellan, *Marketing and Advertising: Harmful to Children's Health, The Lancet;* London, September 28, 2002.

19. From *Brand Loyalty Begins Early,* by Janice Rosenberg and Shirley Henderson (*Advertising Age,* Volume 72, No. 7, February 12, 2001).

20. Ibid.

21. Ibid.

22. Ibid.

23. Sources are Maria Ligerakis, *AANA, AFA Defends Against Child Food Ad Ban Call, B&T Weekly,* September 11, 2002; Maria Ligerakis, *AANA, AFA Weigh In to Child Obesity Debate. B&T Weekly,* September 27, 2002; Tania Mason, *Snack Attack: The Next Ad Ban?. Marketing,* London, February 2002, p. 13; Anonymous, *Selling to—and Selling Out—Children, The Lancet,* September 28, 2002; Faith McLellan, *Marketing and Advertising: Harmful to Children's health, The Lancet;* London, September 28, 2002; Paul Raeburn, Julie Forster, Dean Foust, and Dianne Brady, *WHY WE'RE SO FAT: Fast Food at School, Huge Portions, and Relentless TV Ads Make It Easy, Business Week,* New York, October 21, 2002; Elizabeth Olsen, *Fighting Fat by Going to the Source, New York Times,* November 17, 2002.

24. Olsen, loc. cit.

25. Raeburn et al., loc. cit.

26. Mason, loc. cit.

27. Ligerakis, September 27, 2002, loc. cit.

28. Raeburn et al., loc. cit.

29. Ibid.

30. McLellan, loc. cit.

31. Mason, loc. cit.

32. Ligerakis, September 11, 2002.

33. Ibid.

34. *Fox Sports* is the sports program shown on Foxtel Cable TV in Australia.

35. Source is Sarah Bryden-Brown, *Flogging Kid's Products All Part of the* Show, *The Australian,* November 18, 2002.

36. The following sources are used for this case study: Peter Gotting, *Ads Come Dressed as Entertainment, Sydney Morning Herald,* January 13, 2003; Peter Gotting, *You Can Run, Ski or Skate but You Can't Hide,* January 13, 2003; Peter Gotting, *Hi Pitch, Low Pitch or Just Sales Pitch,* January 13, 2003; Naomi Klein, *No Logo* (London: Harper Collins, 2001).

37. Naomi Klein, *No Logo* (London: Flamingo, 2001, p. 30).

38. Ibid.

39. Sources are Melissa Marino, *20 Years Of Slip, Slop, Slap: How a Bird Provoked a Sea Change, Sunday Age,* November 4, 2001, p. 3; Evelyn Tsitas, *Safely Shaded by Vanity, Herald,* January 13, 2000, p. 18; Dinah Oh, *SunSmart Uses Gore to Shock, AdNews,* January 14, 2000, p. 2; Paula Moyer, *Skin Cancer Program Targets Australians; Many Re-examining Value of a Suntan, Changing Their Behavior in Favor of Sunscreens, Protective Clothing, Dermatology Times,* May 1, 1994.

40. Dr. Alan Cooper quoted in Paula Moyer, loc. cit., 1994.

41. Marino, loc. cit.

42. Ibid.

43. Klein, loc. cit., p. 29.

44. Ibid., p. 30.

45. Suzanne Livingstone, *Next Generation Branding, Brand Strategy,* June 26, 2002, p. 32.

46. Ibid.

47. Sources are Paul McCann, *Branson Fails to Shoot Down BA's Favorite Slogan, The Independent,* June 9, 1999; *OPINION—ASA's Position on BA Is a Threat to Self-regulation, Campaign,* May 7, 1999; Advertising Standards Authority Adjudications, British Airways plc, June 9, 1999, www.asa.org.uk, accessed October 23, 2002.

48. Cited in ASA Adjudication Report, June 9, 1999, www.asa.org.uk.

49. Sources are Advertising Standards Authority Adjudications, Daewoo Cars Ltd, May 10, 2000, www.asa.org.uk, accessed October 23, 2002; Advertising Standards Authority Adjudications, Fiat Auto (UK) Ltd t/a Fiat Auto (U.K.), April 4, 2001, www.asa.org.uk, accessed October 23, 2002; Kathy Lipari, *Target Told to Correct Sale Ads, Daily Telegraph,* July 9, 2001, p. 4; James Madden, *Target Admits to Customers It Led Them Astray, The Australian,* July 9, 2001, p. 5.

50. Sources are *The Weekend Australian,* January 9–10, 1999; *B&T Weekly,* January 15, 1999.

51. Mark Dolliver, *Truth or Consequences—or Lack Thereof, Adweek,* May 24, 1999.

52. For examples of this strategy in action, see Jim Aitchison, *Cutting Edge Advertising: How to Create the World's Best Print for Brands in the 21st Century* (Singapore: Prentice Hall, 1999, pp. 126 and 177).

53. Excerpts taken from the tenth edition of the British Codes of Advertising and Sales Promotion, which came into force on October 1, 1999, with Addendum 1 added on April 23, 2000. It replaces all previous editions. www.asa.org.uk.

54. See Paul D. Colford, *Feds Target Ads for Miracle Diets, New York Daily News,* October 18, 2002, p. 44.

55. FTC Policy Statement on Deception, Federal Trade Commission, October 14, 1983, http://www.ftc.gov/bcp/policystmt/ad-decept.htm.

56. Ivan L. Preston, *Regulatory Positions toward Advertising Puffery of the Uniform Commercial Code and the Federal Trade Commission. Journal of Public Policy & Marketing,* Fall 1997.

57. Sources used for this case study are the following: *Portrayal of Women in Outdoor Advertising Report,* February 2002, Department of Premier and Cabinet Office of Women's Policy www.women.vic.gov.au; Maria Ligerakis, *Agency Anger at Govt Portrayal of Women Pressure, B&T Weekly,* April 15, 2002; Lara Sinclair, *Self-regulation: Haven't We Been There?, B&T Weekly,* August 10, 2001; Portrayal of Women in Outdoor Advertising Policy, February 2002, accessible at http://www.women.vic.gov.au/owa/owasite.nsf/pages/projects#outdoor.

58. Cited in Portrayal of Women in Outdoor Advertising Report, loc. cit.

59. Ibid.

60. Sources used for this case study are the following: Jane Sancho and Andy Wilson, *Boxed In: Offence from Negative Stereotyping in Television Advertising,* Independent Television Commission, June 2001, accessed at www.itc.org.uk; David Lister, *Viewers Protest at "Racist" Stereotypes in Adverts, The Independent,* June 18, 2001, p. 5; Yasmin Alibhai-Brown, *Stop Making Such a Song and Dance about Stereotypes in Advertisements, The Independent,* June 19, 2001.

61. Cited in Jane Sancho and Andy Wilson, *Boxed In: Offence from Negative Stereotyping in Television Advertising,* Independent Television Commission, June 2001, accessed at www.itc.org.uk, p. 9.

62. The title of the case study refers to a line from the refrain in the song "Mother's Little Helper" by the Rolling Stones.

63. Kevin Goldman's description of the Doritos chips commercial appears in "Growing Old in Commercials: A Joke Not Shared," by Ted Curtis Smythe, in Paul Martin Lester (Ed.), *Images That Injure* (Westport, Connecticut: Praeger Publishers, 1996, p. 113).

64. The following sources are used for this case study: David Lister, *Viewers Protest at "Racist" Stereotypes in Adverts, The Independent,* June 18, 2001, p. 5; Jane Sancho and Andy Wilson, *Boxed In: Offence from Negative Stereotyping in Television Advertising,* Independent Television Commission, June 2001, accessed at www.itc.org.uk.

65. See Jane Sancho and Andy Wilson, *Boxed In: Offence from Negative Stereotyping in Television Advertising,* Independent Television Commission, June 2001, accessed at www.itc.org.uk.

66. ITC Advertising Standards Code: Section 6 Harm & Offence, *http://www.itc.org.uk/itc_*

publications/codes_guidance/advertising_standards_practice2/section_6.asp#stereotypes.

67. Ibid.

68. Ibid.

69. See the codes at http://www.adstandards.com/en/standards/adstandards.asp.

70. See the Gender Portrayal Guidelines at http://www.adstandards.com/en/standards/gender.asp.

71. See the codes at www.asa.org.uk.

72. See the codes at http://www.advertising standardsbureau.com.au/industry/aana_code_et hics.html.

73. See the codes at http://www.afa.org.au/index2.asp?pid=274.

74. The AAF Mission, http://www.aaf.org/about/index.html.

75. The Advertising Principles of American Business, www.aaf.org/about/principles.html.

76. Howard Lavine, Donna Sweeney, and Stephen H. Wagner, *Depicting Women as Sex Objects in Television Advertising: Effects on Body Dissatisfaction. Personality and Social Psychology Bulletin,* August 1999.

77. Robert Gustafson, Mark Popovich, and Steven Thomsen, *The "Thin Ideal," Marketing News,* March 15, 1999, Vol. 33, Iss. 6, p. 22.

78. Jane Sancho and Andy Wilson, *Boxed In: Offence from Negative Stereotyping in Television Advertising,* Independent Television Commission, June 2001, p. 10, accessed at www.itc.org.uk.

79. Ibid.

80. Cited in Melinda Messineo and Scott Coltrane (Eds.), *The Perpetuation of Subtle Prejudice: Race and Gender Imagery in 1990s Television Advertising, Sex Roles,* New York, March 2000.

81. Michael O'Shaughnessy, *Media and Society: An Introduction* (Victoria, Australia: Oxford University Press, 1999, p. 221).

82. "Wog" is a derogatory term used in Australia, a lot less now than in the past, to refer to Australians of Greek, Italian, and Lebanese origin. Greek and Italian Australians ironically and playfully will occasionally refer to themselves as "wogs," but they take great offense when Australians of English origin call them that.

83. The apt phrase "images that injure" is the title of the book by Paul Martin Lester, (Ed.), *Images That Injure* (Westport, Connecticut: Praeger, 1996).

84. Extract from the article Long Jump from Glory to a Life of Pain that appeared in the English newspaper the *Sunday Times,* June 27, 1999.

85. See *Lewis: My Fight with Arthritis* In *The Observer,* June, 20, 1999.

86. See *Runners World Daily News,* June 23, 1999.

87. Sources are Rick Lyman and Stuart Elliott, *Sony Admits It Used Employees as Bogus Fans, New York Times,* June 16, 2001; Michael McCarthy, *Recent Crop of Sneaky Ads Backfires: Regulators Step in, Saying Advertisers Crossed the Line, USA Today,* July 17, 2001.

88. Cited in Lyman and Stuart, 2001.

89. Sources are John Markoff, *Apple Ad Campaign Stars Former Microsoft Users, New York Times,* June 10, 2002; Joellen Perry, *What's Really "Real"?; Apple's New Ad Campaign Features Ordinary Folks, but Some Wonder Just How Ordinary They Are, U.S. News & World Report,* August 19, 2002; Stuart Elliot, *Apple Endorses Some Achievers Who "Think Different," New York Times,* August 3, 1998.

90. Cited in Markoff, 2002.

91. Steven E. Landsburg, *The $10 Billion Man?, New York Times,* January 14, 1999, p. 21.

92. Figure taken from *Finance and Economics: A Tiger Economy, The Economist,* April 14, 2001, p. 70.

93. Taken from *FTC Guides Concerning Use Of Endorsements and Testimonials in Advertising,* http://www.ftc.gov/bcp/guides/endorse.htm.

94. Terence Shimp, *Advertising Promotion: Supplemental Aspects of Integrated Marketing Communications,* 5th ed. (Orlando, Florida: Harcourt, 2000, p. 335).

95. U.S. Federal Trade Commission Advertising Guidelines, http://www.ftc.gov/bcp/guides/endorse.htm.

96. ASA's British Codes of Advertising and Sales Promotion, www.asa.org.uk.

97. Advertising Standards Authority Adjudications, British Sky Broadcasting Ltd, April 5, 2000, www.asa.org.uk.

98. The "standard view" is provided by Michael Davies in Michael Davies, *Encyclopedia of Applied Ethics,* Vol. I (Orlando, FL: Academic Press, 1998, p. 590).

99. See ibid.

100. For what is wrong with conflict of interest, see ibid., p. 591. To the extent that conflict of interests usually also involve conflict of interest, the same reasons regarding the moral wrongness of conflict of interest apply also to conflict of interests.

101. Sources are Sylvia Brownrigg, *Your Ad Here, The New York Times,* November 4, 2001, p. 38; Sally Patten, *Bulgari Steals a March with Novel Ploy, The Times of London,* October 13, 2001, p. 51; Arthur Hirsch, *Writer's Call Weldon's New Book an Ad, The Baltimore Sun,* October 2, 2001; Gail Edmonson, *From Lord of the Rings to Hotelier: Can Jeweler Bulgari Succeed at Renting Rooms?, Business Week,* September 17, 2001, p. 21; Kim Campbell, *Death of Literature? Not Just Yet. Concern in the Book Industry over Ads in Novels and Tracking, Christian Science Monitor,* September 20, 2001.

102. Hirsch, loc. cit., p. 51.

103. Brownrigg, loc. cit., p. 38.

104. Sources are Suzanne Vranica, *Universal Music Seeks Ties to Marketers to Raise Sales—Vivendi Unit's Intention Is to Have Advertisers Pay For Artists' TV Promotion, Wall Street Journal,* July 8, 2002; Barbara Lippert, *The Fame Game, Adweek,* May 22, 2000; Lori L. Tharps, *Hollywood Shills, Entertainment Weekly,* September 8, 2000.

105. Sources are Tom Leonard, *Sophie Dahl Poster Tops Advertising Complaints, The Daily Telegraph,* April 24, 2001; Senay Boztas, *Public Complaints Soar on Shock Ads, Sunday Times,* April 22, 2001, p. 11; Rebecca Allison, *"Offensive" Opium Posters to Be Removed, The Guardian,* December 19, 2000; Larissa Kaye, *Opium Given the All Clear, B&T Weekly,* February 26, 2001 www.bandt.com.au; Advertising Standards Authority Adjudication Report, January 10, 2001, www.asa.org.uk/adjudications.

106. Leonard, loc. cit.

107. The following sources are used for this case study: Stephen Brook, *Brands Should Give Bond Film Oscar, The Australian,* December 5, 2002; Tim Jamieson, *Bond Market, Herald-Sun,* December 14, 2002; Suzanne Carbone, *Using the Hard Sell, with a View to Making a Kill, The Age,* December 12, 2002; Gary Maddox, *Movies That Try to Make You Buy Are Stealing the Show, Sydney Morning Herald,* January 14, 2003. All the sources refer to Australian newspapers.

108. The following sources are used for this case study: Elizabeth Winding, *Immersed in Child's Play, Financial Times,* June 10, 2002, p. 17, accessed via ProQuest September 9, 2002; Marc Weingarten, *As Children Adopt Pets, A Game Adopts Them, New York Times,* February 21, 2002, p. G7, accessed via ProQuest October 12, 2002; Anonymous *Advertisers Reach Generation Y through NeoPets Web Community, Direct Marketing,* March 2001, p. 65, accessed via ProQuest October 12, 2002.

109. A cover story in *Business Week Online,* February 15, 1999, describe them as "born during a baby bulge that demographers locate between 1979 and 1994, they are as young as five and as old as 20." http://www.businessweek.com/datedtoc/1999/9907.htm.

110. Sources for this case study are Tobi Elkin, *TiVo Inks Pacts for Long-form TV Ads, Advertising Age,* June 17, 2001, p. 41; Tobi Elkin, *Getting Viewers to Opt In, Not Tune Out, Advertising Age,* November 4, 2002, pp. 10–12; Randall Rothenberg, *Smart Marketers Embrace Personal Video Recorders, Advertising Age,* June 24, 2002, p. 30; Paul Gough, *TiVo Does Advertainment, Media Daily News,* Mediapost.com, July 10, 2002; Wayne Friedman, *72.3% of PVR Viewers Skip Commercials,* AdAge.com Interactive News, July 2, 2002, accessed December 10, 2002.

111. As cited in Friedman, loc. cit.

112. Sources used for this case study are Pamela Paul, *Television Gets Started, American Demographics,* September 2002, pp. 22–26; Paul Gough, *VOD Ads Ready to Take Off, Media Daily News, Mediapost.com,* August 30, 2002, accessed December 10, 2002.

113. As cited in Gough, loc. cit.

114. Ibid.

115. Fuyuan Shen, *Banner Advertisement Pricing, Measurement, and Pretesting Practices: Perspectives from Interactive Agencies, Journal of Advertising,* Fall 2002.

116. Figures taken from www.nua.ie, accessed December 9, 2002.

117. Kate Lyons, *Global Revolution as TV Learns to Interact, B&T Weekly,* October 6, 2000.

118. Figures taken from Centre For Media Research—Daily Brief, *Digital TV Gains Popularity in Europe,* www.centreformediaresearch. com/cfmr_briefArchive.cfm?s=113516, Archived Brief from April 16, 2002.

119. Cara B. DiPasquale, *Direct Marketing Rose 3.6% in 01, Advertising Age,* June 10, 2002, p. 8.

120. Hudson Bawden, *Embrace Interactive TV and Prosper, B&T Weekly,* October 29, 2001.

121. Larissa Kaye, *Interactive Play for Brands, B&T Weekly,* March 9, 2001.

122. Conversation is a two-way consensual process between people, and perhaps sometimes between people and animals or other sentient beings capable of holding a conversation. Inanimate objects, like brands of products, are incapable of "conversations" simply because they do not possess the cognitive apparatus and ability to communicate, which humans and other animals possess, a cognitive capacity that perhaps in the future some computers with artificial intelligence might also possess. What is more accurate to say is that advertisers conduct a one-way communication with consumers through the various advertising modes of communication at their disposal. When that communication is unsolicited, it is an invasion of privacy and ethically unjustified. When it is solicited, it can become interactive communication; but to call it "conversation" is to misname the process and pervert the meaning of the concept of "conversation," something that advertising has a tendency to do in the paradoxical and ethically problematic practice of anthropomorphizing consumer products by associating them with human values or issues and commodifying people through such advertising practices as stereotyping and the branding of cultural and social institutions, such as health, education, sport, public spaces, and entertainment (see Chapters 5 and 11).

123. Like "conversations," "interactive," and "brand loyalty," "immersion" is yet another ad buzz word that amounts to no more than a euphemism to misdescribe a process that is inherently ethically problematic. Like the strategies of concealment that advertising uses in advertorials and immersive advertising, the terms used to describe these ethically problematic practices are also designed to conceal their true meaning and purpose. Like the naked emperor, advertising, in these instances, pretends to be fully clothed through verbiage that has no correspondence to reality. Insofar as it is misleading, it is ethically unjustified and should thus be avoided.

124. Foxtel is one of the two prime cable TV Networks in Australia; and *Rugby,* Aussie Rules, Rugby League and Rugby Union, is as popular in Australia as American football is in the United States.

125. Sources are Craig Smith, *Real Shock Is That Disturbing Ads Fail to Surprise Public, Marketing,* July 5, 2001, p. 15; Sheridan Rhodes, *Ten Years of TAC Success. B&T Weekly,* December 17, 1999, p. 5; Katrina Strickland, *Road Safety Campaign Too Subtle for Some, The Australian,* October 10, 1996, p. 28; Marcus Casey, *Ads Disgust and Offend—That's Why They Work, Daily Telegraph,* July 21, 1997, p. 11; Robert Williamson, *Commercials and Billboards Depicting Grim Scenes Have Sharply Reduced Road Fatalities Down Under, The Globe and Mail,* April 26, 1993.

126. Sources are James Thomson, *Foot Off the Gas, Business Review Weekly,* April 24, 2002;

Sarah Plaskitt, *Car Ads New Code Drives Forward, B&T Weekly,* April 22, 2002; Sarah Plaskitt, *New Code Puts Brakes on Fast Car Ads, B&T Weekly,* August 19, 2002; Advertising Standards Authority, Background Briefings: Motoring, www.asa.org.uk, accessed November 27, 2002.

127. Lesly Brydon, AFA Executive Director, in *B&T Weekly,* April 22, 2002.

128. Advertising Standards Authority, Background Briefings: Motoring, www.asa.org.uk, accessed November 27, 2002.

129. Sources are Tania Mason, *Marketing for a Better World?—Should Brands Shout about Their Focus on Sustainability or Does This Strategy Tend to Expose Them to Cynicism? Marketing,* June 6, 2002; Ben Bold, *Social Responsibility—Kia Selects a Novel Manoeuvre, PR Week,* January 5, 2001, p. 12.

130. Sources are Paul Bloom, Patti Yu Hussein, and Lisa R. Szykman, *Benefiting Society and the Bottom Line, Marketing Management,* Winter 1995; William F. Arens, *Contemporary Advertising,* 8th ed., (New York: McGraw-Hill, 2001).

131. Bloom et al., loc. cit.

132. Ibid.

133. Ibid.

134. Ibid.

135. Ibid. The authors cite 1993 research by the Cone/Roper Benchmark Survey on Cause-related Marketing, which demonstrated that 78 percent of those surveyed were more likely to buy a product that is associated with a product that they care about, and 66 percent would switch brands to support a cause that they care about.

136. Sources are John Heinzl, *Advertisers Take a Serious Stand Against Bullying, The Globe and Mail,* May 10, 2002, p. B9; Concerned Children's Advertisers website http://cca-canada.com/index.htm, accessed December 12, 2002.

137. Heinzl, loc. cit.

138. Source is Jennifer Whitehead, *St Luke's Founder Launches Ethical Shop, Brand Republic,* September 17, 2002 (accessed via Factiva December 3, 2002).

139. Insofar, however, that even the member of the Mafia must recognize that he too has rights to his freedom and well-being, which he needs in order to enable him to engage in the fulfillment of his amoral and criminally orientated goals or purposes, he too is rationally and ethically committed, on pain of self-contradiction, to the requirements of the Principle of Generic Consistency (see Chapter 1) and, by extension, the demands of Universal Public Morality, which the PGC supports.

140. Often when I mention that I teach advertising ethics, the response is invariably "that is an oxymoron," or "is there such a thing?" or even, "that must be a very short course." This attitude indicates to some extent that advertising has a bad ethical reputation, an issue that the advertising industry needs to acknowledge and to take effective measures to address.

Index

K

Kant, I., 9
   moral laws, 10
Kantian Contractarianism, 8
Kingdom of Ends formulation, 35, 37
Knowledge, definition of, 48

L

Legislative regulation, 5

M

Manipulation, 39
Marketing
   basic strategies, 58
   environment, 88
   expertise, 111
   mass, 100
Media, 24, 88
   advertising, 99
   organizations, 26
   traditional, 88
Mediated communication, 99
Message strategy, 44
   and advertising claims, 44–45
Metaethical justification, 13
Misconceptions, damaging, 59
Misinformation, 80
Misrepresentation, 64, 121
   symbolic, 67
Mobile communications, 99
Mobile laptop, 102
Mobile phone, 102
Model in action, 22–23
Moral behavior, 3
Moral integrity, 116–17
Moral obligations, 35
Moral problem, 80
Moral responsibility, personal and
      collective, 113
Moral sentiments, 116, 117
   cultivation of, 116
Moral wrong, 3
Motivation, 4, 112
   internal, 115
   psychological, 4, 116
   rational, 4, 117
Multibranding, 92

N

National Advertising Division (NAD), 23
National Advertising Review Board
      (NARB), 23
National Association of Broadcasters
      (NAB), 24
Noise/unwanted communication, 96
Noncommercial advertising, 109
Nonharm principle, 3

O

Office of Fair Trading, 23
Omission, 65, 115, 116
One-dimensional individuals, 64
One-sided communication, 103
Outside-in strategies, 97
Overload argument, 93–94

P

Paid endorsements, 80
Palm Pilot, 102
Personal role morality, 35
Personal Video Recorder (PVR), 98, 100
Personal virtues, 3
Personal Worldview Imperative (PWI),
      15, 121
Persuasion, 106, 121
   principle of, 51, 80
Persuasive communication, 86, 103
Persuasive strategies, 107
   effective, 49
Pop-ups, 104
Portrayal of Women Advisory Committee,
      55, 60
Portrayals
   of women and men, 55
   stereotypical of women, 55
Practical ethical problems, 66
Principle of Generic Consistency (PGC), 7,
      9–10, 11, 12, 14, 16, 35, 39, 68, 94,
      115, 116, 117, 121
   as worldview friendly, 16
Privacy
   argument, 90
   invasion of, 104, 106
   right to, 90, 94
Private government, 22